D1072110

THREE
FACES OF
REVOLUTION

THREE FACES OF REVOLUTION

Paris, London and New York in 1789

Derek Jarrett

GEORGE PHILIP

British Library Cataloguing in Publication Data

Jarrett, Derek
    Three faces of revolution: Paris, London and New
    York in 1789
    1. French Revolution, 1789–1799
    I. Title
    944.04

ISBN 0–540–01186–X

© Derek Jarrett 1989
First published by George Philip Ltd,
59 Grosvenor Street, London W1X 9DA

Printed and bound in Great Britain by
Butler & Tanner Ltd, Frome and London

Contents

1 Revolution defined   7
2 Revolution anticipated   23
3 Revolution celebrated   41
4 The wider hope   62
5 The long delay   82
6 In the name of the people   103
7 The four horsemen   120
8 Making a constitution   143
9 The year's end   160
10 Revolution reconsidered   175
References   189
Index   201

CHAPTER ONE

Revolution defined

A wise man once remarked that all history is contemporary history. We may imagine, as we turn the pages of a history book, that what we hear is the authentic voice of the past. This is a delusion. The voice of the past is the voice of the dead and it has been silenced for ever. All we can ever hope to hear is the voice of the present as it interprets or distorts or remodels what it thinks was the past. It would be comforting to think that there are great and unbiassed historians who are exceptions to this rule but unfortunately there are none. The best we can say is that all historians are trapped in their own time but some are less firmly trapped than others. All of them, of necessity, have to put their shoes on the wrong way round so that they can stride away from us across the sands of time and still give the impression, when they come to write up the results of their inquiries, that they have been advancing towards us bringing with them truths about the past. What they are in fact carrying is a selection of preconceived ideas and accepted attitudes of mind from their own time. During their retrospective journey they will apply these to the evidence left by previous centuries in such a way as to make it seem that they have been marching from the past to the present rather than the other way about.

These harsh facts of life are particularly harsh when historians try to seek out and study those great upheavals which we know as revolutions. Inevitably they will be tempted to carry back into the past the standard twentieth-century concept of revolution, the disadvantage of which is that it is only a concept of half a revolution. We tend to think of a revolution as a turning of the tables. In our eyes such a change is complete when those who were up are down, when those who were in are out. But this is not a revolution at all: it is a movement through one hundred and eighty degrees, a turning of the clock's hand from midnight to six o'clock. A true revolution is through three hundred and sixty degrees, from midnight to high noon, and the seventeenth and eighteenth centuries knew this better than we do. Their dictionaries defined revolution as 'a full compassing; rounding, turning back to its first place or point; the accomplishment of a circular course'. The word was most often used to describe either the movement of the heavens or the workings of providence. Even when it came to be applied to political events it still meant a natural process which was divinely approved, even divinely ordained, and therefore working for good. The seventeenth-century historian Arthur Wilson saw all revolutions as part of God's plan for the world: 'He hath set times for changes which often tend to the imbettering of it'.[1]

Others might well argue that God had committed himself to working by means of half rather than whole revolutions. 'He hath put down the mighty from their seat and hath exalted the humble and meek,' men read in their prayer-books, 'he hath filled the hungry with good things and the rich he hath sent empty away.' This was clearly revolution through a hundred and eighty degrees, not three hundred and sixty. There was no question here of accomplishing a circular course: the tables had been turned once and for all. But was it the sort of revolution that men could hope to mould, the sort that could be expected to take place within human history? Was it not rather a vision of Christ's kingdom on earth, an apocalyptic event which would take place at the end of time? If so it was blasphemous and sacrilegious for mere mortals to try to bring it about. Until the new dispensation arrived, until such time as time itself should be no more, they must play their allotted parts, whether mighty or humble, hungry or rich, and cope as best they could with the only kind of revolution which fitted the existing dispensation.

This was not entirely a doctrine of despair: although God saw to it that revolutions ended where they had begun he also used them, as Wilson insisted, for the imbettering of the world. Hence the comparison with the clock is a useful one, if only because midnight and noon are not the same thing. There has been progress, movement from darkness into light, even though the face of the clock looks the same as it did twelve hours ago. In the same way the traditional idea of revolution as a series of self-completing cycles arranged by God for the good of the world managed to combine the concept of restoration, a return to the old ways after a period of imbalance, with the notion of the overall progress of mankind under the watchful eye of providence. 'In the many revolutions which have been seen in this kingdom,' wrote John Locke in England at the end of the seventeenth century, 'the slowness and aversion of the people to quit their old constitution has still brought us back to our old legislature of king, lords and commons'. But he did not doubt that all these revolutions, all these successive changes in government and society between 1640 and 1688, had eventually made things better. The greatest of them was the so-called 'Glorious Revolution' of 1688, when catholic James II's attempts at change had been frustrated and the old ways had triumphed under protestant William III. And the victims of this revolution, supporters of the exiled James, hoped in their turn for a similarly reassuring process which would bring back their version of the old ways. 'I did all I could to get the King and my Master reinstated in his kingdom by a revolution and not by fire and sword,' wrote one of them.[2]

But which kingdom? It was easy in an English context to think of revolution as a reassuringly natural and acceptable happening to be contrasted with the horrors of fire and the sword. It was not so easy in the case of Scotland and Ireland. The Glorious Revolution was made by Englishmen for English reasons: the propertied classes were determined to save themselves from the social and political consequences of two rival religions, catholicism and presbyterianism. The Church of England was very much a landowner's church, giving the squire control both over the parson and over the parish structure of local government which kept tenants and labourers in order. While catholicism threatened to submit this comfortable system to the rule of priest and monk and pope the presbyterians had wild and subversive ideas about congregations electing their own ministers. And there was no mistaking where these dangers came from: catholicism was the dominant religion in Ireland and presbyterianism held sway in Scotland. Consequently the noblemen and gentlemen of England, having resisted such extremes in their own country, voted supplies to enable William III to bring Scotland and Ireland to heel by force. North of the border and across the Irish Sea fire and the sword were all too often the handmaidens of revolution rather than its opposites.

If the full glory of the 1688 revolution was hard to discern in the context of the British Isles it was even more elusive in the wider context of the British Empire. The keystone of the much-vaunted constitution of 1688 was the coronation oath: all British monarchs since the Glorious Revolution had sworn to govern 'England and the dominions thereunto belonging according to the statutes in Parliament agreed'. During the 1760s and 1770s, as America's resistance to parliamentary taxation became increasingly violent, George III behaved impeccably. He defended the supremacy of statute, the right of Parliament to legislate for the colonies, and he disregarded the possibility of bypassing Parliament and dealing with his American subjects through their colonial assemblies. Opposition politicians tried to pretend otherwise – one of them told the King that his government was unconstitutional because it 'was not based on revolution principles'[3] – but the truth was that the breach with the American colonies came not from any betrayal of the principles of 1688 but from their being too scrupulously observed. Even though George III has been dubbed 'the King who lost America' it remains true that there was no way in which he could have placated the Americans without breaking the solemn promise he had made to the English. It was the Glorious Revolution itself that had led inexorably to a very different and far more dramatic revolution on the other side of the Atlantic.

Just how different was it? Certainly the Americans seemed to have shown precious little of that 'slowness and aversion to quit their old constitution' which Locke had thought to be the very essence of man's political being. Instead they had asserted boldly in the Declaration of Independence that if an existing form of government ceased to protect basic human rights 'it is the Right of the People to alter or to abolish it, and to institute new Government, laying its foundations on such principles and organizing its powers in such form, as to them shall seem most likely to effect their Safety and Happiness.' But throughout the troubles leading up to the Declaration the colonists had based their resistance not on some abstract concept of the rights of man but on the quite specific rights of Englishmen and the equally specific protection provided by the laws of England. It was only when Parliament in London denied these rights and redefined these laws that the Americans found themselves talking in terms of natural rights and natural law. But once they started to use these terms they began to be pushed inexorably towards the alternative concept of revolution, towards putting down the mighty from their seats and perhaps even towards filling the hungry with good things.

There was no doubt that some Americans were glad to turn their backs on the safely circular revolutions of the past in order to prepare a man-made apocalypse. Benjamin Rush, a Pennsylvania radical whose aims included the abolition of slavery and the education of women, was typical of those who were searching for a way forward to a new world rather than a way back to the old one. 'Nothing but the first act of the great drama is closed,' he cried in 1787. Meanwhile George Washington, commander of the revolutionary armies, was appalled to hear of the demands being put forward by extremists in Massachusetts. 'Their creed is,' he wrote in horror, 'that the property of the United States has been protected from confiscation of Britain by the joint exertions of all and therefore ought to be the common property of all.' He was particularly shocked to learn that these same radicals were determined to 'annihilate all debts public and private', so that the rich would be sent empty away when they tried to collect from the poor.[4]

In the spring of 1787 Daniel Shay led an armed uprising against the Massachusetts state legislature, which was trying to extract high taxes from the impoverished farmers who had actually fought the War of Independence in order to pay off the speculators who had made money out of it. Shay's rebellion was easily and energetically put down but it made the ruling groups in Massachusetts and other states realize the need for concessions, especially where debts were concerned. Seven out of the thirteen state legislatures agreed to allow the payment of private debts in depreciated paper currency, thus going some way towards that annihilation of all debts which so shocked Washington.

But not all debtors were poor, any more than all creditors were rich, and very soon the flood of paper money swept away the livelihood of the very people who had hoped to gain by it. In the autumn of 1788 Jacques-Pierre Brissot, who was soon to lead France towards a new and apocalyptic vision of revolution, was appalled by the misery he found in the state of Rhode Island.

'Paper money, or rather dishonesty, was the main reason for this poverty. Nothing is sold and no work is done, for fear that payment may be made in this discredited currency. Newport resembled a graveyard where living skeletons fought over a few blades of grass.'[5] He cannot have been surprised to learn that a few months earlier, in a popular referendum, Rhode Island had refused by an enormous majority to ratify the new constitution of the United States.

This did not necessarily mean that states where destitution and disaffection were rife, where neither God nor man seemed able to fill the hungry with good things, were the ones most likely to push the revolution towards extremism and apocalypse. 'In the four provinces of New England,' wrote another French visitor, 'they are so weary of the government that they sigh for monarchy and a very large number of persons in several counties would like to return to English domination.' John Jay told Thomas Jefferson that where law and order broke down 'the more sober part of the people may even think of a king'. Washington declared that levelling principles would open the way to 'monarchical ideas'.[6] During the anxious months between the drawing up of the new constitution in September 1787 and its coming into operation in March 1789 there was a very real fear among the new nation's politicians that Americans might after all show 'slowness and aversion to quit their old constitution', even to the point of bringing the revolution back full circle to British rule.

New Yorkers were particularly suspect. Their city had been the British headquarters during the War of Independence and it was a place where the line between loyalist and revolutionary was difficult to draw. Benjamin Rush declared roundly that at least a third of all New Yorkers were 'American citizens with British hearts' and were 'very complaisant to all the vices of monarchy'. When Senator William Maclay of Pennsylvania arrived in the city he soon realized that supporters of revolution there had had mixed motives. While some had genuinely sought 'the abolishing of royalty, the extinguishment of patronage and dependencies attached to that form of government', others had wanted 'the creation of a new monarchy in America and to form niches for themselves in the temple of royalty'.[7]

Nevertheless it was in New York that the mighty were to have their seats. The City Hall housed the original Congress which had fought the War of Independence and it had also been chosen as the place of assembly for the Congress elected under the new constitution. 'We are assured that the alterations and additions now making to the City Hall will, when completed, render it the most elegant and commodious building for a legislative body in the United States,' reported the *New York Journal*. 'The readiness with which the citizens entered into a subscription for defraying the expense shows that we are sensible of the honor conferred on us by Congress'.[8] Members of the old Congress were rather less enthusiastic about the alterations and additions, which made life increasingly difficult for them until they finally adjourned at the beginning of November, leaving the United States with no central government of any kind. Not until 1789, when President and Senate and House of Representatives met in New York, would the new nation be able to proceed on its way. Then and then only, exactly a century after the completion of the Glorious Revolution in England, the future direction of the revolution it had spawned in America would be determined.

It may seem odd that the centenary of a revolution which took place in 1688 should have fallen in 1789. But until the calendar reforms of 1752 the Englishman's year had begun not in January but in March, so that the Glorious Revolution, which took place between November and February, was completed in the year which was 1688 at the time but would be looked back upon as having been 1689 from 1 January onwards. When the constituted electors met in New York in February 1789 to choose a President they did so exactly a hundred years after the Convention Parliament in London set the seal on its revolution by choosing James II's successor. In New York in 1789 the election was straightforward but in London a century earlier things had been more difficult. While the Whig majority in the House of Commons declared that the throne was vacant and proposed to elect William III as King, the Tory majority in the Lords insisted that Mary, William's wife and James's Anglican elder daughter, was Queen by hereditary right. This head-on collision between the irreconcilable elective and legitimist theories of monarchy was disguised by a face-saving formula proclaiming that William and Mary jointly 'be and be declared' King and Queen of England. It was an absurd phrase, since if they already were monarchs there was no need to declare them so, while if they had to be declared monarchs then they could not have been so before the declaration. But it succeeded in papering over the cracks and bringing about revolution, in the safely cyclical sense, instead of worsening civil strife.

Now, a hundred years later, the cracks had reappeared. George III was mentally ill and there would have to be a regency. Was the Prince of Wales Regent by hereditary right in the way the Tories in 1689 had said Mary was Queen, or must he be made Regent by Parliament in the way the Whigs had wanted to make William King? It was a political crisis, not just a matter of constitutional theory, because everyone knew that if the Prince became Regent without having his powers defined and limited by Parliament he would throw out his father's ministers and establish opposition politicians in office so firmly that his father would be unable to dislodge them if he ever recovered his senses. 'Be and be declared' had no power to resolve this crisis, nor could any other sacrosanct 'revolution principle' provide an answer.

The crisis over the regency was not the end of the matter. In this centenary year there were many who were proclaiming vociferously that the Glorious Revolution had been inadequate, that it had left undone things which ought to have been done and now finally must be done. Chief among these was the granting of civil rights to protestant dissenters. William III, a Dutch Calvinist, had come to save all protestants, not just Anglicans, from the catholic clutches of James II. Why then had the Anglicans been allowed to exclude dissenters from Parliament and from public office? The London Revolution Society made it clear at its centenary meeting on 5 November 1788 that this wrong was at last to be righted.[9] In London, as in New York, 1789 was to be the year in which the safe and secure revolutions of the past would be under threat from the radicalism of the present. It was galling for Anglican conservatives to reflect that this radicalism had been closely linked with the American revolution but it was even more disturbing to think that it might soon be encouraged and exacerbated by unrest on the other side of the English Channel.

For there were already many cities in Europe where revolution was a reality. The Prince of Orange had had to call in foreign troops to put down a rising in Amsterdam and in Stockholm the Diet, Sweden's national assembly, was fighting a fierce battle against increasing royal power. The reforms of the Emperor Joseph II were meeting with stiff resistance in Louvain and Brussels and elsewhere in Belgium, then known as the Austrian Netherlands, while in the Swiss Republic the citizens of Geneva were preparing for their third revolution in the space of seven years.

But all these upheavals were overshadowed by the news from France. Arthur Young, a self-appointed and much-travelled agricultural expert, attended a fashionable dinner party in Paris in October 1787 and found that 'one opinion pervaded the whole company, that they are on the eve of some great revolution in the government.' The reasons for these apprehensions were basically financial: Louis XVI and his ministers had run up a deficit which was 'impossible to provide for without the States General* of the kingdom, yet with no ideas formed of what would be the consequence of their meeting.' However, everybody seemed to be agreed that 'the States of the kingdom cannot assemble without more liberty being the consequence', especially as there already existed throughout France 'a strong leaven of liberty, increasing every hour since the American Revolution.'[10]

Young's Parisian dinner companions could face the summoning of the Estates General and the possibility of 'some great revolution in the government' with perfect equanimity. What alarmed them was the alternative, the possibility that the King might repudiate his debts rather than go cap in hand to the three estates for new taxes. Whenever these things were discussed Young heard the same anxious question asked: 'Would a bankruptcy occasion a civil war and a total overthrow of the government?'[11] Revolution *in* government and overthrow *of* government were very different things. Indeed they were opposites, just as revolution had seemed the opposite of fire and the sword to a Jacobite in the 1700s. In both cases the reason was the same: revolution meant a reassuring return to the past and not a leap into the unknown. So far from being the agent of political and civil collapse it was the surest way of avoiding it. The Estates General was a venerable institution and for more than three hundred years, from the early fourteenth to the early seventeenth century, it had played a vital part in national affairs. If Louis XVI decided to convoke it he would be turning his back on royal absolutism, on the upstart system of government which had ruled France for more than a century and a half, in order to go back to older and better things. London newspapers saw the point and the *Annual Register* declared that the troubles of the French monarchy provided 'a most unexpected opportunity towards the restoration of the ancient Gallic con-

*English-speaking contemporaries translated *Etats Généraux* as States General but historians prefer Estates General, which indicates that it was a meeting of the three estates of the realm – clergy, nobility and third estate.

stitution'.[12] It was to be hoped that in Paris, as in London and New York, men would show that 'slowness and aversion to quit their old constitution' which Locke had so commended.

But it was a long time since the Estates General had met and the French might need help in rediscovering the old ways. They would be well advised to profit from the experience of the English, who had trodden this path more recently and, in their own estimation, with spectacular success. 'Our predominance in the affairs of Europe has given rise to a spirit of imitation,' the *Annual Register* remarked grandly, 'which disposes them to copy us in all things, but principally in that in which we are most distinguished, the form of our government.'[13] Young's comment about 'a strong leaven of liberty' made it clear that there were many in Paris who were disposed to look not to London but to New York and to the much more recent experience of the Americans. America's part in the origins of the French revolution, a topic which has come to exercise historians mightily, was already being dismissed by Englishmen in purely negative terms. One London paper reminded its readers that 'the jealousy natural to rival nations makes us fond to attribute the difficulties in which France is involved to the interference of that government in supporting the rebellion of the British American colonists against the parent country.' It was astonishing, it added, 'that a crown which had for ages been establishing despotism should teach a lesson directly subversive of its own principles.'[14] Americans of course saw things differently and were for the most part confident that their revolution had inspired not just France but the whole of Europe. 'It is a well known fact,' wrote James Madison, 'that this event has filled that quarter of the Globe with equal wonder and veneration, that its influence is already secretly but powerfully working in favour of liberty in France.'[15]

The influence might well be less powerful if Frenchmen came to associate the United States with anarchy rather than liberty. By the middle of November 1787, a month after Young had commented on the leaven of liberty which France owed to America, Thomas Jefferson, American ambassador in Paris, had become convinced that the authorities in London were deliberately putting out exaggerated accounts of Shay's rebellion and other disorders in order to make it seem that the United States was unlikely to achieve a stable constitution:

The British ministry have so long hired their gazetteers to repeat and model into every form lies about our being in anarchy, that the world has at length believed them, the English nation has believed them, the ministers themselves have come to believe them and, what is more wonderful, we have believed them ourselves. Yet where does this anarchy exist? Where did it ever exist, except in the single instance of Massachusetts? And can history produce an instance of rebellion so honourably conducted? God forbid we should ever be twenty years without such a rebellion. What signify a few lives lost in a century or two? The tree of liberty must be refreshed from time to time with the blood of patriots and tyrants.[16]

As far as Jefferson was concerned there was no doubt who were the patriots and who the tyrants. Having allied with the Americans in their struggle for independence the French were now giving their support to the Amsterdam revolutionaries, who called themselves the Patriots. Because the Prince of Orange had close links with the British Royal Family – and also, perhaps more to the point, because the London money market was heavily reliant on the money market in Amsterdam – the British were anxious that the Dutch revolution should be put down. When William Eden, British commercial envoy in Paris, sounded Jefferson as to what the United States would do if Britain and France went to war over the Dutch question, he was told roundly that America saw Britain as her natural enemy, 'the only nation on earth who wished us ill from the bottom of their souls.'[17]

It was significant that this outburst was provoked by the prospect of Britain going to war to protect her financial ties with the Dutch. The French view of things was that the financiers of Amsterdam had been the first to create a credit economy, a bubble of illusory prosperity based on pieces of paper taken as wealth when they were in truth nothing but evidence of indebtedness, and that after 1688, when the then Prince of Orange had become King of England, the London financiers had taken over from the Dutch and swallowed them up. London was now the seat of a sinister financial cancer which threatened to eat into healthy and wholesome countries like France where government and society still rested on the wealth of the land and on the traditional values associated with it. Already a French finance minister had stated authoritatively that because England's national debt exceeded her gold reserves she was in reality one of the poorest nations in the world and sooner or later her economy must collapse, endangering all who had links with it.[18] That had been in 1747 when the debt was little more than £60 million. Now, forty years and two major wars on, it was four times that and the danger was all the greater for being so long delayed. Whether they knew it or not the financial charlatans and tricksters of London were the natural enemies not just of the United States but of all traditional and soundly based societies.

From its inception the Glorious Revolution had posed a political as well as an economic threat to the French monarchy. William III's first act on entering London had been to break off diplomatic relations with France, after which he and his allies had encircled her from the Rhine to the Pyrenees and from the Atlantic to the Alps. Financial backing for his wars had come not only from the bankers of London and Amsterdam but also from the Huguenots, persecuted French protestants who had been forced to flee abroad and were determined to use the 1688 revolution as a springboard for the invasion of France and the humbling of French catholicism. 'Is not this auspicious revolution in England a prelude to our own,' wrote one of their pamphleteers, 'a portent to give us hope and a pathway to give us guidance?'[19] While Paris provided a haven for Jacobites planning to reconquer England, London harboured Huguenots who dreamed, rather less realistically, of returning in triumph to France. And most of them had come to occupy positions of power and influence far beyond anything the Jacobites of Paris could ever aspire to.

In French eyes – and indeed in those of many Englishmen as well – London was the stamping-ground for the mob and the breeding-ground for faction. It was a place where, in the name of liberty, corrupt politicians and venal journalists and scheming financiers were given licence to divide the nation and make good government impossible. In the 1770s this wildly exaggerated view of London's importance played a vital part in securing French aid for the thirteen colonies and thus in ensuring the success of the American revolution. Vergennes, the French foreign minister, was told by his spies in London that the troubles in America were the product of this hotbed of faction: Lord Chatham and other politicians out of office had deliberately incited the colonists to revolt in the hope that the rebellion would overthrow the existing government and bring them back to power. They then planned to join with the Americans in attacking France. Vergennes used these absurd speculations in order to persuade Louis XVI that the quarrel with the colonies was a mere cover for a carefully planned joint attack by the British and the Americans on French and Spanish possessions in America.[20]

For good measure he bombarded the King with memoranda proving that England had been the disturber of the peace of Europe ever since 1578, when she had helped the Dutch to rebel against Spain, and that her present troubles were the direct result of her unnatural and ungodly form of government. He also took up the old charge that her credit economy was against nature. It bore the same relation to proper landed wealth as a man with dropsy bore to a robust and healthy individual. Under the strains of war the great bloated swelling would burst while the stout frame of sturdy France went from strength to strength.[21] From London French agents sent the same message in different metaphorical guise. The English were a race of sorcerers, one of them reported, but now their evil spells were losing their power. They were no longer in control of the forces they had called up and France had her chance to reduce them to bankruptcy and impotence. At a more serious level Accarias de Serionne's celebrated treatise on *The Wealth of England,* based upon an apparently well argued distinction between real and artificial wealth, concluded that England's prosperity was entirely artificial, sustained only by a political system that was becoming increasingly divisive and a credit structure that was on the point of collapse.[22]

Yet it was only five years since the same writer had declared that 'by the conquest of America England has become the most powerful nation in Europe. Her greatness and her power are genuine and are not just the result of success in war. They spring from her extensive commerce, which in its turn is based on flourishing agriculture and industry.'[23] It was not just that the American revolt and French readiness to make capital out of it had produced a sudden change of attitude. There had always been an ambivalence, a triple thread of admiration and distaste and misunderstanding, running through France's view of the achievements and consequences of 1688. In 1779 the comte d'Albon published a series of weighty discourses on the history and political prospects of the nations of Europe. When he came to consider England he spoke admiringly of the Glorious Revolution as 'a great revolution which demanded all the energy and enthusiasm of the whole population'. This was nonsense, since in fact the changes of 1688 were brought about by a few hundred propertied men in London. Equally nonsensical was his idea that those who governed England had to bow to the wishes of all the people. Finally he convinced himself that England's overweening commercialism also sprang from the people as a whole rather than from a few financiers and merchants and politicians in London: 'Tormented cruelly and unceasingly by a burning fever of ambition, this race of people brings about its own ruin and destruction in its attempt to overthrow and smash everything around it.'[24]

This fantasy of a frenetic popular democracy was necessary for d'Albon's argument: he wanted to show what sort of government was desirable and so he created a particularly undesirable one and pinned it on the English to show what must be avoided. Conversely Montesquieu's famous encomium on the English – 'Of all the nations upon earth, this is the one that has made the best of these three great things: religion, commerce and liberty' – served to point up the principles on which he alleged the French constitution had once been based and might yet be based again. Beauties as well as blemishes were in the eye of the beholder. The Parlement of Paris, a privileged body of lawyers who envied the even greater privileges of Parliament in London*, published fulsome eulogies of England as 'the land which liberty seems to have chosen as her refuge.' Voltaire praised English civil liberty and religious toleration in order to attack the tyrannies of church and state in France; and towards the end of his life, as the danger of a collapse of French government credit became apparent, he argued that the British representative system guaranteed financial as well as political stability because government borrowing was underwritten by the wealth of the country represented in Parliament. On the other hand Turgot, a reforming minister who saw strong centralized government as the basis of sound finance, declared that the boasted checks and balances of the English constitution really only represented 'a state of permanent civil war'. Most ordinary Frenchmen agreed with him. 'The French affirm that we are little better than wild untamed savages,' an English traveller in France reported, 'ready at the least provocation to subvert the very foundations of government.'[25]

But when the Americans began to subvert the foundations of British government in the 1760s and 1770s it did not occur to the

---

*Contemporaries misleadingly translated *Parlement* as 'Parliament' and I have retained this in quotations but not in the text.

French to condemn them as wild or untamed. They were seen as victims, not abettors, of the mayhem in London. D'Albon made it very clear that whereas mobs in Britain perverted the principles of 1688 in order to bring the country to the brink of anarchy, those in America made noble use of those principles in order to win the freedom to which they were entitled. Precisely because most Frenchmen were profoundly traditionalist, wedded to what they saw as the simple uncorrupted values of a landed society under threat from the British, they were very ready to see America as a rural paradise peopled by sturdy pioneers who had not yet eaten of the tree of the knowledge of capitalist enterprise and who would prove more than a match for the soulless commercial tyrants in London. 'It is perhaps in America,' wrote Louis Sebastian Mercier, 'that the human race is to be re-created.' The marquis de Chastellux's enormously popular *Travels in North America* portrayed American life in this light, as did St Jean de Crèvecoeur's *Letters of an American Farmer*. The French government rewarded Crèvecoeur with the post of consul at New York, which he held from 1783 to 1790, while the French envoy in Philadelphia advised the ruling groups in Congress to keep ordinary Americans as poor as possible, so that their new nation should have the advantages of a hierarchical society as well as a landed one. Even those who were anything but traditionalists themselves shared this vision of the Americans as paragons of all the rural virtues. When Jacques-Pierre Brissot the unsuccessful lawyer collaborated with Etienne Clavière the international financier in the spring of 1787 to publish a treatise on *France and the United States* they both insisted that America must discourage all manufacturing industries in order to make sure that her life remained a pastoral idyll.[26]

In December 1787, still preoccupied with Shay's rebellion and with his conversation with Eden, Jefferson wrote a lengthy letter to James Madison in which he came to much the same conclusion. 'I think our governments will remain virtuous for many centuries,' he observed, 'as long as they are chiefly agricultural; and this will be as long as there shall be vacant lands in any part of America. When they get piled upon one another in large cities, as in Europe, they will become corrupt as in Europe.' He once again discounted the uprising in Massachusetts, pointing out that both Britain and France had a worse record of disorder and riot, though he nevertheless confessed that 'the instability of our laws is an immense evil.' But unlike Madison he was not primarily concerned about instability discrediting America in French eyes, about some imagined contest between the British and American constitutions for the attention of potential revolutionaries in France. What worried him was the more immediate and more dangerous prospect of a contest between Britain and France for the control of America. New York had been New Amsterdam before the British took it from the Dutch and if the malignant obscenity of London finance was stretching out its tentacles towards the original it might soon threaten the namesake as well. Then Americans would face the dilemma the Dutch now faced, having to choose between domination by the British and domination by the French. Jefferson's fear was that the new constitution would tempt an unscrupulous President to entrench himself, to become 'an officer for life', and to invite either the French or the British 'to interfere with money and with arms'. 'A Gallomane or an Anglomane will be supported by the nation he befriends,' he predicted gloomily.[27]

It was just over four years since Britain had signed treaties of peace with France and the United States in order to end the War of American Independence. They had been concluded 'in the name of the most Holy and Undivided Trinity', as though the signatories had been potentates of a Christendom still united under God, but in fact they had been spawned by a system of independent sovereign states whose only rule of international law was not the Christian ethic but the pragmatic doctrine of 'balance of power'. And this doctrine implied, as the jurist Johann von Justi had pointed out a quarter of a century earlier, that any sovereign state had the right to interfere in the internal affairs of any other. If one nation's government became stronger by crushing internal resistance, or weaker by failing to do so, then its neighbours were entitled to consider how the balance of power had been affected and to take appropriate action.[28] This placed the far from holy and extremely divided trinity of France, Britain and America in an anxious and watchful position. Each of its members was involved with a revolution – France because she was anticipating one, Britain because she was celebrating one, America because she was completing one. And each had cause to fear that her search for her own revolutionary identity might be adversely affected by the competing efforts and influences of the other two.

CHAPTER TWO

Revolution anticipated

In July 1788 the *New York Journal* was optimistic about the course of events in France. 'Opposition to the King's orders advances so rapidly, and has already assumed so formidable a shape,' it assured its readers, 'as to give the most rational hope of his being able to rescue the country from the doom with which it was menaced.' The inference was clear enough: the King had good intentions and the very fact that the country was opposing his ministers' measures would enable him to save France from their clutches. He was said to be determined to give the French a proper representative system and in early August, when news came that he had abolished 'every species of torture', the New York papers were extremely impressed. Louis XVI was personally still very popular in America and his health was drunk enthusiastically by New Yorkers when ships of his navy visited the port. The *Gazette of the United States*, also published in New York, was glad to echo the sentiments of the official French almanac when it spoke of Americans paying homage to 'Louis XVI, Peacemaker of two Worlds'. This was in sharp contrast to a paragraph it inserted about George III being haunted by 'the ghosts of murdered millions ... putrid carcases ... the monumental bones of ravaged America' because of his predilection for 'murder, the royal sport.' 'This piece was written some time before His Britannic Majesty's physicians declared him insane,' it explained, 'but years after the Americans thought him so.'[1]

In the middle of September, after receiving reports that had come out of France two months earlier, the *New York Journal* changed its tune. 'In this unfortunate and unhappy country we cannot depend on anything,' it declared. 'The King of France is now at WAR with his subjects.' 'The affairs of this country become every day more alarming,' it added a week later. London papers also noticed a remarkable transformation of the scene in France at about the same time. 'The nation seemed to have changed its character,' remarked the *Annual Register*, 'a settled and melancholy gloom now seemed fixed in every countenance.' One reason was the great storm of 13 July 1788. 'At about nine in the morning, without any eclipse, a dreadful and almost total darkness suddenly overspread the face of the earth in several parts of France and this awful gloom was the prelude to a tempest or hurricane supposed to be without example in the temperate climates of Europe.' With the wind came hailstones more terrifying and more destructive than anything in living memory. Crops were flattened, livestock killed outright. Only the fact that it was a Sunday, so that there were few people working in the fields, averted a serious loss of human life. A day later men were still finding lumps of ice as big as a man's fist. Peasants crouched in terror, 'concluding it to be the last day and expecting the immediate dissolution of all things.'[2]

It was not the end of all things but it did seem to mark the end of plenty and prosperity, perhaps even of national self-confidence. Harvests were disastrous and as winter drew on things were made worse by floods and frosts. Peasants abandoned their land and became vagrants. In England there was a system of poor relief operating at parish level but in France the best hope for the starving lay in charitable institutions run by monks and nuns, usually in towns. When these came to the end of their resources, or when epidemics threatened, town gates were shut and vagrants were turned away to beg or steal. Many formed themselves into large and threatening bands and by the spring of 1789 these were terrorizing many parts of the country. 'About a dozen arrived in the early hours of Thursday morning,' reported one landowner. 'We cannot go to bed unafraid,' complained another.[3] The spiral of rural and urban distress ran its sinister course: farmers and peasants could no longer sell their produce in the towns because of urban unemployment, which in its turn increased inexorably as towns could no longer find markets for their goods in the starving countryside.

Clearly distress on this scale could not be put down to a single storm. For decades the politics of grain supply in France had revolved round allegations about a supposed *pacte de famine*, whereby hoarders were said to be stockpiling grain in order to create artificial shortages which would enable them to sell at a profit. In this highly charged atmosphere of real or imagined conspiracy the government could not win: if it prepared for emergencies by storing grain it was accused of being in league with the hoarders, while if it did not it was accused of being callously indifferent to the sufferings of the people. There was also a long-running argument between those who said free trade in grain brought down prices and eliminated shortages and those who maintained that it did the opposite. The free traders had had their way in 1787 and so they were now being blamed for the current troubles. Waiting in the wings was their formidable opponent Jacques Necker, a Genevese banker who had been in charge of French government finances from 1776 to 1781 and whose attacks on subsequent administrations had been so vitriolic that Louis XVI had banished him from Paris. The rich and the fashionable had flocked out to visit him and the Queen had persuaded the King to make the terms of his banishment more lenient to prevent him becoming a popular hero and martyr.

On the face of things Necker did not seem to have the makings of such a figure. He was a foreigner and a protestant whose associates in the world of international finance ran banking houses and other enterprises in Geneva, Amsterdam and London and were speculating in everything from American frontier land to the Paris water supply. He had a reputation for secret and shady dealings – he had worked behind the scenes in London to save the French ambassador there when he was charged with dishonest speculation in British government stock – and he had paid for French participation in the War of American Independence by borrowing from his foreign financier friends on terms that were advantageous to them as well as giving them opportunities to make large private profits out of the war.

These loans had been popular enough at the time, since they had avoided the need for new taxes, but now that they seemed to have brought the government to the brink of bankruptcy they were under attack for having sacrificed traditional French values to the false gods of artificial wealth and inflated credit that were worshipped in London. Necker maintained that government finances had been ruined not by him but by his successor Calonne, who had also now been dismissed and was putting out virulent pamphlets against Necker from his fashionable villa outside London at Wimbledon. 'Calonne's *mémoire* has made a very great impression,' wrote the duke of Dorset, British ambassador in Paris, to his friend the duchess of Devonshire. 'Mrs B. is reading it, and she is to tell me what she thinks of it tomorrow. Necker and his friends seemed to be entirely knocked up by it.'[4] 'Mrs Brown', as Dorset called the Queen in his private correspondence, had in his opinion been responsible for Calonne's dismissal as well as for lightening Necker's sentence of exile. The fierce debate between the partisans of the two ex-ministers was now at the centre of the French political stage. 'I am neither for Calonne nor for Necker,' the Genevese Etienne Dumont was at pains to proclaim when he came to Paris in the summer of 1788.[5] He had particular need to declare his impartiality, not only because he was Necker's compatriot but also because he was in the service of Lord Lansdowne, who had been George III's First Lord of the Treasury five years before and had hopes that developments in France might help him back to power.

The domestic situation of Dorset's 'Mr and Mrs Brown' also had international implications. Louis XVI had been married to Marie Antoinette, sister of the Holy Roman Emperor, as part of an alliance with Austria which had become more and more unpopular. The Queen was dismissed as 'the Austrian woman' and her enemies alleged that the King was little more than an imbecile whom she manipulated for her own and for her brother's ends. They also whispered that the children who were supposed to be his had in reality been fathered by her lovers. Now she was dubbed 'Madame Déficit', suggesting that she was personally responsible for government over-spending, and in the weeks that followed Calonne's fall, graffiti appeared on the walls of Paris reading '*Isabeau de Bavière – Madame Déficit*'. The reference was to Isabel of Bavaria, who as Regent for her mad husband King Charles VII had sold France to the English in 1420. In Paris as in London there was talk in the autumn of 1788 of a mad King and of a Queen who must somehow be stopped from seizing power. Mrs Swinburne, an Englishwoman high in favour at Court, reported that Louis XVI was half mad already and that his brothers spoke openly of him as 'tottering on his throne'. 'People talk of the King being put aside as incapable of governing,' she wrote early in October, 'a regency appointed and the Queen in a convent.'[6]

The baron de Besenval, later to be a scapegoat for alleged royal plans to intimidate Paris by force of arms, cast his net wider and claimed that Louis's throne was being undermined by treacherous princely factions subsidized from London by British secret agents. Supporters of the King's brothers the comte de Provence and the comte d'Artois, who had hopes of succession if the royal children were illegitimate, were only too ready to inflate the rumours about Marie Antoinette's supposed infidelities. There was also the threat from the duc d'Orléans, head of the turbulent and ambitious cadet branch of the French royal family. The Orléanists had long had designs on the crown and now Besenval believed that they were conspiring with the British to seize it. He also believed that France was falling prey to British mistakes as well as to British money. The sacking of Calonne was as fatal, he argued, as Charles I's sacrifice of Strafford to the Long Parliament in 1641. In both cases the monarchy had abandoned the only man who could have saved it from ambitious magnates manipulating popular grievances for their own advancement.[7]

Others accused Calonne of allowing London to ruin French industry and so cause the very grievances it subsequently exploited. One of his free-trade measures had been a Commercial Treaty cutting import duties on British manufactured goods coming into France. In Normandy in August 1788 Arthur Young found good quality china and textiles from England selling for less than inferior French imitations. When he asked the shopkeeper whether this meant that the treaty had been a mistake he was told that on the contrary it had had a stimulating effect: 'However poor these imitations may be they are still better than anything produced in France until now. Next year we shall do better and soon our manufactures will be undercutting yours.'[8] Calonne had indeed hoped that exposure to British competition would promote French industrial growth, which he had tried to encourage with government grants and loans, but this policy was now in ruins and few Frenchmen were as optimistic as the one Young met. In November 1787, six months after the Treaty came into effect, Dorset heard that it had put more than a thousand men out of work in one French cloth-producing town alone. Two months later he reported that a deputation from Brittany had told Louis XVI to his face that the province could pay no more taxes 'owing to the great injury it had sustained by the Commercial Treaty with England'.[9]

Nor were the British the only villains of the piece. The Breton deputation also complained of 'permission granted to the Americans to supply the Antilles with stores and provisions, a commerce that had before been carried on solely from the Ports of Brittany'.[10] When a French force had set out from those same ports in 1780 to fight in America the government sending it had had hopes of supplanting Britain as America's trading partner, only to find when peace came that London's transatlantic links were stronger and more resilient than they had seemed. Strenuous but ultimately unsuccessful attempts had been made by the marquis de Lafayette, the most colourful and popular of the French officers in America, to get United States tobacco exports diverted from London to French ports. The *New York Journal* was still campaigning for closer trading ties with France as late as December 1788 – 'France has by her arms contributed to confirm the independence of free America. A treaty of commerce founded on the interests of the two countries must unite them more and more intimately' – but in truth all that remained of the intended partnership was a series of specific concessions such as the one that so infuriated the Bretons. It was individuals who were benefiting, not the French and American economies as a whole. The *New York Journal's* effusion about a commercial treaty was sparked off by news that Brissot and Clavière had founded a Gallo-American Society in Paris, but when Brissot visited America in 1788 to bring greetings from this high-minded body he was also briefed by Clavière to find out how best he and other financiers could extend their speculations from Paris and London to New York.[11]

Before going to the United States Brissot had been a follower of Orléans, suggesting to him that he should head a political party in order to work for the restoration of the ancient French constitution. Orléans was biding his time but Lafayette, the hero of America, had already openly demanded the summoning of the Estates General and was now making trouble for the King in the provinces. 'I have just returned from the Auvergne Provincial Assembly,' he told George Washington in January 1788, 'where I had the good fortune to please the people and the misfortune to displease the government to a very high degree.' He also had the good fortune to please the people of New York. 'At this dinner,' wrote Brissot of his first New York banquet, 'as at almost all the others I attended in America, they drank the health of M.

Lafayette. Americans take pleasure in referring to him as one of their liberators ... they have no warmer supporter in France.'[12]

It was significant that none of this redounded to the discredit of Lafayette or Brissot or Orléans. All three were subsequently accused, along with many others, of being paid by foreigners to bring down the French monarchy. They were the subject of countless scurrilous pamphlets which provided the basis of the 'conspiracy thesis' of the French revolution, whereby all resistance to royal government was the work of plotters and secret agents. Orléans was the principal target of these attacks – he was, in Talleyrand's pungent phrase, the chamber-pot into which all the excrement of the revolution was poured – and all his links with Britain were exploited and exaggerated and misrepresented.[13] Yet no one thought to accuse him or his associates of being suborned by the Americans. It is easy to imagine what the pamphleteers would have made of it had one of Orléans's agents gone to London at the behest of a foreign banker to seek out fields for speculation and had attended banquets at which the health of a prominent Anglophile French opponent of Louis XVI had been drunk while the Anglophile himself was recounting his exploits to a future British head of state. But because these things were associated with America and not with Britain there could be no ground for suspicion. Bretons might complain about the trading privileges of the British and the Americans in the same breath but Parisians could not see London and New York in the same light. The one was guilty until proved innocent, the other innocent until proved guilty. This remained true even when the things they were supposed to be guilty or innocent of changed with the changing situation in Paris.

The situation really began to change after the dismissal of Calonne, when Louis XVI saw that he might have to yield to the widespread demand for some sort of representative body. It was this that turned a credit crisis into a political and constitutional one. 'The King of France became a King of England,' wrote a previously liberal but now disillusioned Frenchman, 'forever obliged to assemble his people to ask them to supply his wants. I regret this, I regret it very much.' When Brissot advised Orléans to campaign for the restoration of the French constitution he added that 'the basis of this constitution is the right not to pay taxes without having consented to them.'[14] But under what form, within what forum, should this consent be given? Since 1614 the lawyers in the Parlement of Paris, backed for the most part by those in the twelve provincial Parlements, had argued that in the absence of the Estates General they were the legitimate representatives of the nation. They were in fact merely magistrates who were allowed to suggest modifications to the laws they were going to have to enforce. When they tried to inflate this into a right to give or withhold consent to taxation the government replied by setting up Provincial Assemblies such as the one in Auvergne that Lafayette wrote to Washington about. The Parlements became even more contumacious and Daniel Hailes, secretary to the British embassy, observed shrewdly that 'the establishment of the Provincial Assemblies throughout the Kingdom (a measure which could not be opposed by them in an open manner on account of its extreme popularity) is the real though concealed motive of their conduct.'[15]

By the spring of 1788 Hailes was convinced that Louis XVI was going to sweep away the Parlements and establish a constitution modelled on that of Great Britain. The French envied Britain's financial and political resilience – 'The example of the very extraordinary and rapid recovery of Great Britain from the wounds she received in the late war has not failed to attract the attention of this people' – and they were determined to seek out her secret. He found the prospect daunting:

In such a point of view there appears without doubt much ground of apprehension for the interests of Great Britain, for it may be reasonably asked, if France, with all the vices of her government, has been for so many ages in a situation to act often so brilliant and formidable a part in the affairs of Europe, what may not be expected of her when those vices shall have been eradicated, and when she shall be in possession of a constitution (as it is pretended she may) similar to that of her neighbour and rival?

The only consolation was that the French were unlikely to do the thing properly. 'Many parts of the English Constitution, it is said, may be adopted with great advantage to this kingdom,' Hailes continued. 'I should rather think that it must be taken whole and entire ... A partial assumption of these great features of freedom would only tend to disfigure the French monarchy without producing any real advantage.'[16]

Three weeks later, on 8 May 1788, Louis XVI announced what many saw as just such a partial assumption. The Parlements were to be abolished and replaced with a Plenary Court which would be 'a supreme tribunal such as existed in ancient days, the court of barons and peers, the highest court of justice in the land and the King's great council'. He might almost have been talking about the House of Lords in London. The proposed body would be more parliamentary than the Parlements and according to one courtier 'there were those who hoped that this court of barons and peers might draw up a Magna Carta of the liberties of the realm, as the great barons of England had done, and become the upper house of a truly representative national legislature.' 'We have good authority for saying,' wrote the *New York Journal*, 'that a negotiation is actually begun between the court and the leaders of the opposition to give to France what it has always claimed but never truly enjoyed, an independent representation in the Plenary Court.' It predicted that each Provincial Assembly would be invited to send two representatives to this new upper house, just as the American constitution allowed each state to elect two members of the Senate.[17]

Dorset told his government there would be little resistance to the new move. 'This country may appear to those who are at a distance to be in a state of actual civil war but I can assure your Lordship that in the capital everything is perfectly quiet and likely to continue so ... It is upon the whole imagined that the storm which seemed to threaten the internal tranquillity of this kingdom will blow over.' For the next fortnight, as the fierce and united opposition of all the Parlements to the Plenary Court increasingly proved him wrong, he remained insistent that 'the discontent of the Parliaments has not yet reached the people at large'. 'Mr and Mrs B. are both a good deal tormented,' he wrote to the duchess of Devonshire, 'but if their ministers are firm it will all end well as the people as well as the King hate all the Parliamenti.' But on 12 June he had to confess that he was 'exceedingly concerned for Mr and Mrs B. The latter is *amazingly* out of spirits,' and on the same day he sent the Foreign Secretary an account of a serious riot in Grenoble, the capital of Dauphiné, in support of the Parlement there. On 2 July, when he had to report further troubles in Dauphiné and Brittany and elsewhere, he added angrily that 'no artifice is left untried to inflame the populace.'[18]

He also mentioned in passing that Jefferson had told him Maryland had ratified the new constitution of the United States.[19] This meant that seven out of the thirteen states had ratified and

Jefferson had been assured by Washington that the remaining six would follow suit. This was more relevant to the French crisis than Dorset may have realized, for in many ways France's constitutional problem bore a closer resemblance to that of the United States than to that of Great Britain. Although George III ruled three kingdoms and the principality of Wales, his Parliament at Westminster had swallowed up Scottish and Welsh representation while the legislative independence recently granted to the Parliament in Dublin had as yet presented no political or constitutional problems. Louis XVI on the other hand ruled a patchwork of territories which his predecessors had stitched together by dint of conquest and judicious marriages. Many provinces, and in particular Dauphiné and Brittany, could cite solemn treaties which set limits to the authority the King of France could exercise over them. A few were entitled to hold their own provincial Estates, instead of merely sending representatives to the Estates General, and several more claimed that this right had been unjustly taken from them and must be recovered. And so the Americans were perhaps forging just the sort of constitution the French looked like needing, one which reconciled the sovereignty of autonomous states with the authority of a federal government.

But they had not forged it yet. Underlying the cheery predictions Washington sent to Jefferson in Paris was a very real fear that the state assemblies might yet prevent the constitution coming into effect. His own state of Virginia was especially turbulent. 'The accounts from Richmond are indeed very impropitious to federal measures,' he wrote anxiously to Madison in New York. Madison for his part feared the scrapping of the constitution and the calling of a second Constitutional Convention which would be dominated by separatists. This he thought would shatter the image France had of America's revolution and sap her will to copy it. 'The prospect of a second Convention would be viewed by all Europe as a dark and threatening cloud over the Constitution just established,' he warned, 'and would therefore suspend at least the advantages this great event has promised us on that side.'[20]

The advantages were not quite what Madison thought they were. The United States constitution was less than a year old and as yet the French knew little of it. They were familiar with the high-sounding phrases of the Declaration of Independence –

Lafayette had had them framed in one half of a double frame, the other half waiting for a French counterpart – and they knew about the various state constitutions, translations of which had run through several editions during the past decade. French noblemen such as Lafayette's friend the duc de La Rochefoucauld took a leading part in the task of translation and in the debate to which it led. The Massachusetts constitution in particular was fiercely attacked and as fiercely defended because it was said to be too Anglophile, being based on the charter granted to the colony by William III in 1691.[21] And this charter, like the treaties cherished by Brittany and Dauphiné, safeguarded the privileges of the few rather than the rights of the many. So far from offering the French an example of a federal constitution which would unite them, as Madison and Washington hoped, America might yet show traditional vested interests in the provinces how they might divide France still further.

Interestingly enough it was a journey through Brittany that led Arthur Young to think that 'the American revolution has laid the foundation of another in France, if government does not take care of itself.' Brittany had its own Estates in which the nobility was powerfully entrenched, working closely with the Parlement in the Breton capital of Rennes. The day after Louis announced the setting up of the Plenary Court they issued a decree condemning in advance anyone serving in any court not sanctioned by the Breton constitution. Dorset sent home a copy of the decree, commenting that 'the language of the nobility is even stronger than that held by the Parliament of Paris.' He was grimly amused to hear that Rochambeau, French commander in the War of American Independence, was to be given command of the troops sent to restore order in Rennes. 'No doubt they think he is as good at putting down rebels as he is at helping them,' he remarked drily. But when Young arrived in Rennes it was the maréchal de Stainville who was camped outside the gates with four regiments of infantry and two of dragoons because of the continuing unrest. Young was amazed at the blind readiness of the populace to back the nobility: 'Why the people should love their Parliament was what I could not understand, since the members, as well as the States, are all noble, and the distinction between the *noblesse* and *roturiers* nowhere stronger, more offensive or more abominable than in Bretagne.'[22]

Young's instincts were right: the united front in Rennes was about to fall apart and very soon the Breton nobility's confrontation with an insurgent third estate would be far uglier than that with the royal government. But in Grenoble the three estates were on better terms and they resolved to follow up their opposition to the Plenary Court by pressing for the restitution of the ancient Estates of Dauphiné. Dorset was delighted to be able to tell his government on 24 July that Louis was standing firm against this demand and was sending troops under the aged maréchal de Vaux to restore the situation not just in Dauphiné but throughout the south of France:

"The high opinion entertained of the maréchal de Vaux induces people to conclude that he will soon bring the southern provinces to obedience, this experienced officer is a severe disciplinarian, one of his first steps has been to forbid the wearing of cockades, which had become universal at Grenoble, this order extends to persons of both sexes of whatever condition, and some of the lower class of women have been punished for persisting to wear cockades in defiance of it. In consequence of the maréchal de Vaux's taking upon himself so extensive a command most of the governors in those provinces avail themselves of the opportunity to leave their governments: M. de Clermont Tonnerre has, it is said, left Grenoble and M. de Camaran (governor of Provence) is already arrived at his country house in this neighbourhood.'[23]

A week later Dorset learned that 'the maréchal de Vaux could not prevent the Nobility of Dauphiny from assembling' and that they had issued a decree which was 'more dangerous to the authority of the Court than any that has appeared'. So far from southern France being cowed into submission it was now moving towards open revolt: from the head waters of the Rhine to the mouth of the Rhône, from the Mediterranean to the Atlantic, the fiercely separatist provinces of Dauphiné, Provence, Languedoc and Béarn had all declared against the King's policies. 'Nothing but an absolute promise of assembling the nation at an early period can restore tranquillity to this country,' Dorset concluded. The defiant Parlements brought the law courts of the kingdom out on strike so that Hailes, left in charge of the British embassy while Dorset went home on leave, was seriously worried by 'the immense number of offenders of all descriptions that crowd the gaols of this city'.[24] The great storm of 13 July had by now taken its toll and this ominous increase of untried criminals in the prisons of Paris reflected the desperate state into which the labouring classes had been driven as well as the disastrous divisions among those who should have been governing them.

Many thought these divisions could only be healed if the King agreed to call the Estates General. Little more than a year ago this had been a wild suggestion made by a few hotheads like Lafayette; now it seemed to be the burden of a nation's song. The Parlements led the clamour, abdicating not just their professional responsibilities but also their claim to have a representative rôle. Essentially their tactic was to declare their own incompetence. They insisted that they could no longer perform either their legal or their constitutional functions. There was a financial crisis to be faced, new taxes to be raised, and neither they nor any other court, new or old, plenary or otherwise, had the authority to sanction them. Only the whole nation assembled in the Estates General could do that. This argument was echoed by courts and constituted bodies throughout the realm and it was also in the mouths of most of those who passed for political or intellectual radicals.

Most, but not all. The marquis de Condorcet, who had made a close study of the American revolution, thought that the Estates General, like the federal constitution of the United States, would open the way to aristocratic ascendancy. Nor could he see why it should be venerated just because it was old: 'If, for several barbaric centuries, usage could make this form legitimate, why should not a century and a half of disuse, in a less barbaric age, make it legitimately extinct?' 'What is this Estates General that is being recommended to you?' wrote Malesherbes to the King. 'It is a vestige of ancient barbarism; it is a battlefield where three factions of the same people come to fight each other ... Take this old structure for what it is, a ruin.' The abbé Morellet, a friend of reformers in London and a stern critic of the British parliamentary system in its existing form, told Lord Lansdowne that the Estates General was 'the most vicious and false representation any nation ever had'. France should stick instead to the Provincial Assemblies, 'whose deputies would later become true and perfect representatives, much better than yours'.[25]

One man who thought the Estates General could be reconciled both with the present needs of France and with the past traditions of Britain was Jean-Joseph Mounier, secretary to the assembly which met at Vizille near Grenoble on 21 July. This was not just a meeting of 'the Dauphiny nobility' as Dorset imagined, but of all three estates gathered together in a single chamber and voting as a single body. The first and second estates were represented by 50 clerics and 165 noblemen respectively, while there were 276 members of the third estate.[26] In the Estates General, on the other hand, the three estates had normally had equal representation and had met separately, each taking its own decision – which had meant, of course, that the first two estates, the so-called 'privileged orders', had always been able to prevail over the third. The Vizille assembly was based on *doublement* and on *vote par tête*, the two vital changes needed to end the dominance of the privileged orders. The representation of the third estate must at least be doubled – at Vizille things were even more favourable – and decisions must be made by counting heads in a united assembly, not by counting orders in a divided one. These two requirements formed an indissoluble whole: neither was any good without the other. A doubled third estate – or a tripled or quadrupled one for that matter – would still be outvoted if voting was *par ordre*, while a third estate that was not doubled would still be swamped even if voting was *par tête*.

As well as being a model, a prototype of all that the progressives hoped for and the conservatives feared, the Vizille assembly was also a resounding success. It persuaded the government to allow Dauphiné to elect a further consultative assembly which met in September to draw up a constitution for the resurrected Estates. These met at the beginning of December and constituted themselves electors of the deputies to the Estates General before adjourning in January 1789 and leaving behind a provisional commission to deal with any further business. Mounier was in charge throughout, acting as secretary to the assembly in all its successive forms and dominating its debates with his forceful speaking and his clear vision of what needed to be done. He was now known all over France as spokesman for the Anglophiles, those who sought a limited monarchy along British lines and wanted to replace France's triple division into three estates with a simpler division into Lords and Commons. To be Anglophile was inevitably to be anti-clerical, since the intention was to strip the French clergy of its place in the nation's legislative. 'Amidst all this appearance of anarchy,' wrote Hailes, 'the clergy, who at first had presented strong remonstrances to the sovereign ... began to prove in how clear a light they saw their interests to be inseparable from that of the throne, and of consequence endangered by a national assembly.'[27]

Archbishop Loménie de Brienne, Calonne's successor as Controller-General of Finance, had so far stood firm against the demand to assemble the nation. He said he was prepared for anything, even for civil war, and he was not daunted by 'the appearance of anarchy'. What did daunt him was the prospect of bankruptcy. At the beginning of August, just as the government was agreeing to the consultative assembly in Dauphiné, a treasury official informed him that the royal coffers were now empty. Against a background of heavy falls in government securities on the Paris bourse the King consulted urgently with his ministers and decided that the time had come to give in. On 8 August a royal decree was published convoking the Estates General for 1 May 1789 and postponing the establishment of the Plenary Court until then. 'His Majesty already entertains consoling hopes,' the decree went on, 'that serene and tranquil days will follow those of storm and stress and that harmony will be restored among all the contending parties.'[28]

Unfortunately not all the contending parties viewed the calling of the Estates General in the same light. The decree itself pointed to one potential difficulty when it said that the Estates General could not meet until provincial Estates had been assembled or in some cases restored. Did this mean that it would rest on their shoulders, as Mounier and his friends in Dauphiné intended, or that provincial Estates would reject its authority just as the Assemblies of the American colonies had rejected that of the Parliament in Westminster? The Estates of Burgundy had already declared that their objective was to steer clear of France's difficulties and avoid being dragged down by her, while in Brittany there was talk of boycotting the Estates General altogether and insisting on the royal government dealing directly with the Breton Estates. The accounts from Rennes, like the accounts Washington received from Richmond in Virginia, were 'very impropitious to federal measures'. The revolution whose first rumblings Arthur Young had detected there might yet prove a closer copy of the one in America than he had anticipated.

In Paris there were ominous signs that the days of storm and stress were not over. A brief rally in government stocks soon petered out, after which the fall became even more disastrous. When Loménie de Brienne tried to shore up the finances by making payments in interest-bearing treasury bills, rather than in cash, Hailes reported that 'this operation is considered as a forced loan' and that 'a refusal to pay all taxes is talked of as likely to be the consequence of so many exertions of authority'. The price of bread in the city was rising inexorably and the resulting discontent led to demonstrations in support of the Parlements, which were still in open revolt. 'The tide of popular opinion continues to run strongly in their favour,' Hailes commented.[29]

It ran even more strongly in favour of Necker, who was credited with almost magical powers. He alone, it seemed, would restore government credit, bring down the price of bread, pacify the Parlements and hasten the convocation of the Estates General. 'This idea, that only Necker could regenerate France, was injected into the public mind by the party of the duc d'Orléans,' declared an anti-Orléanist writer.[30] There was no proof for this assertion but it was as good an explanation as any of one of the least explicable phenomena of that unruly summer. On 25 August Louis XVI bowed to the inevitable and appointed Necker as finance minister in place of Loménie de Brienne. Government stocks rose immediately and excited crowds ran through the streets of Paris proclaiming that their troubles were over. Two weeks later Necker issued a decree reimposing controls on the movement of grain and after another fortnight the King reinstated the Parlements and brought the date for the meeting of the Estates General forward from May to January. It seemed that Necker had performed all that had been expected of him.

But his magic wand was waving without much conviction. He believed in general terms that assembling the nation might regenerate France but he insisted that it was his return to power, not the prospect of an Estates General, that was the best guarantee of financial recovery. Any minister worth his salt would have taken a decision on the key issues of the time – on *doublement*, on *vote par tête*, on the relationship between national and provincial Estates, on the measures to be put before the Estates General when it met – but Necker could decide nothing. 'To give your Lordship any detail of the proceedings of government at this juncture with accuracy would prove a very difficult task,' Hailes told the Foreign Secretary, 'plans that were adopted yesterday are rejected today and there is nothing invariable but a constant change of measures and projects.' The ministry had lost the initiative and all the King could do, as one conservative remarked bitterly, was to ask his subjects: 'What is to be done? What can

I do? What powers will they deprive me of? Which will they leave me?' The answers came not from his counsellors but from hundreds of publicists and pamphleteers who rushed in to profit from the recent lifting of censorship and to fill the vacuum left by ministerial indecision. 'Every day brings forth some new publication,' wrote Hailes.[31]

At last on 5 October something was done. A royal decree was issued ordering the Assembly of Notables, a select body of prominent men first called in January 1787, to reconvene and advise the King on the forms under which the Estates General should be summoned. Paris gossip could not believe that Louis intended to take the advice of the Assembly of Notables, a mere talking-shop, and it was whispered that his real motive was to delay the calling of the Estates General or perhaps even put it off altogether. These rumours were assiduously cultivated by the Parlement of Paris, which had issued a decree ten days earlier saying the Estates General should be constituted as in 1614 and was furious to find its pronouncement snubbed. Hailes, in his last despatch home before Dorset's return from leave, produced a masterly survey of the prospect before the French and of its significance for the British:

But if so many obstacles and difficulties present themselves respecting the mere form of this meeting your Lordship will, I dare say, as well as many here who now begin to examine the measure more nearly, foresee no very favourable result of it to any party. Many years of trouble and distress appear to lie in prospect, and since it unfortunately so happens that the interests of the two countries must continue divided, and that the prosperity of the one must excite the jealousy of the other, it is a matter of great satisfaction to me to be able to congratulate your Lordship, on closing my correspondence with you here, on a situation of affairs that is so little likely to give any serious cause of disquiet to His Majesty's Government.'[32]

Only six months ago he had feared that the French might make themselves more formidable by looking outwards to the British constitution; now he was delighted to find that they were to make themselves less effectual by turning inwards to their own institutional complexities. If he appreciated the finer points of historical coincidence he might draw additional satisfaction from the fact that they were approaching their introspective intricacies just as the constitution they should have been copying was approaching its hundredth birthday. If the Notables had met on the first Monday of November as planned they would have been well launched into their discussions by the time the British centenary commemoration began on Wednesday 5 November. But their opening session was postponed for three days and so on that Wednesday morning, as the workmen in the palace of Versailles finished putting up hangings and nailing down carpets, the cooks in the London Tavern in Bishopsgate were already putting the finishing touches to the Revolution banquet. The centenary of the most famous of all revolutions had overtaken the halting preparations for the birth of its progeny. Soon it would be the progeny that would be doing the overtaking.

CHAPTER THREE

Revolution celebrated

Even though its records only went back a few years the London Revolution Society, 'consisting partly of Members of the Established Church and partly of protestant dis-senters', proclaimed that it had been founded 'soon after the Revolution'. It asserted the continuity not only of its 'revolution principles' but also of its devotion to the dissenter cause. At the centenary meeting held before the banquet the chair was taken by Earl Stanhope, close relative of the Prime Minister, and beside him sat the Foreign Secretary. Several members of the House of Commons were present, most of them at the same time radicals and government supporters. One, William Smith of Clapham Common, was soon to declare himself a dissenter even though he sat in a Parliament which was supposed to be restricted to Anglicans. The meeting decided to celebrate the Revolution's hundredth birthday by bringing two Bills into Parliament, one to remove dissenter disabilities and the other to force Anglican clergymen to commemorate the achievements of 1688 regularly from their pulpits every year. Both Bills were entrusted to Henry Beaufoy, who had been brought up a dissenter and was still their spokesman in the Commons even though he had conformed to the Church of England. Then eight hundred of the most distinguished noblemen and gentlemen in London sat down to the banquet, for which the tavern was 'elegantly illuminated'. At St Paul's Cathedral there was a service of thanksgiving attended by the Artillery Company and by several Revolution Clubs who could claim to have taken part in the events of a hundred years before.[1]

More impressive and very different in its political significance was the service in the little village church of Whittington in Derbyshire, close to the tiny inn known as the Revolution House, where the earl of Devonshire, head of the great Whig family of Cavendish, had drafted the invitation to William III a century earlier. The *Annual Register* pointed out the significance of the scene:

The descendants of the illustrious houses of Cavendish, Osborne, Booth and Darcy (for the venerable duke of Leeds, whose age would not allow him to attend, had sent his two grandsons, in whom the blood of Osborne and Darcy is united); a numerous and powerful gentry; a wealthy and respectable yeomanry; a hardy, yet decent and attentive peasantry; whose intelligent countenance shewed that they understood, and would be firm to preserve that blessing, for which they were assembled to return thanks to Almighty God, presented a truly solemn spectacle, and to the eye of a philosopher the most interesting that can be imagined.[2]

The philosopher's eye would quickly see that this was not the commemoration of a great social upheaval. Whatever else revolution may have meant to these illustrious nobles, these powerful gentlemen and respectable yeomen and attentive peasants, it clearly did not mean the putting down of the mighty from their seats. This was a congregation giving thanks for the preservation of the social order, not for its overthrow. It was not for nothing that the Cavendishes and the other great Whig political dynasties of England were called 'the Revolution families'. They had been powerful enough to defy catholic James II in 1688; lesser men must be grateful and realize that their own liberties only existed because of what the great men had done once and might be prepared to do again. The social order had made revolution possible and only its maintenance would ensure continued blessings. Whig propaganda of this sort conveniently forgot that 1688 had been a compromise between Whigs and Tories. For the Whittington worshippers that morning their Glorious Revolution, their social and constitutional holy of holies, was safe only in Whig hands.

When the service in the church was over the company went to the Revolution House to view the actual chair in which the earl of Devonshire had sat a hundred years earlier. 'Every one was then pleased to partake of a very elegant cold collation, which was prepared in the new rooms annexed to the cottage', after which they formed ranks to march in procession to the nearby town of Chesterfield. The great cavalcade was led by eight separate Revolution Clubs, over two thousand persons in all, with flags flying and banners waving. Then came the Derbyshire county militia, with its band playing suitably patriotic airs, and over forty carriages bearing local noblemen and their ladies. They were followed by four hundred gentlemen on horseback and more than a thousand humbler folk on foot. In the evening there were fireworks and a grand ball. A hogshead of ale was given to the populace at Whittington and three hogsheads at Chesterfield, while the duke of Devonshire gave three guineas to each of the eight Revolution Clubs.[3]

The fifth duke of Devonshire, head of the house of Cavendish and a direct descendant of the revolutionary earl whose chair had been so venerated, was thirty-nine years of age. He ruled Derbyshire from his palatial home at Chatsworth, a few miles to the west of Chesterfield, and he had another residence at Hardwick Hall on the other side of the town. It was entirely natural that he should be at the centre of the Whittington and Chesterfield spectacle but in national politics he was of less account. The duchess, Dorset's friend and correspondent, was a leader of fashion and had made Devonshire House a focal point of the London season but the duke himself was somewhat overshadowed by his distinguished uncle Lord John Cavendish, Chancellor of the Exchequer for a few brief months in 1783, and by the duke of Portland, who had been Prime Minister at that time and was Devonshire's brother-in-law. And even they had now been in opposition for five years without making much headway. It was beginning to look as if Devonshire's devotion to inherited revolution principles would never be demonstrated by anything more dramatic than riding in processions and handing out largesse.

In any case the great British political crisis of 1783, as a result of which Portland's ministry had fallen, had made many people wonder just what these famous principles really were. By means of consummate wheeling and dealing Portland and his lieutenant in the House of Commons, Charles James Fox, had pieced together a coalition of great men with a parliamentary following large enough to dominate the Commons and force out of office the King's chosen Prime Minister the marquis of Lansdowne.* George

*In fact in 1783 he was still earl of Shelburne, only becoming marquis of Lansdowne in the following year. But here, as elsewhere, I have tried to avoid giving two names to the same person.

III had been furious with Lansdowne for deserting him and even more furious with the Portland gang for pushing its way into office against his wishes. He had taken the first opportunity to dismiss them, even though they still had a Commons majority, by getting their measures defeated in the Lords. They declared indignantly that their dismissal was unconstitutional because they controlled the Commons; their successor William Pitt insisted that it was the right and proper way to restore the balance of a constitution threatened by oligarchic domination of a corrupt and unrepresentative House of Commons. He described the King's prerogative of appointment and dismissal of ministers as an essential defence for the people against an overmighty House of Commons and it seemed that the people were inclined to agree: the King received well over two hundred loyal addresses thanking him for taking a stand against the forces of faction. Orthodox exponents of the Glorious Revolution did their best, proclaiming that 'a misguided people had been taught to desert their natural guardians and fly for protection to the crown',[4] but it was clear that the constitution of 1688 no longer belonged to the Revolution families in spite of the ecstasies in Whittington church.

The French had been shocked by the 1783 crisis and one English visitor to Paris reported that 'sensible thinking people here all concur in wishing this Mr Fox at the devil, as he seems to them always embroiling matters without advantage to the kingdom or to himself'. Lady Clermont, whose husband was a close friend of Fox's patron the Prince of Wales, wrote to say that Marie Antoinette and the French Court seemed obsessed by events in London. 'They are all sure there will be a revolution and that Fox will be King,' she continued, 'it was quite ridiculous the questions the duc d'Orléans asked about the English Parliaments'.[5] Most Frenchmen would not have deigned to ask questions at all, being convinced that Parliament was an unrepresentative and corrupt mockery. The House of Commons was elected by a tiny minority of George III's subjects and even those who did have the vote were only concerned to use it to put in men who would pass a share of the spoils of office down to them. Patronage and corruption, the unseemly scramble for appointments and pensions and other royal favours, made a nonsense of limited monarchy. It put into the King's hands a key with which to open the door that was supposed to have been slammed in his face in 1688.

Many commentators, British as well as French, saw this state of affairs as some kind of distortion or debasement of the constitution, a foul accretion of greed and venality which had overlaid its pristine purity. They were much mistaken. By accepting that sovereignty lay with King in Parliament the men of 1688 had brushed aside the question of what was to happen if King and Parliament differed. The King had sworn to govern according to statutes in Parliament agreed and so if his policies were to go forward, if his measures were to become law, he had to have a following in the two Houses. Whatever men might think of the patronage structure it was the only available means of achieving this, the only possible way of cementing a union between the two parts of the sovereign body. Without patronage and corruption there would have been no government. The constitution did not require the King to choose ministers who had existing majorities and he did not need to do so because he was normally able to provide any minister he chose with a suitably subservient Parliament. And so in 1784 Pitt had won a triumphant election victory, just as every government in office had won every general election it had fought since the Glorious Revolution. It was the electors who respected the wishes of the King in eighteenth-century British politics, not the other way about.

This had made it easy for foreign critics to dismiss the British constitution as a sham, an elegant facade masking an unsavoury reality, but it had not always been easy to decide what sort of a sham it was. Sometimes it had looked like royal despotism working through a weak and corrupt nobility, sometimes like aristocratic oligarchy making use of an enfeebled monarchy. The Whigs who had been excluded since 1783 alleged that it was degenerating into the first – hence the eagerness of the great families to reassert their revolutionary principles on that first Wednesday in November – while the Pittites who had excluded them claimed to have saved it from becoming the second. Dr Milne, chosen to preach the Revolution sermon in St Margaret's at Westminster, used the occasion to attack the Whig opposition as 'Pseudo-Patriots' and to insist that revolutionary principles meant that the King was the essential pillar of the constitution. 'If you loosen this pillar, nay if you violently shake it, the annals of our country too lamentably evince that a demolition of the fabric will be the certain consequence. All is then anarchy and wild commotion.'[6]

Within hours of the words being spoken it seemed that God himself was doing the shaking and that anarchy and wild commotion could not be long delayed. 'At the jubilee for the centenary of the Revolution we were at Chesterfield,' wrote the duchess of Devonshire, 'and we heard the first reports of the King's insanity.' The public was still kept in ignorance but for those in the know there was confirmation of earlier rumours: George III's mental illness was now so serious that he was incapable of ruling. At Windsor, where the King was in residence, it was a day of anxious dread – one lady of the Court recorded 'horror on every face I met' – but for the Revolution families the prospect was exciting and even exhilarating. At last the tabernacle of revolution might be about to pass back into their keeping. Urgent letters arrived at Chatsworth from the duke of Portland in London, asking the Devonshires to come to town, and soon the duchess was writing excitedly in her diary about the new ministry which the Prince of Wales would appoint as soon as he became Regent. It would be made up, needless to say, of Cavendishes and other Revolution families.[7]

Meanwhile Dorset, now back at his post in Paris, was assuring his government that Louis XVI and Marie Antoinette felt 'a very sincere anxiety' about George III's illness. But no amount of polite sympathy could disguise the fact that the tables had been turned. Instead of conducting their deliberations in the shade of a British constitution from which they might be expected to learn the Notables saw only a neighbour reduced to constitutional chaos. 'Parliament cannot proceed to business without the session being opened by the King or by some commission authorized by him,' admitted a colleague of Pitt on 8 November, 'and no Regent can be appointed but by Act of Parliament.'[8] Neither branch of the constitution could move without the other. Nor did difficulties end there. When opposition politicians said the Prince was Regent by hereditary right, whatever Parliament might or might not do, nobody knew whether they were right. The constitution of 1688, so recently and so publicly celebrated, had nothing to offer on either point. The vacuum which ministerial indecision had produced in Paris dwindled beside the void which Geroge III's incapacity threatened to produce in London. Perhaps most ironic was the changed attitude to the past. For months the British, secure in the knowledge that for them all constitutional wisdom began only a century ago, had looked on in pity as lawyers and archivists throughout France searched through ancient records in an attempt to establish the forms under which different Estates

General had met. Now constitutional experts in London had to embark on a similar voyage of antiquarian discovery.

In both cases the mediaeval wisdom which was turned up brought forth scorn from those who considered themselves progressives. Just as Condorcet had spurned the Estates General as the product of 'several barbaric centuries', so when Pitt outlined what had been done in 1454, at the time of Henry VI's insanity, Fox angrily refused to consider 'precedents drawn from so dark and barbarous a period of our history'.[9] But whereas for Fox the darkness of the remote past only served to make the effulgence of 1688 still brighter, Condorcet wanted to consign most of human history to oblivion. For him the enactments of the past were mere distillations of ignorance: modern rational man should be able to cast them aside as an author tears up his earlier drafts once his final manuscript is complete. Nations must base their constitutions not on what had been done but on what ought to be done, on immutable natural laws revealed by the philosophers of the new-born age of reason. Although these philosophers had been widely read in Britain as well as in France there were few people in either country who wanted to live within a constitutional framework constructed according to their designs. But such frameworks did supposedly exist, or at any rate would soon exist, in America. In the home of the Declaration of Independence, where political institutions were based on self-evident truths and unalienable rights, it should be possible to find a government painting rational signposts to the future instead of carving contentious pathways back into the past.

Unfortunately no central government of any kind, rational or otherwise, was yet to be found in America. And so on that first Wednesday in November, as London celebrated one revolution and Paris prepared for another, the French ambassador to the United States, the comte de Moustier, was to be found not in New York but at Mount Vernon in Virginia, where he was visiting George Washington. Moustier had arrived in New York some months earlier and had succeeded in infuriating many of its citizens. 'If France had wished to destroy the little remembrance that is left of her and her exertions,' wrote John Armstrong to Horatio Gates, 'she would have sent just such a minister – distant, haughty and penurious – and entirely governed by the the caprice of a little, singular, whimsical, hysterical old woman whose delight is in playing with a negro child and caressing a monkey.'[10] The little old woman was Moustier's sister-in-law the marquise de Bréhan, who travelled with him and managed to give even more offence than he did. 'Some ladies have thought she rather undervalued them,' wrote one observer tartly, 'when she appeared in a considerable company with a three-cornered muslin handkerchief tied round her head, nearly in the fashion of the negro women'.[11]

Mme de Bréhan could not understand why her attempts at 'plainness of dress and simplicity of manners' should be so resented. Like many fashionable Frenchwomen she had filled her head with romantic nonsense about the pastoral idyll of American life and she had come to the United States determined to live it out. 'She is furiously displeased with America,' said Jefferson. 'Her love of simplicity and her wish to find it had made her fancy she was going to Arcadia, in spite of all my warnings to the contrary.' From New York she wrote him a reproachful letter, which Moustier also signed, complaining of the 'formalities, pretensions and foppery, remains of English rust' which prevailed there. With the old Congress disbanded and the next one not yet arrived Moustier found the city very depressing. He was impatient to meet the new congressmen and he wrote rather wistfully that he hoped at least some of them would be prepared to accept him. He was also very anxious about the new-born United States government and he was certain it could not survive unless George Washington became President. 'He must be the keystone of the arch of your federal edifice,' he told Jefferson.[12]

So he and his sister-in-law had turned their backs on the political vacuum of New York and made their way to the home of the prospective keystone. It was a beautiful day, calm and warm, and Washington took his visitors for a seven-mile walk round his plantations to watch the slaves at work. 'Everything there is enchanting,' recorded Mme de Bréhan. She found a rural paradise cultivated by slaves preferable to the urban foppery of New York. Indeed, she had already shocked New Yorkers by buying a negro girl and then shopping round for a boy 'in order that they may breed'.[13] Brissot visited Mount Vernon ten days later and was rather more worried by it because he was a founder member of the Paris anti-slavery society. He admitted that his host owned 'large numbers of negro slaves' but added that 'They are, however, most humanely treated. Well fed, well clothed and required to do only a moderate amount of work, they continually bless the master God gave them.' He also convinced himself that Washington and other Virginia plantation owners wanted to give up growing tobacco, because it needed slave labour, and turn instead to the potato, a crop which Brissot invested with an almost mystic significance: 'The potato is a food admirably suited to the man who seeks liberty and knows how to be free. It grows everywhere and is both easily raised and easily prepared as food. The more such chores can be eliminated, the less is the need for money and work to satisfy private wants and the greater the time that can be devoted to public service.'[14]

Within hours of Brissot's departure Washington was putting on paper, in a letter to James Madison in New York, the fears he had about Virginia's future. They centred not on the potato but on the politics of the state Assembly. 'The whole proceedings of the Assembly it is said may be summed up in one word,' he told Madison anxiously, 'to wit that the edicts of Mr Patrick Henry are enregistered with less opposition by the majority than those of the Grand Monarch are in the Parliaments of France.' Patrick Henry was a man of strong and even violent convictions – he was said to have predicted 'rivulets of blood throughout the land' if those he disliked were elected to the Senate – and the measures Washington described as his edicts were for the most part directed against the new United States constitution, of which he said: 'Among other deformities it squinted towards monarchy.... If your American chief be a man of ambitions and abilities, how easy is it for him to render himself absolute!'[15] He wanted Virginia to take the lead in a nationwide anti-federalist campaign to get the constitution radically amended or perhaps jettisoned altogether.

Patrick Henry was so successful that in the middle of November George Turberville, another of Madison's informants in Virginia, concluded that 'the triumph of anti-federalism is complete'.[16] In several states, including both New York and Virginia, assemblies were making endless and perhaps deliberate difficulties over choosing the congressmen and presidential electors without whom the constitution could not come into force. And New York, where the new governing machinery would have to be forged and put together, was a city torn apart by ferocious party conflicts. In addition to the British sympathies Benjamin Rush and William Maclay claimed to detect,* New Yorkers also seemed to have a thoroughly British capacity for factious and divisive politics. By

*See above, p.12.

the beginning of December Washington, who thought the anti-federalists would 'throw everything into confusion', was professing his extreme reluctance to 'go from home in a public character again'. 'At present I see nothing but clouds and darkness before me,' he added.[17]

As the year drew to its close his uncertainties about what would happen in New York and what part he might have to play there became more acute. One moment he was looking forward to 'the prospect that a good general government will in all human probability be soon established in America', the next he was lamenting that 'the future is all a scene of darkness and uncertainty to me ... nothing but a conviction of the indispensable necessity of the measure can ever induce me to make the sacrifice.' Few now doubted that he would be elected first President of the United States and on all sides he was told that his acceptance was essential for the survival of sound revolutionary principles, not only in the United States but throughout the world. He took pride in the fact that the United States was the inspiration of other countries – 'The American revolution, or the peculiar light of the age,' he claimed, 'seems to have opened the eyes of almost every nation in Europe and a spirit of equal liberty appears fast to be gaining ground everywhere' – and he saw it as his duty to ensure that this inspiration was not marred by the confusion and possible breakdown threatened by the separatists.[18]

He had still not got over the shock of being accused of marring it himself. 'We have been virulently traduced,' he wrote indignantly on 7 September, 'for not discouraging an establishment calculated to create distinctions in society and subvert the principles of a republican government.' The establishment in question was the Order of the Cincinnati, a league of French and American officers which Washington had helped to found. Because of its insignia and rituals, above all because it intended to allow membership to pass from father to son, the Order was attacked on both sides of the Atlantic as an attempt to export the aristocratic principle from France to America. 'Tell us about the Society of the Cincinnati, which is a real cause for concern to political philosophers,' Clavière urged Brissot when he set off for the United States. Brissot found one major-general who 'bears no love for the American Cincinnati; he thinks their eagle is a gewgaw fit only for children to play with,' but another major-general, the baron de Steuben, militia commandant in New York, was happy to be elected President of the Cincinnati there and to lead it in a string of toasts to the monarchs of Europe and to 'the Companions of our Order in France and America'.[19]

There were many Americans who had no interest either in importing monarchy and aristocracy or in exporting republican and democratic notions. 'Consider that we live three thousand miles from the nations of Europe,' Benjamin Rush told a friend who was starting a newspaper, 'and that we have but little interest in their domestic parties or national quarrels. The less therefore you publish of them the better.' There were also those who saw all the nations of Europe, and France in particular, as a threat. 'I wish to God we had paid our debts to our good ally and were well rid of her,' wrote John Armstrong, 'for there's some danger in remaining the connection of a power whose character it is to destroy her friends, not her enemies ... 'tis obviously our interest to be but the distant acquaintance, not the intimate friend, of any European power.' The *New York Journal*, commenting in a leading article on 'the extreme proneness of nations to make war on each other', saw both the British and the French as propagators of fruitless conflicts from which America must at all costs stand aloof. Idealism and political philosophy might preach involvement, either to bring the American revolution to completion or to bring the French revolution to birth, but common sense was more cautious and more isolationist.[20]

Not all Americans saw events in France as heralding some great change: some regarded them as an end rather than a beginning. 'I hope the late troubles in France are nearly over,' Benjamin Franklin told Morellet on 10 December 'it is a country I dearly love and in whose prosperity I feel myself deeply interested.' Three weeks later a Massachusetts newspaper gave its readers an account of 'the late French Revolution'. Even Jefferson in Paris thought, as late as July, that the struggle between the monarchy and the Parlements could only result in things getting worse rather than better. 'The danger is that the people, deceived by a false cry of liberty, may be led to take side with one party and thus give the other a pretext for crushing them still more.' By November he was more cheerful, predicting that the Estates General would become a permanent part of the constitution, with the right to grant taxes and initiate laws, though he still thought the form the Notables were proposing to give it 'augurs ill to the rights of the people'.[21]

Furthermore Jefferson was not at all sure that the French were capable of living in a free country. 'The misfortune is,' he told Madison, 'that they are not yet ripe for receiving the blessings to which they are entitled.' John Adams, soon to be elected Vice President of the United States, had said much the same thing in his *Defense of the Constitutions of the United States*, a comparative study of European and American political systems which gave great offence in France by praising the British constitution as 'a stupendous fabric of human invention' and dismissing the idea that the French could ever produce anything as good. 'It was impossible to meet Mr Adams, who is so familiar with European constitutions,' wrote Brissot bitterly, 'without discussing with him the one which seems to be being prepared in France. I do not know whether he does not have a high opinion of our character, or of our stability, or of our enlightenment; in any case, he does not believe that this new constitution can establish in our country a liberty comparable to that enjoyed by the English.' In late November Brissot heard the news of the convocation of the Estates General and decided to play his part in the preparing of the constitution and the establishing of liberty. He hurried back to New York and sailed for France on 3 December.[22]

In Paris it was becoming clear that the Notables would advise the King against doubling the third estate. When at the opening session the Paris Parlement repeated its demand for the forms of 1614 it provoked a fierce reaction from those Parisian journalists and would-be politicians who were beginning to call themselves the Patriot party. There was a flood of angry pamphlets denouncing the so-called 'privileged orders' and calling for the doubling of the third estate and its merger with the other two. 'A general dissatisfaction prevails among the Tiers Etat in consequence of the resolution respecting them which they foresee is likely to be passed in the Assembly of Notables,' Dorset reported, 'many provinces, and particularly Normandy, refuse to send delegates upon those terms'. 'I have reason to think M. Necker begins to repent his having so hastily decided upon the measure of assembling the Notables,' he continued, 'finding that he would have done better if he had adopted the ideas of the Parliament'. Dorset was shocked to the depths of his aristocratic Whig soul at the idea of a government minister pandering to the third estate and encouraging what he called 'unpleasant discussions' about its increasingly insolent demands.[23]

The third estate's representatives in the Notables pointed out that if numbers were taken into account it would be entitled to more than ten times as many members as the other two orders put together. On the basis of its contribution to taxes it could claim that its representation should be quadrupled rather than merely doubled. But the Notables were divided into committees, each under the chairmanship of a royal prince, and in each of these the commoners were outnumbered by the clergy and nobility. Dorset heard that the committee headed by the comte de Provence, the elder of the King's two brothers, had voted narrowly for *doublement*, Provence himself giving the casting vote, but he could not believe that either the Notables as a whole or the government would follow suit. 'It is a wise measure of administration to keep the nobles attached to the sovereign,' he reflected, 'they are the natural or at least the near supporters of the crown.'[24] He was right about the Notables but wrong about the government. After Louis had been advised against *doublement* both by the Notables and by the majority of the royal princes he called a meeting of the Royal Council which debated the matter for several days and finally decided, on 27 December, that the forthcoming Estates General would consist of at least one thousand members, the number of deputies for the third estate being equal to those for the other two orders put together. The decision, together with Necker's report on it, was published in Paris on New Year's Day.

The story went round that when the King returned to his private apartments after the Council meeting he found that the portrait of his grandfather which normally hung there had been replaced by a painting of King Charles I of England, whose fate had long fascinated and horrified him. After gazing at the picture for some minutes he remarked that he understood perfectly well what was being said to him but that nevertheless the decision was irrevocable. Marie Antoinette, who was said to have boasted that she was 'Queen of the Third', took the exceptional step of attending the Council meeting. Although she remained silent most of those present concluded she was in favour of *doublement*.[25] Two months earlier and three thousand miles away in New York James Madison had said that the French monarchy would soon be 'endeavouring to counteract the aristocratic policy by admitting the people to a greater share of representation'.[26] Now those endeavours were open and avowed. It might be a bad joke to suggest that Louis XVI was imitating Charles I but he certainly seemed set on a more dangerous kind of revolution than the one his nobles and his Parlements had envisaged when they had pressed for the restoration of their ancient rights and liberties.

On the other hand it could be argued that *doublement* pointed to a far more respectable sort of revolution, one which would preserve the balance of the constitution just as George III had preserved it five years earlier by making a stand against the Portland Whigs. In practical political terms an Estates General without a doubled third estate would be a single force dominated by the privileged orders, even though it might sit in three separate chambers. But one with a doubled third estate would have five hundred commoners to balance out five hundred members of the privileged orders, even though the latter might sit in two separate chambers. George III had used the Lords in order to bring down an oligarchy which controlled the Commons, but it was conceivable that things might have been the other way round. The important thing was to ensure a balanced legislative and in France's case this could only be done by 'admitting the people to a greater share of representation'. George III had no intentions of this kind but the man who made his victory possible certainly had: Pitt had supported parliamentary reform from the moment he entered politics so that in 1783, when his opponents said he did not have the confidence of the Commons, he was able to retort that the Commons did not have the confidence of the country.

But now the rôles were reversed. When George III fell ill Pitt needed Parliament desperately, however unrepresentative he might consider it, because it was his only shield against an immediate and unrestricted regency. Conversely the theory of divine hereditary right was the only shield for the Portland Whigs against the possibility that Parliament might delay or limit the Prince's power to bring them back into office. On the day the Notables began their deliberations the Prince took charge at Windsor Castle and summoned Lord Thurlow, who was Lord Chancellor and the highest legal officer in the kingdom. Thurlow was determined to stay in office whatever happened and so he began to play a double game, assuring both the Prince and Pitt that they had the law on their side. Lesser men also felt the need to face both ways. 'If the King dies I lose a good friend, but I am in hopes I may still be employed by his successor,' the banker Thomas Coutts wrote to the duchess of Devonshire from Paris. 'I should wish much Your Grace would speak to the Prince in case the melancholy event proves true.' After a week of uncertainty Pitt decided to play the parliamentary card and bring in a Regency Bill. He was by no means assured of success: six months earlier his party in the Commons had been reckoned at fifty-two, of whom 'were there a new Parliament, and Mr Pitt no longer Minister, not above twenty would be returned.' A fortnight later the *Morning Post* listed the members of the new administration which would shortly replace him.[27]

When Parliament met at the beginning of December there was talk of the Prince dissolving it in the hope that Pitt's majority would be slashed when the voters realized that patronage was no longer in his hands. But the mood of the country was to prove more important than the calculations of party managers or the intentions of venal electors. The merchants and financiers of London led a campaign of support for Pitt and *The Times* hailed him as 'a minister who deserves so well the thanks and reward of the nation at large'. Five of the King's doctors were called before the Privy Council and four of them said that he would recover. The fifth, Dr Warren, was politically committed to the duke of Portland. The Whig leaders insisted that the King was a dangerous lunatic – the duchess of Devonshire told how he pushed a candle into the Queen's face and tore his attendants 'almost to pieces' – and when he was put in the care of Dr Willis, 'a clergyman who is used to the care of madmen and treats them with kindness, even keeping a pack of hounds for them and allowing them to hunt and shoot', they shook their heads over such rash indulgences. But Dr Willis's reports on his patient were 'full of promise and hope', so that by the time the crucial debate began in the Commons on 10 December there seemed every chance that the King would recover.[28]

Whig hopes in the debate were pinned on Charles James Fox, who had been urgently recalled from an Italian holiday because of the crisis. He arrived in London on 24 November, 'his body emaciated, his countenance sallow and sickly, his eyes swollen', and was too ill to attend the conference at which the Whig lords discussed their tactics. In the Commons, when Pitt moved that the House appoint a committee to find out what had been done on such occasions in the past, Fox retorted that there was no need to look for precedents because 'the Prince of Wales had as clear, as express a right to assume the reins of government, and exercise the power of sovereignty during the continuance of the illness and incapacity with which it had pleased God to afflict His Majesty, as in the case of His Majesty's having a perfect and natural demise.' Later in the debate he alleged that to appoint a Regent by Act of Parliament would be to overthrow the balanced constitution of 1688 and replace it with an elective monarchy.[29]

Fox seemed to be preaching Tory legitimism rather than the orthodox Whig doctrine of the supremacy of Parliament which he had asserted so vigorously in the 1783 crisis. Pitt accused him of 'treason to the constitution' and Henry Beaufoy, warming up for his campaign in honour of the Glorious Revolution, charged him with slandering that great event and reducing it to 'a profligate act of deliberate robbery and consummate injustice', since the legitimate successor at the time had not been William but Mary.[30] *The Times* deplored the violence of the debate and one of Pitt's supporters said later that it ushered in 'a period, comprising more than two months, of greater agitation, violence and mutual animosity than any other that I have witnessed in my time.' There was general agreement that the Whigs had overplayed their hand and the debate ended in victory for Pitt in both Houses. The *St James's Chronicle* told the Prince of Wales sternly that 'he has seen a very singular Phenomenon, a Man who was deemed a falling Minister supported by a decided Majority in Parliament. He must necessarily conclude that no regal Power can possibly support an Administration in Opposition to that Majority.' Addresses of thanks were showered upon the Prime Minister: one paper listed fifty four, including one drawn up at the London Tavern in Bishopsgate where the Revolution banquet had been held. It seemed that Pitt had saved the constitution in the nick of time so that it could move triumphantly into its centenary year.[31]

In Whig eyes he had done nothing of the kind. Edmund Burke, reputedly the party's constitutional expert, declared that by questioning the Prince's hereditary right Pitt had emerged as a dangerous usurper who wanted the regency for himself, 'one of the Prince's competitiors'. All such questioning was unwarranted because the makers of the Revolution had provided for everything. 'Our constitution was framed with so much circumspection and forethought that it wisely provided for every possible exigency,' Burke proclaimed.[32] This was nonsense: the men of 1688 had certainly not indicated what should be done if the King went mad.

They had simply stated that William III and Mary were joint sovereigns and they had then listed the ancient and undoubted rights of Englishmen. And those rights were undoubted because they were ancient, not just because they had been reasserted. In some cases they were even more ancient than those mediaeval precedents which the Whigs now rejected as dark and barbarous. For Burke 1688 was the only possible constitutional starting point, the beginning and end of all wisdom – 'Then comes the Revolution,' he cried, 'a memorable period in the history of this kingdom – full of light – full of instruction – never to be blotted out of the memory of mankind'[33] – but if this was so it was difficult to see how 1688 could at the same time be hailed as a revolution not made but prevented, an assertion of ancient rights against the innovative tyrannies of James II. If nothing before 1688 was worth considering what was it that 1688 had restored?

There was worse to come. In February 1789 the Irish Parliament met in Dublin and accepted the Whig doctrine of the Prince's hereditary right. 'We beg leave humbly to request,' it asked in a formal address to him, 'that Your Royal Highness will be pleased to take upon you the government of this realm under the style and title of Prince Regent of Ireland.'[34] By that time Pitt's Regency Bill had been passed by the Commons at Westminster and was going through the Lords. Under its terms the Prince was appointed Regent in Britain by the authority of Parliament, which placed important restrictions on his powers. The constitution of 1688 had become the plaything of factious politicians and while the interpretation of one faction had triumphed in Britain the totally different view of the other had won the day in Ireland. As well as being unable to decide between hereditary and elective monarchy, as well as having the two faces of a fresh starting point and a restoration of ancient liberties, the Glorious Revolution was now unable to disguise the fact that it had been exported to a reluctant Ireland and had suffered further schizophrenia as a result. And all this just as it reached its hundredth birthday, just as it was being held out as a model for supposedly eager Frenchmen to copy.

The Times was undismayed. 'Mr Pitt is to Great Britain what the celebrated financier Mr Necker is to France, but while Mr Pitt has the favour of a free and spirited people, Mr Necker is the only hope of salvation in a distracted nation galled by the iron fetters of despotism,' it declared on New Year's Day, as Pitt gave the

Prince details of the regency limitations and as Necker gave the French details of the Estates General. 'Should the liberty of the press be established in France,' it added next day, 'no fresh taxes levied but by the consent of the States of the kingdom, and the Monarch restrained from issuing *lettres de cachet*, the French would only want trial by jury to enjoy all the advantages of the British constitution.' It was also convinced that the British crisis was the chief concern not just of the French but of all other nations: 'The important question that engages the attention of all Europe is whether a King universally allowed to be one of the best that ever swayed the sceptre should be dethroned by a set of abandoned, desperate men.'[35]

The thing that did engage the attention of all Europe that January was the weather, which was ferociously cold. In London the Thames was frozen and a group of enterprising thieves broke the ice by the steps down to the river and then put planks across, charging people a penny to cross them. The planks were deliberately made slippery so those using them could fall in and be charged to be rescued, as well as having their pockets picked at the same time. 'Hundreds were robbed, but what is worse, above ten people have actually lost their lives.' The Prince of Wales gave the city authorities £1000 for the relief of the poor and in Paris the duc d'Orléans arranged daily distributions of bread as well as giving firewood, broth and meat to women in childbirth. 'The great distress of the poor during the uncommon inclemency of the weather excited the attention and compassionate relief of many,' reported Dorset, 'but Their Serene Highnesses the Duke and Duchess of Orleans have, far beyond all others, eminently distinguished themselves'. This ostentatious display of charity was soon to be portrayed by Orléans's enemies as the first stage in his campaign to win popularity in Paris and make political use of discontent and possible insurrections there.[36]

It was now certain that Parliament would make the Prince of Wales Regent in a matter of weeks but it was by no means certain who would be his ministers. The *St James's Chronicle*, as well as telling the Prince that he could not govern without Pitt, also adjured Pitt to stand firm against any invitation to join the Prince's men: 'Be this then your great political commandment – Thou shalt not coalesce!' There was in any case no sign that such an invitation would be forthcoming, for Fox was pressing on steadily with arrangements for a Whig administration, even

though he was still a sick man. 'Mr Fox's complaint is a sup-
puration in the neck of the bladder, for which his friends are much
alarmed,' reported a government newspaper blandly.[37]

When the Regency Bill came before Parliament in February
Burke attacked the proposed limitations on the ground that there
was no prospect of George III ever ruling again. 'They were
talking of a sick King, of a monarch smitten by the hand of
omnipotence,' he warned, 'the Almighty had hurled him from his
throne and plunged him into a condition which drew upon him
the pity of the meanest peasant in his kingdom.' Two days later
he talked darkly of lunatics who had apparently been cured and
who had then 'butchered their sons, done violence to themselves
by hanging, shooting, drowning, throwing themselves out of
windows, and by a variety of other ways,'[38] The Whigs were now
confident that they would be in office within a few days and letters
dismissing Pitt and his colleagues had already been prepared when
it became known on 19 February that George III was in a state
of convalescence. Eight days later, as delegates from the Dublin
Parliament presented the Prince with their address asking him to
be Regent, it was officially announced that the King was fully
recovered and no further bulletins on his health would be issued.

A quarter of a century later Sir Nathaniel Wraxall declared
that 1789 was 'one of the most important years that took place
in the eighteenth century. First, as in it we witnessed His Majesty's
happy recovery.... Secondly, as having originated, a few months
later, the calamity of the French revolution.' The order in which
he placed the two events may cause surprise now but it caused
none then. For years to come the British would look back on the
period of George III's illness as one of the most critical and
dangerous they had known. It seemed to threaten not merely
danger at home – constitutional and political breakdown, perhaps
even civil war – but also danger from abroad. 'With little better
than anarchy during the present calamitous situation of a good
and watchful sovereign, and with little less than civil discord,'
wrote *The Times* in the middle of January, 'is it not reasonable to
suppose that our insidious neighbour is not regardless of the
advantage she might take?'[39]

The British embassy in Paris had long been worried because
'Madame de Champaretz, a Dutch woman of intriguing spirit,
receives in her house all the refugees of the Patriot party'. Dutch
revolutionaries, previously supported by France until crushed

by Anglo-Prussian intervention, were trying to get the French government to challenge the Triple alliance of Great Britain, Prussia and the Dutch Republic which had driven them into exile. In November 1788 Prince Henry, brother of the King of Prussia, visited Paris. He was known to be an opponent of the alliance with Britain and so British suspicions were immediately aroused when special arrangements were made for him to observe the deliberations of the Notables. 'A gallery is erected purposely for him and his suite,' Dorset reported, 'but no other foreigners were to be allowed to be present.'[40]

Now, a fortnight after *The Times* voiced its fears, Dorset told his government that 'every advantage will be taken of Prince Henry's present residence in this capital to endeavour to weaken our alliance with the Court of Berlin.' At first even *The Times* thought that French attempts to take advantage of Britain's 'calamitous situation' would be limited to diplomatic initiatives – in mid-February, writing gloomily about tensions which 'threatened to throw all Europe into a conflagration', it assured its readers that France could take no active military part because of her financial problems – but on 26 February, the day before the King's recovery was announced, it claimed to have irrefutable evidence that the French were about to march into the Austrian Netherlands on their way to invade the Dutch Republic. One army would advance on Brussels, where arrangements had already been made to receive it, while another would make for the Channel coast and take Ostend and Nieuport. Nobody would believe in these invading forces until they were actually on the move, it concluded somewhat irritably, but 'certain however it is that quarters are preparing for their reception.'[41]

On the same day and on the same page, as if to demonstrate the impartiality of its chauvinism, *The Times* gloated over the fact that 'the states of North America are said to be yet unsettled in regard to their form of constitution'. Jefferson in Paris knew full well that continuing constitutional wrangles in New York could weaken the United States and so he hoped fervently that those in London would also continue and perhaps get worse. 'For the peace of Europe,' he wrote, 'it is best that the King should give such gleanings of recovery as would prevent the Regent or his ministers from thinking themselves firm, and yet that he should not recover.'[42] Meanwhile Paris was full of stories of conspirators suborned by British gold, of food shortages deliberately created by speculators holding French grain in British and American ports. Each of the three nations seemed to have a boundless capacity for maligning the other two and wishing them ill. Against this background of distrust and suspicion a few idealists set out to make 1789 a year of international co-operation and bring together the differing revolutionary aspirations of Paris and London and New York.

CHAPTER FOUR

The wider hope

'I am very glad to hear that you intend taking up the cause of the people in France,' wrote Lansdowne to Jeremy Bentham on 3 January 1789. 'Nothing can contribute so much to general humanity and civilization as for individuals of one country to be interested for the prosperity of another; I have long thought that the people throughout the world have the same interest – it is governments that have different ones.'[1] Bentham's efforts on behalf of the French people so far consisted of a pamphlet against the Paris Parlement for trying to revive the forms of 1614 and an attack on the Breton nobility for its reactionary demands. He had not succeeded in getting either of them published. Now he was busy with a work on political tactics which he hoped would enable the third estate to give France a permanent national assembly. His ultimate aim was much wider. Perhaps the most ambitious thinker of his time, he had taken up a phrase of Priestley's about 'the greatest happiness of the greatest number' and was determined to make it 'the foundation of morals and legislation'. He saw himself as the Newton of the moral world: just as Newton had discovered the laws which governed the physical universe so he would lay bare those which governed the behaviour of societies and the organization of political systems.

Lansdowne was the friend and patron of Bentham and of many other radical thinkers. Grandiose theories circulated freely both at Lansdowne House in London and also at Bowood, his country home in Wiltshire. In the House of Lords at the end of December he had swept aside the arguments for and against the Regency

Bill and declared that kings and princes had no rights while those of the people were 'born with every man in every country and exist in all countries alike, the despotic as well as free, though they may not be equally easy to be recovered in all. Kings have at times different interests and great calamities have followed on their differences; but the People can have but one interest throughout the world'.[2] If Bentham could help the French discover and proclaim that interest it might revolutionize British policy as well as French, foreign policy as well as domestic. It might also restore the fortunes of Lansdowne himself, the most cosmopolitan as well as the most progressive of Britain's leading political figures. Tom Paine, the radical English publicist whose pamphlet *Common Sense* had helped to bring about the American revolution, told Washington in March 1789 that Lansdowne still hoped for a reunion of Britain and the United States and that he would also be 'a good minister for England, with respect to a better agreement with France.' On this last point Paine was echoing Vergennes, who had always said that Lansdowne was the only British minister he could work with, the only one who shared his vision of international co-operation.[3] Lansdowne had tried to lay the economic foundations for a reunion of Britain and America when he was in office in 1783, only to have his work undone by the Portland Whigs when they defeated him.

Now the Whigs themselves were not merely defeated but discredited. By asserting the Prince's hereditary right over that of Parliament they had made nonsense of their alleged revolutionary principles and by branding his father as a hopeless lunatic they had offended and infuriated the whole nation. 'His popularity is greater than ever,' a lady at Court wrote of the King. 'Compassion for his late sufferings seems to have endeared him to all conditions of men'. *The Times* claimed on 9 March that Whig slanders on the King amounted to treason and two nights later angry London crowds broke unlit Whig windows when the city was illuminated in honour of his recovery. A pamphlet entitled *The Fall of Faction; or, Edmund's Vision, which soars to the Beautiful and Sublime* turned Burke's lurid utterances about madness against their author: 'Edmund, inflamed by the rage of faction and rendered almost delirious ... became furiously mad, and was invested with the strait waistcoat.'[4] Before the King's illness Burke had been the leading intellectual of the Whig party, a thinker whose speeches and treatises celebrated both the British and the American revolutions and whose *Inquiry into the Sublime and the Beautiful* broke new ground in aesthetic theory. Now he was a figure of fun, an object of contempt, and Lansdowne saw a chance for his own very different brand of intellectualism to take the field. If Burke and the Whigs could not mount an opposition then he and his radical friends would do so instead.

It had to be admitted that Lansdowne's following in the Commons was small, even though it was no smaller than that which the party managers had attributed to Pitt only a few months earlier. He was also heartily disliked by the King, who regarded his resignation in 1783 as rank desertion. However even Pitt was now said to have incurred royal displeasure: George resented the Regency Bill almost as much as he resented the Whig attempt on his throne. Perhaps the most significant thing about Lansdowne as a politician was his declared opposition to patronage, the system which the regency crisis had shown up in such a bad light. Pitt's father the earl of Chatham had said that politics should be about 'not men but measures' and Lansdowne gave substance to this slogan, claiming to rely not on the support of a confederation of office-seekers but on his own reforming intentions. He was the man most distrusted by patronage politicians but he was also the man best placed to take over from them if they finally became discredited. The *Rolliad*, a current satire on Pitt's followers, depicted Lansdowne waiting in the wings as 'the sylvan sage, Whom Bowood guards to rule a purer age'; and if the British could be persuaded to learn from the French or from the Americans, if revolution could acquire a new meaning other than the tired corruption which 1688 had made necessary, then the purer age would come all the quicker. Lansdowne might yet have a political future in London if either New York or Paris would usher it in for him.

Sixteen years earlier he had taken the dissenter scientist and reformer Joseph Priestley into his service. 'My office was nominally that of librarian, but I had little employment,' Priestley wrote. 'I was with him as a friend.' Other friends included Richard Price – like Priestley a campaigner for the removal of dissenter disabilities – and the abbé Morellet, a distinguished French philosopher of whom Lansdowne wrote that 'he liberalized my ideas'. It was at Bowood that Morellet met the great American sage Benjamin Franklin. All these things might yet bear fruit. At the end of February, as the King's recovery left the way clear for the initiatives Lansdowne's men were planning in the Commons, Bentham sent part of his unfinished *Political Tactics* to Morellet. Further instalments were to be brought over by Lansdowne's son Lord Wycombe, who would be in Paris to observe the elections. A week later a letter went off to Benjamin Franklin from Benjamin Vaughan, who edited for Lansdowne a London journal called *The Repository* in which Franklin's discoveries rubbed shoulders with the anti-slavery campaign in France and 'animadversions on Dr Priestley's sentiments concerning the use of torture'. Now Vaughan had an even wider and grander vision of international co-operation which he called 'the new system of general politics'. 'These people understand faction, and even that but ill,' he wrote bitterly of British participants in the regency affair, 'but seem to know nothing of the new system of general politics. I wish that your country may set them proper examples.'[5]

Proper examples might perhaps be forthcoming from Franklin's own state of Pennsylvania but they were not plentiful in New York where the political system of the new-born United States was about to be inaugurated. Journalists there were quick to condemn the squabbles in London, dismissing both Pitt and his opponents as factious and scurrilous, but they had to admit that their own city was 'convulsed by party strife'. Originally it had been a clash between the Federalists, who wanted to ratify the constitution of the United States, and an Anti-Federalist party led by George Clinton, Governor of the state of New York for the past twelve years. Clinton was immensely popular in rural areas of the state and his men dominated the convention which met at Poughkeepsie in the summer of 1788 to decide for or against ratification. But many of them lost heart as news of acceptance by other states came in, so that late in July the bells were rung in New York city to celebrate a Poughkeepsie vote of thirty to twenty-seven in favour of ratification. Unfortunately their clangour also rang in an increasingly bitter confrontation. In the elections for the House of Representatives early in March the Federalists won by 2342 votes to 373 in New York city, while in the state's other five constituencies they either lost or scraped home by narrow margins. This was a party conflict which echoed the one in London, rather than a new general system which might transcend it.[6]

In some ways it was even more violent. The contending parties at Westminster were at least agreed on the need to keep the lower orders in their place and preserve the supremacy of propertied men, but in New York there was open and avowed class conflict. Clinton's supporters called their opponents Tories, over-rich and arrogant would-be aristocrats – 'their manners are haughty and their estates and those of their connections are immense and beyond all proportion to a popular government and therefore dangerous' – while styling themselves 'the old-fashioned Whigs of the Revolution, representatives of the yeomanry'. The Tories said the Whigs were 'the scum of society', men so poor that Clinton had been able to buy their loyalty and 'perpetuate himself in office by scandalous appointments of men destitute of capacity'. A Federalist newspaper accused him of being in league with subversive Massachusetts rebels. On one occasion, it asserted, he had deliberately walked across a room in an Albany tavern to greet Daniel Shay. St Jean de Crèvecoeur, French consul in New York, told Jefferson in January 1789 that Robert Yates – soon to change sides and become a Tory – was the only Whig he could stomach, 'all the rest being illiterate and ignorant'. 'Let them say here what they will,' he added, 'the bulk of mankind are incapable of governing themselves'.[7]

The French government appeared to have no such reservations. The electoral regulations published on 24 January gave increased representation to commercial and industrial centres and laid it down that every Frenchman over twenty-five who paid taxes should have a vote unless he was a bankrupt, an actor or a domestic servant. This meant an electorate of nearly six million, far wider than anything ever seen in the world before. Arthur Young had feared that the French 'know not how to value the privileges of the people' and James Madison had expressed cautious hopes about Louis 'admitting the people to a greater share of representation'. Now the fears were confounded and the hopes exceeded. The plans put forward by the dissenters and other parliamentary reformers in London were cautious and timid compared with this. It remained to be seen whether this vast electorate could produce an Estates General capable of succeeding where both Britain and America seemed to be failing, whether it could at last make the representation of the people into a workable reality unsullied by corrupt and factious politicians.

But who were the people? When Englishmen used the word they usually meant the existing electorate, which was about one twentieth of the population. In the United States the proportion was about the same, though the franchise varied widely: some states gave the vote to all freemen who paid poll tax, others restricted it to men who owned a certain amount of land. And in both countries it was agreed that only the free could vote. In America this meant the exclusion of the unfree, of slaves and indentured servants, while in England it normally meant the enfranchisement of the propertied classes. Men of a certain status, freeholders in the counties and freemen in the boroughs, had the right to vote because of that status. Freedom was not the heritage of all men but the property of some. It was not for nothing that towns and cities presented it to honorary freemen in a gold box while freeholders kept their title deeds to it in a safe place. Freedom was an extremely valuable privilege which brought with it membership of the political nation. When Arthur Young talked about the French not valuing the privileges of the people he only meant that they should give more weight to untitled men of property. He certainly did not mean that they should enfranchise mere labourers.

Yet this was what Louis XVI had done. Instead of following the example of the British and the Americans and setting up an electoral system which would represent property he had set up one which represented mere numbers. Who then were these six million Frenchmen to whom he had so rashly given the vote? Most were members of the third estate, ranging from rich and powerful merchants and professional men down to impoverished peasants and labourers who paid just enough taxes to qualify. And it was the range that was important: there was a far wider gulf between the rich merchant and the poor peasant than between the merchant and the nobleman. Indeed, the gulf between the merchant and the nobleman existed in the propagandist writings of Patriot publicists rather than in reality. It was comparatively easy for men who had grown rich in commerce or industry to buy patents of nobility and also to buy estates which gave them feudal rights and made them into *seigneurs*. Most of the complaints made by peasants about the abuse of feudal rights were directed either against newly ennobled *seigneurs* or against those who were still *bourgeois*. For at least two centuries France had been undergoing what one historian has called *l'embourgeoisement progressif du sol* — the turning over of the land to the middle classes.[8]

This had not happened to anything like the same extent in England, where the availability of mortgages ensured that landowners rarely had to sell off their estates. The highly fluid land market, which gave the French *bourgeois* the chance to buy their way into the landowning nobility, simply did not exist in England. Nor was it possible to buy noble status as it was in France. It had to be earned by years, even generations, of political activity. Families had first to get their feet onto the parliamentary ladder, building up an 'interest' at constituency level and then pushing their way into Parliament. The high road to the House of Lords lay through the House of Commons. Even those who looked for peerages as rewards for successful careers in the law or in the armed services had little hopes of getting them unless their families had parliamentary influence. 'To be out of Parliament is to be out of the world,' observed Admiral Rodney.[9] In spite of the myths that were cherished at the time and have been cherished since, the eighteenth-century English aristocracy was more secure, more integrated, more powerful and better entrenched than its French counterpart.

It was also more sure of its grip on the lower classes. Most Englishmen were hired labourers with little or no land of their own, living in tied cottages which went with their jobs. They themselves, as well as their wives and children, were totally under the control of the lord of the manor. They were employed either by him or by his tenant farmers, so that if they displeased him he could get them dismissed and evicted from their homes. He could mete out summary punishment in his capacity as Justice of the Peace and he could oversee their lives by means of his control over the parish officers. Things were very different in France. Feudalism might mean that French peasants were poor and over-taxed and over-worked but it also gave them a claim to land. It was not a very good claim, certainly not to be compared to the security of English freehold, and the land itself was seldom enough to keep them in any sort of comfort. Nevertheless they enjoyed an independence from local control which made lawlessness endemic in many areas. As historians uncover the extent of this lawlessness it is beginning to look as though 1789 saw the culmination of years of turbulence rather than the breakdown of years of repression.

The British embassy in Paris was shocked both by the threat of violence and by the King's apparent indifference to it. 'Several insidious hand-bills in the Breton language have been distributed about the country to stir up the peasants,' reported Dorset on 5

March. 'None of the authors of these inflammatory papers has yet
been discovered, nor do I understand that government has taken
any measures to that effect.'[10] Indeed, Louis could be said to be
encouraging the peasants to produce their own hand-bills, for he
was inviting them to give their elected representatives detailed
lists of their complaints so that he would know what needed
putting right. These lists of grievances or *cahiers de doléances*, a
time-honoured part of the Estates General procedure, had no
parallel in Britain or in America. Both Parliament and Congress
had steadily resisted the idea that members could be dictated to
by their constituents. The House of Commons liked to think of
itself as 'the grand jury of the realm', a body of independent men
free from pressure of any kind, and the House of Representatives
followed the same doctrine. Both were aware that the patronage
of kings and presidents undermined independence and produced
powerful pressure, but at least it was pressure from above. Pressure from below, giving those outside not only a voice but an
agreed script, could endanger the very foundations of society. 'The
demands of the Tiers Etat are extraordinary beyond measure, not
to say ridiculous,' Dorset said later in March, 'at Tours in particular the people went so far as to require an equal partition of
property.'[11]

More reassuring in Dorset's eyes was the pressure which great
men exerted over the elections and over the *cahiers*. 'I send your
Lordship the Instructions which His Serene Highness the Duc
d'Orléans has transmitted to his Representatives at the several
Bailiwicks where His Highness presides,' he wrote, 'in which not
only His patriotic principles are displayed, but the strongest proof
is given of his disinterestedness'. The proof which so impressed
Dorset was an offer to give up certain hunting rights. This was a
shrewd move, as these rights were coming under attack in *cahiers*
throughout France, not so much because they stopped the peasant
from eating the lord's game as because they failed to stop the
lord's game from eating the peasant's crops. The *cahiers* contained
one or two other complaints which were fairly widespread, such
as those about venality of offices and about inequalities in
taxation, but on the whole they were remarkably conservative
documents. In most areas the numbers of clergy and nobility were
small enough to allow them to meet in one assembly to elect
deputies and draw up *cahiers*, but the third estate was too numerous for this to happen: the voters elected electors to elect their

deputies and they drew up preliminary *cahiers* to form the basis of the general *cahiers* which were formal instructions for deputies. Indirect elections may have helped to get moderate men chosen as deputies but indirect composition of *cahiers* does not seem to have blunted the edge of popular discontent, since most of the preliminary ones were even less subversive than the general ones.

The process of indirect composition did however graft an appearance of national intent onto a hotchpotch of local grudges and grievances. In the preliminary *cahiers* suggestions for reform were all too often swamped by complaints about horse thieves, about the state of the roads, about neighbours getting away without paying taxes. In the general *cahiers* a serious attempt was made to outline the sort of constitution the Estates General should give to France. The instructions which Orléans sent out, said to be by the abbé Sièyes, were especially influential in this respect and they won the approval of the press in London as well as of the duke of Dorset in Paris. After listing the demands they put forward *The Times* added: 'This is what is generally intended to be proposed at this great National Assembly; and in perusing them we shall discover that the fundamental principles of our own are very nearly discovered.'[12] Yet a few weeks earlier Sièyes had published *What is the Third Estate?*, one of the most influential books in French history, in which the British constitution was dismissed as not worth copying. 'I am afraid that this much vaunted masterpiece cannot survive any impartial examination which is based on the principles of true political order,' he wrote. 'We should recognize perhaps that it is much more a product of chance and circumstance than of enlightenment.'[13]

The reason for the apparent contradiction was simple: *The Times* was confusing tactics and objectives, means and ends. The demands it mentioned – freedom from arbitrary arrest, liberty of the press, no taxation without representation – were certainly things that the British constitution was supposed to guarantee, but this did not mean they could best be achieved by an assembly based on the fundamental principles of the one at Westminster. It was not yet clear what would be the principles on which the Estates General would be based, since no decision had yet been made as to whether it was going to debate as one body or three, and in this uncertain situation Sièyes aimed to set out in *What is the Third Estate?* the tactics the deputies for the third estate should adopt.

These depended on the tactics likely to be adopted by the government. Its primary objective, Sièyes pointed out, was to get the Estates to sanction new taxes, which would best be done by counting heads in one single assembly where any resistance from the privileged orders would be swamped by the third estate. But the second objective was to head off demands for reforms, such as the ones *The Times* listed, and this would obviously be easier if the three orders met separately. Just as the King of England drew advantage from the supremacy of the Commons in matters of taxation while at the same time being able to play them off against the Lords, so the King of France was refusing to decide between vote *par tête* and vote *par ordre* because he wanted to keep his options open. The third estate must therefore speak for the whole nation and resist any attempt to set up the other orders as a counterbalance to its own absolute and indivisible sovereignty. Having rightly rejected the Plenary Court, recognizing it only too clearly as a potential House of Lords, France must also reject any attempt to turn the Estates General into a divided legislative. Precisely because British constitutional practice was likely to favour the government it must be spurned by the assembly.

If this analysis was correct – and thousands of Frenchmen thought it was – then the most vital decision made in France in the early months of 1789 was the result of looking to the British example. By deciding not to decide, by giving no lead on the vital question of one assembly or three, the King made *doublement* ineffective and thus sacrificed the popularity which agreeing to it had brought him. He made well-nigh inevitable not only the initial deadlock in the Estates General but also the violent manner in which it was later to be broken. The two alternatives for which French precedents could be found, an Estates in one chamber and an Estates in three, were both rejected in favour of an open-ended situation which promised to offer some at least of the advantages George III had enjoyed in 1783.

It was certainly assumed in Paris that spring that when the Estates met the King would tell them what measures they were to discuss and whether they were to discuss them as one assembly or three. The Parlement had invited him to announce a programme of legislation in advance and his ministers had been bombarded with advice as to what that programme should be. The debate on the respective merits of the British and American constitutions took place in this context, in the context of what the government should do. What made Sièyes's contribution so different and so important was that he turned the context on its head and suggested what the deputies should do in reply.

In *What is the Third Estate?* Sièyes expressed a hope that someone would write an impartial account of the British constitution, comparing it with that of the United States and relating both to French needs. He was delighted to report in a subsequent note that such a work had now been published in Paris.[14] It was supposedly a French translation of *Observations on Government* by John Stevens of New Jersey, which had appeared two years earlier, but it contained so much additional material that the book's original argument was obscured. Even though Stevens had been writing before the United States constitution took final shape he had thought it should provide for a legislative divided into two chambers and an executive with an effective veto. His French editors rejected both these things, arguing in favour of one all-powerful assembly, and all that was left of the original book was its attack on Jean Louis de Lolme's *The Constitution of England*, which Stevens considered to be at fault because of its defence of monarchy and aristocracy.

De Lolme, a Genevese writer who had made his home in England for many years, was certainly a great admirer of kings and lords. The first English edition of his book had been dedicated to Lord Abingdon, head of a Tory family turned Whig, and in May 1784, when George III and Pitt won their great general election victory, a new edition appeared which was dedicated to the King himself by 'Your Majesty's most humble and devoted servant and these many years subject by choice'.[15] This was reprinted in 1789 and a new French edition was brought out by Buisson of the Rue Hautefeuille, the Paris bookseller whom Bentham had already approached in vain. In January 1789 it was given a glowing review in the *Mercure de France* by Jacques Mallet du Pan, another Genevese with English connections, who had agreed to act as foreign correspondent for Lansdowne's *Repository*. As if to counteract the use which had been made of John Stevens's book Mallet du Pan was careful to point out that de Lolme's approval of the British constitution had been endorsed by John Adams, 'one of the most enlightened authors of the American revolution'.[16]

It was not the best time to cite de Lolme as the acknowledged interpreter of the British constitution. On 23 January he published

The Present National Embarrassment Considered, which proclaimed that the debate over the regency was unnecessary and misguided. 'The fact is,' he declared grandly, 'that at this present time there is no occasion for a Regent or business for a Regent. Parliament possesses powers fully sufficient, more than sufficient, for the governing of the nation.' This extraordinary doctrine, a total contradiction of his earlier emphasis on the monarchy as the vital element in the balance of the constitution, provoked a very angry response. Englishmen did not relish having their crisis described as a national embarrassment and they relished even less being told that they had brought it on themselves by their inability to understand their own constitution. There were infuriated protests at 'the indecency of a stranger thrusting himself forward and deciding peremptorily on a question deemed by many to be of great legal intricacy.'[17] As well as exposing the weaknesses of the British constitution the regency crisis also discredited its most famous apologist.

A more powerful advocate of the British constitution was Mounier, still riding the wave of national acclaim which his exploits in Dauphiné had earned him. His *New Observations on the Estates General*, published late in February, denied that the upper chamber at Westminster had anything in common either with the Plenary Court or with the order of nobility as it existed in France. Many members of the House of Lords had sat in the Commons before succeeding to their titles, while their sons and brothers in all probability still sat there. Nor were there any social distinctions in the Commons: scions of noble families sat alongside baronets and knights and untitled gentlemen as representatives of the people. The French, torn between the desire for a balanced constitution and the need to assert popular sovereignty, should recognize that only the British had managed to reconcile the two. Nicholas Bergasse, regarded even by Brissot as an ardent revolutionary, was prepared to go further still. He dismissed both vote *par ordre* and vote *par tête* and suggested instead an Estates General divided into an upper chamber, where royal princes and bishops and heads of great families sat as of right, and a lower house to which voters could elect either commoners or noblemen as they pleased.[18]

On this last point Bergasse was pushing at an open door. The electoral regulations of 1789 already allowed the third estate to elect nobles and this was giving rise to some concern. Early in

April, as the elections drew to a close, *The Times* listed constituencies in which it had happened and reported fears that the third estate might be swamped by noblemen. Many people even in Britain were worried by the fact that the Commons was 'a parcel of younger brothers', its independence called into question because it was a cadet branch of the House of Lords. The other British worry about Parliament, the fear that its independence was being undermined by government patronage and the election of office-holders, had also been exported to France. 'The nobility of lower Normandy have testified their disapprobation of electing any one holding an office or who is otherwise connected at Court,' wrote Dorset on 26 March, 'and have even gone so far as to declare that no one having a commission in the army shall be considered as eligible'.[19] The British example was raising more problems than it solved.

It was unfortunate that the comte de Mirabeau, the man through whom Lansdowne and Bentham hoped to influence the course of events in France, was also the man who most typified those problems. 'A late publication by the comte de Mirabeau entitled *L'Histoire secrète de la Cour de Berlin* has made so much noise here that I am induced to send it to your Lordship,' wrote Dorset on 22 January. 'The Prussian minister has made a formal complaint to the French minister of the scurrility and abuse exhibited in this work'.[20] Mirabeau had long had a reputation for scurrility and abuse: his works ranged from a compendium of erotica to a series of pamphlets on stock-jobbing. Calonne had used him in an attempt to rig the Paris bourse and he had also sent him on a diplomatic mission to Berlin. Mirabeau had ratted on Calonne, publishing details of his stock-jobbing and helping to get him dismissed, and now it seemed he was ratting on the government as well. The Parlement of Paris ordered the book to be burned by the public executioner and the nobility of Mirabeau's constituency in Provence expelled him. He stood as a candidate for the third estate and was elected. As well as being a nobleman in the ranks of commoners he was also a government agent, secret as well as open, financial as well as diplomatic, and for good measure he was an agent capable of betraying his masters. It was hard to imagine anyone who gave more grounds for the fears that were being entertained about the independence of the third estate.

Four years earlier Mirabeau had also managed to make himself notorious in London. His manservant Jacques-Philippe Hardy

had threatened to sue him for arrears of wages and Mirabeau had
got in first by bringing a case against him for theft. When the case
was tried at the Old Bailey it emerged that one of the things
Hardy was said to have stolen was a volume of scabrous Court
gossip which Mirabeau had presumably intended to publish in
London. Mirabeau lost his case and lowered his reputation but his
English friends stood loyally by him. Lansdowne and two dukes,
as well as Edmund Burke and other prominent members of the
House of Commons, were at the Old Bailey to support him. In
France such readiness on the part of aristocrats and politicians to
rally round a shady pamphleteer was a matter for surprise and
even suspicion. Now, in the wake of the *Secret History* scandal,
the surprise and suspicion were even greater. Morellet was shocked
to learn, from Bentham's letter of 25 February, that Lansdowne
and his friends regarded Mirabeau as a possible mouthpiece for
their ideas in France. He left the letter unanswered for several
weeks and when he did reply he said coldly that he could not have
dealings with such a man.[21]

It was to take another revolution, this time in Geneva, to bring
Mirabeau and the Lansdowne set into some sort of collaboration.
'The people of Geneva have mutinied,' Dorset reported on 1
February. 'The rise of bread was the pretence for this tumult, but
the real cause was a desire of forcing the magistrates to alter some
laws'.[22] The magistrates agreed to repeal the laws banishing the
leaders of the short-lived 1782 revolution, which had been crushed
by French intervention, but they were again supported by the
French government in refusing to readmit the returning exiles to
public office. The exiles determined to take their case to the
Estates General and at the end of March Jacques-Antoine Duroveray and Etienne Dumont left London for Paris in order to
spearhead this campaign. They hoped for the support of Necker,
who was a fellow Genevese and whom they thought to be an
advocate of liberal policies and an opponent of the 1782 intervention. But they would also need allies in the Estates General
itself and it was already clear that Mirabeau would be one of the
leaders there. He might disgust the fastidious and philosophical
Morellet but to Dumont and Duroveray, who needed forcefulness
rather than integrity, he seemed worth cultivating, especially
since he had already worked closely with many of the Genevese
exiles for several years.

'I hope when you have given France a legislature you will suffer nothing to interfere and prevent your pen from enforcing these triumphs,' Lansdowne told Bentham airily two days before Dumont and Duroveray left London.[23] Since all Bentham's approaches to France had been rebuffed it seemed that his only chance of fulfilling this hope lay in the two Genevese. Their proposed international co-operation was at a lower level than his, a matter of revolutionaries in one country helping those in another rather than a vision of all nations following immutable Benthamite principles, but it nevertheless qualified as a wider hope and a pointer to a purer age. Lansdowne certainly seemed to think so, for he gave Dumont indefinite leave from his job as his son's tutor so that he could go to Paris. There was a minor detail about this tutoring job which might grow into a major difficulty: instead of paying Dumont a salary Lansdowne had obtained a government pension for him. Duroveray was also in receipt of a government pension which had been settled on him as a consolation when Lansdowne's scheme to settle the Genevese exiles in Ireland had foundered. It would be unpleasant and perhaps dangerous if Mirabeau's enemies discovered that his friends from Geneva were pensionaries of the King of England. It might also be unfortunate if Lansdowne, hammer of the patronage system and prophet of the purer age, was shown to be using government funds as a way of paying for his son's education.

When Dumont and Duroveray arrived in Paris Mirabeau was in Provence on his election campaign and they were in no hurry to contact him. They stayed for several weeks with Clavière, another Genevese exile, sometimes at his country house outside Paris and sometimes in the city.[24] In the past Clavière had used Mirabeau to write pamphlets to assist his shady dealings on the Paris bourse and he had also had Mirabeau used against him by his enemies. Now he wanted to put stock-jobbing behind him but one enormous financial adventure still fascinated him. It was the prospect of buying up the American debt. A few years earlier, because it had been widely assumed that the Americans would never be able to repay in full the debts incurred in fighting the War of Independence, debt securities had sunk to little more than an eighth of their face value. Prices were so low that European speculators began to buy and the New York partnership of William Duer and Daniel Parker made great profits hawking American debt stock in Amsterdam and Antwerp and Paris.[25] In 1788 prices began to harden, partly because so many European syndicates were in the market and partly because of renewed confidence as state after state ratified the United States constitution. It was to test the strength of this rise, as well as to find out what stock was available and on what terms, that Clavière sent Brissot to America. Now Brissot was back in Paris and the reports he brought were encouraging. Clavière had his own international visions, just as compelling in their way as those of Lansdowne and Bentham and Dumont and Duroveray.

There was unease in America about the activities of the European speculators. Jefferson had done his best to stop stock passing into French hands and in 1786 the then Congress had blocked an attempt by a Dutch syndicate to buy a controlling interest in America's debt to France. But now there was no Congress, no central authority, and those who would later constitute the government of the United States had to act unofficially. Financiers in New York had come to dominate the market in debt securities and it was there that bid and offer prices for the whole country were fixed. So it was a New Yorker, Gouverneur Morris, who arrived in France in February 1789 with the intention of re-establishing American control of the overseas market. He was not what he sounded, for he had never been governor of anything – his unusual first name was the maiden name of his Huguenot mother – and he was not related to Robert Morris, the New York financier and land speculator for whom he was acting. He brought with him an impressive bundle of letters of introduction from George Washington to eminent men in Paris, London, Dublin and Amsterdam but none gave details of his mission. 'Mrs Washington joins me in wishes that you may have a prosperous voyage,' Washington told him guardedly, 'and that when your objects shall be accomplished you may have an equally happy return to your friends'.[26]

Morris's objects were very different from those of Dumont but they had one thing in common, the need for a confidential interview with Necker. Dumont later claimed he had such an interview as soon as he got to Paris but Necker denied seeing anything of him until the month of May. Morris dined with Necker on 27 March, while Dumont and Duroveray were still in London, and although he had no opportunity for a private talk he judged him to be dull and self-important, a hard worker but certainly not a financial or political genius. 'Mr Necker, who thinks that he directs everything, is perhaps himself as much an instrument as any one of those which he makes use of,' he wrote. 'His fall is I think decreed but it will not happen as soon as his enemies expect. It will depend much on the chapter of accidents who will govern the States General or whether they will be at all governable.' With ill-disguised impatience Morris concluded that 'it is not until after the meeting of the States General that solid plans of any kind can be formed'. Meanwhile there was an air of unreality about Paris, a feeling that there was much to do but little point in doing it: 'I have seen enough to convince me that a man might in this city be incessantly employed for forty years and grow old without knowing what he had been about.'[27] The Estates were officially supposed to meet on 27 April but there were bound to be delays – Dorset said that nobody thought they could open before the middle of May – and in Paris even the primary assemblies, the elections to elect electors, had been put off until 21 April. It was a city trapped in suspense and uncertainty.

Morris was glad to know that in America the suspense was almost over and that only one thing was needed to resolve the remaining uncertainties and enable New York to show the world how a revolution should be brought to fruition. 'Our new constitution has greatly raised our reputation in Europe,' he told Washington, 'but your appointment and acceptance would go far to fix the general opinion. I will not in this place discuss the question whether mankind is right or wrong in that universal idea.' Towards the end of March Washington became convinced that 'the event which I have long dreaded, I am at last constrained to believe is likely to happen' and he began to make preparations to go to New York. Governor Clinton offered to make over his house to him but Washington thought it wiser to take lodgings. On 2 April the *New York Journal* announced that he would be unanimously elected President. 'Ye little great ones of the world!' it proclaimed in triumph. 'How might the man who floats upon the full tide of universal approbation look down on hereditary right!'[28] The House of Representatives was already quorate and the Senate became so on 6 April, after which the votes cast in February could at last be counted and the result announced. Washington was officially informed of his election on 14 April and two days later he set out for New York.

His arrival there on Thursday 23 April was marked by the most splendid pageantry the American revolution had yet seen. A ceremonial barge rowed by twenty-six liveried oarsmen brought him across the bay from New Jersey and as he approached Staten Island he was greeted by a naval parade and a thirteen-gun salute. Then a sloop under full sail slipped gracefully alongside his barge and from its decks there came an anthem which went to the tune of the English *God save the King* and described Washington as 'crowned with glory'. He noted in his diary that 'the loud acclamations of the people rent the skies as I passed along the wharves'. He landed at Murray's Wharf at the foot of Wall Street, where magnificently carpeted steps flanked with crimson upholstery led to a waiting carriage. He spurned it and insisted on making his way on foot through the dense crowds: it took him half an hour to walk half a mile to the house in Cherry Street which had been 'fitted up for the reception of His Excellency' and he was moved to tears by the ecstatic reception he received: 'the General was obliged to wipe his eye several times before he got to Queen Street.' 'The scene was superbly great, beyond any descriptive powers of the pen to do justice to,' wrote the *Gazette of the United States*. 'Many persons who were in the crowd on Thursday were heard to say that they should now die contented – nothing being wanted to complete their happiness previous to this auspicious period but the sight of the Saviour of his Country.'[29]

On the same day Great Britain's salvation was celebrated with equal pomp and even greater emotion. Before Parliament adjourned for the Easter recess it was informed that Thursday 23 April, St George's day, had been proclaimed a day of general thanksgiving: the King would go in solemn procession to St Paul's Cathedral to give thanks for his restoration to health. When the two Houses met again on 20 April they were immediately plunged into the practical problems this raised. Humphrey Minchin, member for Okehampton, told the Commons that he had just walked along the processional route and seen rickety scaffolding erected outside houses that were themselves aged and in need of repair. Once the scaffolding was filled with spectators it would undoubtedly tumble into the street and bring the houses down with it. The Commons then appointed a committee to ensure that there was no loss of life. Seats on the scaffolds cost between a guinea and three guineas and it was possible to hire a whole frontage of four windows, with breakfast and refreshments thrown in, for forty-five guineas. 'Numbers of people of consequence in France have ordered apartments to be taken for them to see the procession on the 23rd, when they purpose being present,' reported *The Times*.[30]

The spectators were not disappointed. 'The universal joy and loyalty which pervaded the Cities of London and Westminster; the grandeur of the spectacle exhibited in the more than triumphal, the religious entry of our beloved Sovereign, fill the mind with such awful ideas as scarcely leave it room to enter into the minutiae of grandeur,' said the *Gentleman's Magazine* breathlessly before entering into the minutiae of grandeur for seven closely printed columns. The hushed excitement in St Paul's itself was almost unbearable until 'the happy moment arrived when the congregation were rejoiced with the sight of their beloved monarch, whose long absence from them had almost driven them to despair.' The accounts closed with the comforting reflection that 'the utmost possible decorum was preserved and that which was so much dreaded, tumult and bloodshed, did not occur in any one instance that has come to our ears.'[31]

That same Thursday, as George Washington stood in his ceremonial barge and George III knelt in St Paul's Cathedral, Louis XVI sat in a council meeting seeking ways of averting tumult and bloodshed in the French capital. Because of what Dorset called 'the ungovernable spirit of the populace of this city' it had been decided – against Necker's advice, so it was said – to hold the Estates not in Paris but at the royal palace of Versailles fourteen miles away. It was generally considered, because of the police and troops quartered in the capital and because of the fortresses which ringed it round, that 'dangerous rioting has become a moral impossibility in Paris', but Louis was taking no chances. Morris's assertion in the middle of April that 'ten thousand men are ordered into the neighbourhood of Paris' was an exaggeration but orders were certainly given for large detachments of cavalry and infantry with artillery support to move to positions around Paris and Versailles. Siméon-Prosper Hardy, a law-abiding Parisian bookseller, was horrified to find angry crowds and patrolling soldiers in every street. 'If we have an insurrection it will be warm work,' wrote Morris apprehensively.[32]

In an attempt to prevent the bread riots which would be the most likely signal for such an insurrection the royal council on 23 April issued an edict requiring farmers to bring all their grain to market and sternly forbidding any disorders at the point of sale. In London that morning *The Times* reported that France was facing the worst grain shortage ever known and that it was being attributed to government negligence. In Paris there were uglier rumours, stories of farmers and bakers receiving secret instructions to withhold food supplies from the city in order to provoke an uprising. Hardy heard that agitators were going to release criminals from the prisons and march on Versailles to disrupt the opening of the Estates General.[33] Revolution in Paris might soon have a face very different from the comforting countenance it wore in New York and London.

CHAPTER FIVE

The long delay

On the last Sunday in April, the day before the Estates General had originally been supposed to meet, the new arrangements for its opening were at last announced. The Royal Family and the deputies were to join in a solemn service at the church of St Louis in Versailles on Monday 4 May and the opening session was to be held the next day in the presence of the King and his ministers. After that the deputies would have their credentials checked to make sure they had been properly elected – a process known as 'verification of powers' – and then business could begin. But what business? At the end of the previous year Mirabeau had written to the Foreign Secretary, the comte de Montmorin, warning him that the monarchy was in danger and could only be saved if ministers took the initiative and put definite proposals before the Estates rather than allowing deputies to decide for themselves what their business would be. In case the ministry had no such proposals he offered his services to draw up a master plan for the defence of the throne. The offer was not taken up and a few weeks later the publication of *The Secret History of the Court of Berlin* ended any hopes he might have had of government employment.[1]

In Mirabeau's view the danger to the throne came principally from the upstart lawyer nobility of the Parlements, whom he described contemptuously as 'black-robed aristocrats'. Together with Clavière and Sièyes he sought to guide the debates of the Society of Thirty, a Parisian political club in which leaders of the Paris Parlement tried to agree tactics with men from the so-called 'high nobility' including the duc de la Rochefoucauld-Liancourt, the duc d'Aiguillon, the duc de Lauzun and of course the indefatigable Lafayette. In May 1788 Lafayette had said that true liberals like himself must use the Parlement as a stalking-horse in their campaign to get the Estates summoned. Now that this policy had succeeded the Parlement men must be made to see that they had created not just an opportunity to get their own privileges confirmed but an opportunity for France to win her freedom. But the Parlement men were not easily persuaded and Mirabeau told Lauzun that the Society of Thirty would need all its strength if it was to escape from 'Parlement tyranny'. 'What is very true and can be counted on,' he wrote, 'is that in the national assembly I shall be a very zealous monarchist.'[2] He saw nothing wrong in being a deputy and also a monarchist, any more than he saw anything wrong in being at one and the same time the author of a ministerial master plan and one of those who were to vote on it. The British tradition, whereby ministers and government supporters had seats in Parliament and took the initiative there, seemed to him the best and perhaps the only way to defend the throne.

Dumont later wrote that when he arrived in Paris in April 1789 'the Society of Thirty was continuing to hold its useful meetings'. It had circulated specimen *cahiers de doléances* to many constituencies 'in order to impose uniformity on the demands of the people' and there were also preliminary meetings to try to produce uniformity in the Paris primary assemblies where each district chose its electors. Clavière took Dumont and Duroveray to his local assembly in the Rue Neuve St Marc on 21 April, only to have them denounced as strangers and thrown out. Nevertheless Dumont was impressed by what he heard. 'The French, towards whom I had a prejudiced and scornful attitude because of my republican upbringing and my experience of England, now appeared to me in a new light: I began to think of them as free men.'[3] His mission on behalf of the Genevese exiles was not forgotten but he also determined to help forge the new French constituion. It would of course be modelled on the glories of 1688 – 'my intentions did not go beyond the imitation of the government of England' – but it would take into account the reforms which Lansdowne's supporters were now introducing in the House of Commons. The Society of Thirty had produced a programme and all that remained was for Dumont to convince himself of the trustworthiness of Mirabeau, the man most capable of putting the programme into effect. This he did with remarkable ease: on Tuesday 28 April he wrote to tell his friends in London that the publication of *The Secret History of the Court of Berlin* had been engineered by Mirabeau's enemies in order to blast his career. He insisted that Mirabeau himself was innocent, a man more sinned against than sinning.[4]

There were other shadows less easily dispelled. As Dumont wrote his letter that day a running battle was being waged between rioters and soldiers in the Saint-Antoine district of Paris. There had been some trouble there the previous afternoon and evening but Tuesday's rioting was a great deal more serious and was widely believed to have been politically instigated. The target was an employer named Réveillon who had said that although he now paid his men more than the fifteen sous a day which used to be the standard rate they still could not make ends meet. This was alleged to mean that he thought the poor should live on fifteen sous a day. The mob attacked and burned his house but his own workmen had no grievance against him and refused to take part in the attack. In the course of the day's fighting Réveillon was largely forgotten and when the mobs were called upon to surrender they replied not with jeers against him but with shouts of 'Down with the nobles and clergy!' and 'Long live the third estate!' An interrogator who questioned wounded rioters claimed to have heard men in their death agonies cursing themselves for having agreed to this 'for twelve miserable francs'. Many of those arrested were said to have six-franc pieces on them, each equivalent to more than a week's wages. Dorset reported that as Orléans drove through the faubourg Saint-Antoine that night there were repeated cries of 'Long live the House of Orléans!' The baron de Besenval, who put down the riot, described it later as 'the explosion of a mine laid by enemy hands'. 'I judged that it must be the work of the English,' he went on, 'since I did not at that time dare to suspect the duc d'Orléans.'[5]

Others did, in spite of the total lack of evidence, and Duval d'Eprémesnil was said to have asked the King to let the Parlement of Paris put Orléans on trial and hang him. D'Eprémesnil was the hero of the Parlement, a man who had once been imprisoned for defying royal authority, and he was Mirabeau's chief rival in the Society of Thirty. In his view all his opponents were in the pay of Orléans or the English or both. It was alleged that Orléans planned to make use of English institutions as well as English money: 'He promised those whom he knew to be diseased with Anglophilia that he would support the setting up of two chambers modelled on the English Parliament.'[6] Poor Dumont had no idea that his intentions were being misrepresented in this way, any more than the English knew they were supposed to have inspired the Réveillon affair, by which they had in fact been deeply shocked. 'It was in this insurrection that women were first seen to forget all the timidity natural to their sex,' wrote the *Annual Register*, 'and to mix with more than masculine fury in scenes of blood and destruction. It was here too that men were taught to disguise themselves in the dress of women, thereby to evade the punishment due to their crimes'. Those who did not evade punishment were hanged with great solemnity two days after the riot. The *Gentleman's Magazine* was impressed by the ceremony and Gouverneur Morris commented on 'the magnificence of the hanging match'.[7]

The greater magnificence at Versailles was now getting under way. During the last days of April the deputies gave in their names to the marquis de Brézé, the master of ceremonies, and on Saturday 2 May they were presented to the King. There were some angry outbursts when the third estate was kept waiting longer than the other two and then denied access to the room in which they were received. However it was decided that it was beneath the dignity of the representatives of the nation to worry about mere matters of etiquette and so no formal complaint was made. It was another matter two days later when the third estate led the procession into the church of St Louis only to find the front seats reserved for the first two orders. Several deputies sat in these seats and there were undignified scuffles when the clergy and nobility came to claim their places. 'The sermon was generally much approved,' reported Dorset, 'and a particular passage in it addressed to the members was received with clapping of hands which, as may well be imagined from the novelty of the circumstance, interrupted for some time the devotion of the congregation.'[8] The passage applauded was not an invitation to give France a constitution but a reminder that taxes were already too burdensome. In spite of all the fine talk about the regeneration of France the deputies were still hard-headed men determined to drive a hard bargain before agreeing to new taxes.

They were therefore disconcerted to be told next day that there might be no bargain to be struck. In his speech at the opening session Necker first warned them not to imagine that they were France's only hope of solvency. 'Everybody is shocked,' wrote Dumont, 'at his indecent enumeration of the criminal means by which the King might have avoided calling the States'. Necker went on to insist on the need to keep things as they were, to check the passion for change, and he recommended separate sessions of the three orders as the best way of doing this. But he also suggested that debating as one single assembly might make it easier for the King to control the Estates General. It looked as though Sièyes had been right to predict that the government would deliberately refuse to settle the matter of vote *par ordre* and vote *par tête*. *The Times* commented that Necker was 'floating between two contending parties, undetermined which side to take' and that his failure to put forward proposals for a new French constitution would lead to his downfall.[9]

Notices were posted in the streets of Versailles saying that the King expected the three orders to meet on the following day to verify their powers and that 'the place destined for their meeting will be ready to receive them by nine o'clock in the morning'; but inside the palace separate chambers were prepared for the clergy and nobility in addition to the large hall in which all three orders had met for the opening session. And so on the Wednesday morning the third estate gathered in the great hall while the other two went to their own rooms. Nobody could say who was obeying and who was flouting the King's commands because nobody knew for certain what those commands were. The clergy decided by a narrow majority to verify their powers immediately and the nobility decided by a much larger majority to do so on the following Monday. The third estate could not decide anything because to do so would be to recognize its existence as a separate assembly. It could neither proceed to verification nor send deputations to see whether the other orders were doing so. Any action of any kind might be taken as an admission that one estate could legally debate without the others being present, which was precisely what the third estate was determined not to admit. In the end it was decided that a dozen deputies should go as private individuals to find out what was going on in the other two orders. They returned to say that the nobility had adjourned until Monday and the clergy had verified their powers but not yet constituted themselves as a separate order. And so the first week in the life of the Estates General came to its inconclusive end.

The Times had gone to some trouble to ensure that it was well informed on the great events that were to take place in France. 'No limit has been placed on expense,' the editor claimed, 'to procure the earliest and most authentic information.... A gentleman at Versailles is engaged by this paper to transmit us every particular on this important business, who will attend the proceedings regularly whenever the Assembly meets'. Now the gentleman was being paid good money for attending proceedings which were proceeding nowhere. 'There is no further particular news from France of a political nature,' the paper reported wearily towards the end of May. 'This assembly has now met sixteen days without having brought forward any business of the nation, or even concluded on the mode in which it is to be transacted.'[10] Most of its readers were equally weary and found it hard to admire or even understand the policy of inaction which the third estate had adopted. What chance would there have been of a Glorious Revolution in 1688 if the House of Commons had refused to do anything unless it was joined by the Lords?

Henry Beaufoy was determined to make sure the Glorious Revolution was not forgotten at Westminster even though its triumph at Versailles might be delayed. At the end of March he had been given leave by the Commons to bring in the Bills with which the London Revolution Society had entrusted him, one to complete the work of 1688 by removing dissenter disabilities and the other to provide for its annual commemoration. On Friday 8 May, as the three orders at Versailles reached deadlock, he introduced the first of these. Fox and other opposition members supported it but Lord North, with whom Fox and the Portland Whigs had allied in 1783, said it was 'an attempt to sap the foundations and destroy the fabric of the British constitution'. Pitt said that although toleration was a good thing in principle the Bill should be rejected because it might disturb 'the quiet and regularity which prevailed at present in relation to religious differences.' After a short debate the Bill was thrown out by a majority of twenty votes.[11]

That day Edmund Burke wrote an extraordinarily fierce letter to Richard Bright, a Bristol dissenter who had asked him to be sure to vote for Beaufoy's Bill. He flatly contradicted Bright's assumption that toleration for dissenters was the logical fulfilment of the Glorious Revolution. On the contrary, James II's challenge to the Anglican supremacy had itself been mounted in the name of toleration, dissenters joining with catholics to support him. Burke pointed out angrily that the dissenters had played a similar part in 1783, approving and applauding George III's unconstitutional attack on the Whigs. He said he did not propose to take part in the debate and he added a postscript to his letter reporting with some satisfaction that the Bill had been defeated. In fact his absence from the Commons had nothing to do with the dissenters: he thought it wise to stay away because the House had recently passed a vote of censure on him.[12]

It was in any case a black Friday for Burke because it saw the appearance of *Cooling the Brain*, the first of many caricatures in which he was portrayed as a lunatic. He was shown raving not only about George III's illness but also about the impeachment of Warren Hastings, the reason for the vote of censure.[13] The House of Commons had sent Hastings for trial before the House of Lords on charges of misgovernment in India; Burke, managing the impeachment, had gratuitously added unauthorized accusations to the indictment. None of this had much to do with what was going on in France but it had a lot to do with the way in which Burke later reacted to it. Isolated and unpopular, bitterly opposed to Lansdowne's dissenter allies and their brand of 'revolution principles', desperately in need of a way to make himself politically respectable again, he was already forging the weapons with which he was to fight his immensely effective crusade against the French revolution.

There were well over two hundred votes in the division on Beaufoy's Bill but as members left London to spend summer in the country the House of Commons thinned. The following week, when William Wilberforce brought up the question of the slave trade, he became so exasperated by poor attendances that he demanded a call of the House in order to nail the absentees. This was fiercely resisted, constantly postponed and finally abandoned altogether. On several occasions the House met only to adjourn because it did not have the required minimum of forty members.[14] But a sufficient number of office-holders and other ministerial supporters could always be relied upon to turn up when essential government business was under discussion. While more than twelve hundred deputies at Versailles were unable to do anything at all a handful of men could keep things going at Westminster. It seemed that the British had indeed found the secret that Necker sought in vain, the way of holding change in check and still making sure that the government got what it wanted. It was to some extent a matter of what the constitutional theorists called bi-cameralism, the effective management of a legislative divided into two as opposed to the difficulties of managing one which argued as to whether it was divided into three or not divided at all. But it was also a matter of numbers. Maintaining an effective government presence in two poorly attended Houses of Parliament was one thing but it was quite another to do so in an Estates General consisting of over twelve hundred deputies most of whom turned up regularly and conscientiously.*

The task should have been at its simplest in New York, where Congress consisted of a mere twenty-six senators and sixty-five members of the House of Representatives.[15] What made it more difficult was the idea of the separation of powers, the theoretical proposition that no member of the executive should be allowed to pollute the ranks of the legislative. This notion had been abandoned at Westminster, where attempts to exclude members of the government from Parliament were regularly and decisively voted down, but the Americans and the French still cherished it. George Washington decided in advance that he would not use his powers of patronage to dominate Congress in the way George III used his to dominate Parliament. 'Should it become inevitably necessary for me to go into the chair of government,' he told an applicant for a government post, 'I have determined to go into it free from all positive engagements of every nature whatsoever. This is the answer I have already given to a multiplicity of applications.' But there were those who feared that constitutional theory might lead to chaos unless the President's administration took a firm grip on Congress. From Charleston in South Carolina Senator Ralph Izard wrote to Jefferson in Paris complaining of 'the humiliating state into which we are plunged' and attributing it to 'the want of an energetic and efficient government'. 'The federal business has proceeded with a mortifying tardiness,' Madison told Jefferson some weeks later, 'we are in a wilderness without a single footstep to guide us'.[16]

Washington saw only one source from which guidance could be sought. In his inaugural address he reminded Congress that they had always been in God's hands – 'every step by which they have

*The King's original estimate of a thousand deputies had been exceeded: the final total was 1232, of which 648 represented the third estate.

advanced to the character of an independent nation seems to have been distinguished by some token of providential agency' – and that the final consummation, albeit republican in form, must not depart from ancient and hallowed traditions. 'The propitious smiles of Heaven can never be expected on a nation that disregards the eternal rules of order and right,' he warned. Even the sermon in the church of St Louis in Versailles could hardly have produced sentiments more pious or more conventional. The House of Representatives replied on 5 May and the Senate two days later. Both echoed the President's devout aspirations, the House committing the United States to 'the Invisible Hand which has led the American people through so many difficulties' and the Senate paying its respects to 'the Great Arbiter of the Universe, by whom empires rise and fall'.[17]

These high-sounding phrases had been hammered out in debates as ferocious as any at Versailles or Westminster. The Vice President, who took the chair in the Senate, was the same John Adams who had described the British constitution as 'this stupendous fabric of human invention' and now he wanted its rituals observed in Congress. There was talk of providing a throne and a canopy for the President, of thanking him for his 'most gracious speech', of making the members of the House of Representatives stand at the bar of the Senate in the way the Commons stood at the bar of the House of Lords. Adams wanted the Senate to say that the President alone had rescued the United States from 'anarchy and confusion' and Ralph Izard spoke of the necessity for kingship. A Senate committee set up to decide the title by which the President should be addressed suggested that it should be 'His Highness the President of the United States and Protector of the Rights of the Same.'[18]

The House of Representatives did not care for this extraordinary formula with its echoes not only of British kings but also of Lord Protector Cromwell who had once replaced them. 'Does the dignity of a nation consist in the distance between the first magistrate and his citizens?' asked Thomas Tudor Tucker of South Carolina. 'Would it add to his fame to be called after the petty princes of Europe?' demanded James Jackson from Georgia. Congress rejected all attempts to give the President the trappings of monarchy but the press was still reluctant to let the vision go. The *Massachusetts Spy* spoke of the United States 'espousing in the presence of the King of Kings the darling object of her choice,

His Highness the President General of United Columbia,' and even in the middle of June, weeks after Congress had decided that the President should be plain Mr Washington, it was still referring to him as 'His Excellency' and to his wife as 'Her Ladyship'.[19]

'Titles to both the President and Vice President were finally and unanimously condemned by a vote of the House of Representatives,' Madison told Jefferson on 9 May. 'This I hope will show to the friends of Republicans that our new government was not meant to substitute either Monarchy or Aristocracy.' Jefferson was waiting anxiously in Paris for the new government to be set up because he wanted to go home on leave and could not do so until there was a properly constituted authority in New York to give him permission. Madison's letter took six weeks to reach him but in the mean time he heard from other sources that the federal government was already organized and that 'public affairs wore a very promising appearance'. This was over-optimistic, because on 27 May Madison had written again to say that Jefferson could not hope to get his leave permit until 'auxiliary officers to the President shall be established'.[20] There were proposals to set up a finance ministry, a foreign office and a war department but these had yet to be approved by Congress. At Versailles an executive waited for a legislative to constitute itself while in New York a legislative struggled to constitute an executive. Political delay and constitutional deadlock was the prelude to revolution on one side of the Atlantic and the aftermath of revolution on the other.

'It is utterly impossible in the present situation of things for the States General to proceed upon business,' Dorset declared on 14 May. There had been a suggestion that the bishops and higher clergy should merge with the nobility to form a House of Lords while the parish priests joined the third estate to form a House of Commons. 'It is not however likely,' Dorset reported, 'that Government will adopt a plan by which the Commons would gain too great a preponderance'. Jefferson thought resistance to the idea came from the third estate rather than from the government: 'some think the nobles could be induced to unite themselves with the higher clergy into one house, but the tiers etat are immovable'. Benjamin Vaughan could not see why the third estate should oppose such a scheme. 'If the clergy and nobility will not coalesce with the Tiers Etat,' he asked Jefferson, 'will they coalesce with each other and form one house as with us? This would be a popular gain.'[21] In the context of existing institutions he was right: it was clearly more advantageous for the third estate to contend with one rival than with two. But most third estate deputies had ceased to think in terms of existing institutions. They might have been prepared to accept a government policy within the existing context if one had been put forward but since it had not they were now ready to change the context, to give France her first National Assembly rather than her last Estates General. The French revolution was already taking place, its visions and its aspirations implanted in men's minds during the long days of frustration and delay.

Nobody saw this more clearly than Dumont and Duroveray and Clavière, now established at Versailles together with Etienne Salomon Reybaz, another Genevese, as Mirabeau's unpaid assistants. 'All the seeds of unrest were sown and took root during this interval,' wrote Dumont, 'the historian of the revolution should pay particular attention to this period.'[22] Few historians have taken his advice but nevertheless the interval he was speaking of, the five seemingly uneventful weeks from the first Wednesday in May to the second Wednesday in June, saw the passing of old attitudes and the emergence of new. Men ceased to talk about balance and equilibrium, about initiatives from the executive and responses from the legislative, about bi-cameralism and the separation of powers. Instead they talked of the rights of the nation and the sovereignty of the people. They were no longer interested in regeneration and restoration, in revolution through three hundred and sixty degrees to return to some fabled happiness that was supposed to have been lost by the French in 1614 or found by the British in 1688. These were the weeks when revolution began to change its meaning.

The third estate did not bring about the change on its own. Accounts of the opening session of 5 May spoke of galleries from which more than two thousand people were able to watch the proceedings and these galleries were still available when the third estate took over the great hall. But the other two orders found themselves in rooms so small that they would not have had room for themselves if they had admitted spectators. 'Neither the clergy nor the nobles suffer any strangers to be present at their meetings,' Dumont wrote, 'while the commons have thrown open their doors to the public. At first few persons had curiosity enough to profit by this advantage, but the number begins to increase very considerably and in the same proportion the influence of the commons increases.'[23] Instead of being a mere abstraction dreamed up by philosophers the sovereign people was a real flesh and blood presence, at first applauding the action and later coming near to controlling it.

As a result the action was not always edifying. Dorset reported that 'the confusion and disorder that have prevailed are scarcely to be imagined' and the Keeper of the Seals told the King that reactions from the galleries made third estate debates dangerously heated. Mirabeau's journal *The Estates General*, to which no fewer than 12,000 Parisians were said to have subscribed, compared the deputies to unruly children just let out of school. It was so scathing that it was suppressed after only two issues, even though Necker had promised that there would be no censorship. 'As to Mirabeau,' wrote one of Bentham's Lansdowne House friends, 'he is, I fear, an incorrigible blackguard and also very deficient in common sense. What could be more foolish than to publish anything at this time which should give a pretence to say that the liberty of the press was dangerous? They would not have dared to suppress a journal which had given a fair account of the proceedings of the States.' Yet this same incorrigible blackguard had sufficient common sense to petition the King to preside in person over a joint session of the Estates and decide the matter of vote *par ordre* or vote *par tête* once and for all. It was certainly one of the last sensible suggestions the government received.[24]

But the government was still determined not to govern. When the nobles met again on Monday 11 May the Keeper of the Seals informed the King that they seemed set against verification in common but he had no orders to try and influence their decision. The clergy and the nobility sent deputations to the third estate only to be told that it could not receive them because it was not a separate estate but merely 'an assembly of citizens lawfully convoked in order to wait for other citizens'. It would not admit its own existence by electing a President but it did ask its senior member to act as Dean. On Wednesday further deputations from the other two orders were told that their suggestions for con- ciliatory talks would be considered if and when the assembly constituted itself. The next day another new word joined 'assem- bly' and 'citizen' and 'patriot' in the burgeoning vocabulary of revolution. One of the Breton deputies, Isaac-René-Guy Le Chap- elier, proposed that 'the Commons of France' should reject any idea of a conference with the other two orders and simply tell them that if they did not come and have their powers verified in the great hall they were not legitimate representatives of anyone or anything. He was opposed by Jean Paul Rabaut St-Etienne, a protestant minister from Nîmes whose election had been questioned on religious grounds until the other deputies for the city refused to serve without him.[25] Rabaut wanted to accept the idea of a conference and nominate sixteen commissioners to attend it.

Instead of debating one or other of these motions as the House of Commons would have done the assembly submitted both to a procedure called 'nominal appeal', so that each of the 648 deputies could first comment on them and then say which he favoured. This took until the following Monday, when Mirabeau intervened and proposed a different tactic altogether. 'Send to the clergy, gentlemen,' he cried, 'but do not send to the nobles, for the nobles command while the clergy negotiate.' The suggestion was brushed aside and Rabaut's motion was accepted after he had agreed to two amendments, one insisting that the commissioners should not discuss anything other than verification and another requiring them to keep minutes of the conference. The sixteen commissioners were elected the next day – they included Le Chapelier and Rabaut but not Mirabeau – and seven of them went to see the other two orders. They returned to say that they had been well received and that nothing now stood in the way of conciliation.[26]

They deceived themselves. The nobles welcomed them with great courtesy, inviting them to be seated and remaining standing themselves when the invitation was refused, but as soon as they had left there were fierce protests against their use of the word 'Commons'. It was said that it was entirely unconstitutional and that the nobles should not agree to confer unless it was withdrawn. Commissioners for the nobility were finally appointed but their powers were so hedged round with limitations that the conference was foredoomed to failure. After two abortive sessions it was adjourned indefinitely. The nobles then voted decisively for separate verification but the clergy began to show signs of splitting down the middle. When the Archbishop of Arles read out his report on the conference some of the parish priests called him a liar and insisted that their alternative version be heard. That evening several of the lower clergy met deputies from the third estate and said they would join them if an invitation was forthcoming.[27]

By now the third estate was in turmoil, its debates ungoverned and its members ungovernable. 'The inconveniences of debating in so tumultuous a manner are terrible,' wrote Dumont's friend Samuel Romilly, another of the radical thinkers patronized by Lansdowne, 'they render me quite impatient that the papers I sent the Count de Sarsfeld should be published.' At Sarsfeld's request Romilly had compiled a manual of English parliamentary procedure for the use of the deputies but Sarsfeld was now dead and Dumont was having trouble finding another translator and publisher.[28] In any case the chances of having these or any other rules of procedure accepted seemed remote. Formal attempts to regulate debates had begun soon after the conference commissioners were appointed but all had been rejected. Always the answer was the same: set procedures implied a constituted chamber and this was what the assembly could not admit to being. Members who tried to copy the House of Commons were scorned – 'a ridiculous and puerile imitation of the English prevails in the assembly' wrote Adrien Duquesnoy angrily – and reputations were made by demonstrating 'patriotic zeal' rather than by obeying rules. Some of these demonstrations were about remarkably trivial things, as when deputies were attacked for accepting complimentary tickets for theatrical performances at the royal palace. Even Duquesnoy, a moderate and later a rank conservative, declared that such slavish dependence on royal charity was 'infinitely indecent' and the extremists tried in vain to get the performances cancelled and the cost of them given to the poor.[29]

Having attached themselves to Mirabeau, writing his speeches and helping to edit his *Letters to Constituents*, successor to the banned *Estates General*, the Genevese did not like to see control of the assembly slip from his hands into those of Le Chapelier and the Bretons. 'They constitute an inseparable phalanx,' wrote Dumont. 'They prepare their opinions at private meetings, give one another mutual support, and do not neglect the policy of forming themselves into a party. The quarter of the hall which they occupy is more active, more animated and more tumultuous than the rest.' 'Brittany has forty-four deputies and we have joined with them,' wrote Maximilien Robespierre, a deputy from Artois, 'most of them are men of talent and full to the brim with courage and energy.' In his opinion Mirabeau was as nothing in the assembly because of his reputation for immorality. Dorset had already reported that 'M. de Mirabeau, who was considered by many people as the leader of the Tiers Etat, has lost much of his consequence' and even Dumont admitted that 'he is listened to by the assembly in profound silence but it is rather as an actor, on account of the pleasure which his speeches afford, than as an eloquent politician'.[30]

In Brittany the third estate had come near to open rebellion and its representatives at Versailles were sworn enemies of monarchy and aristocracy. Dumont on the other hand wanted to see the verification question settled in a way which would persuade the French to copy the British constitution and he also wanted to reconcile the assembly with Necker so that both could work together to help the Genevese exiles. Now it seemed that both these objectives might be within his grasp and he determined to make Mirabeau play his part in defeating the extremism of the Bretons. In the course of a long conversation in the gardens of Versailles he told him frankly that he had made a bad start in the assembly and must now make a fresh one under the guidance of his Genevese friends.[31]

On 27 May, when the intransigence of the nobility and the divisions within the clergy seemed to be opening the way to a House of Lords and a House of Commons, Dumont was glad to find that 'the comte de Mirabeau, who is naturally hot, violent and impetuous, upon this occasion very wisely recommended moderation to the Commons.'[32] The extremists wanted to break off the conferences altogether and keep the assembly as it was but Mirabeau argued that it would be immensely strengthened by the accession of the lower clergy. A solemn deputation was sent inviting the clergy to the great hall for verification in common. They promised to debate the matter and another deputation was then sent, saying that the Commons would remain in continuous session, all night if necessary, until they got an answer. The clergy refused to be pressurized in this way and they adjourned until the following day, when a very angry debate took place. One priest said bitterly that the clergy was no longer one order but two, all the higher clergy wanting to support the nobles and all the lower wanting to accept the third estate's invitation.[33] Just when it seemed that the parish priests were getting the better of the argument the doors opened and the master of ceremonies entered with a letter from the King. At last the government had decided to act.

'There is every reason to believe that M. Necker is extremely embarrassed at this moment,' Dorset wrote that evening, 'for as his popularity has hitherto been his chief support the decline of that minister's credit, which is already wavering, will unavoidably be attended with a national bankruptcy.' He went on to say that all officers from the rank of major upwards had been ordered to join their regiments forthwith. Prices of government securities had been falling for a month and whatever Necker might have said at the opening session it was clear that France would not be solvent much longer if the deadlock continued.[34] The government must try to break it by political means and if those failed it might have need of the officers and their regiments. And so on Thursday 28 May the King sent letters to all three orders commanding them to resume their conferences at six o'clock the following evening in the presence of the Keeper of the Seals and other government ministers.

'The clergy yielded to this demand with the devoutest gratitude,' reported Dumont. 'The nobles consented, but haughtily and with an ill grace. Among the Commons many deputies thought they had discovered, in this dangerous intervention of the crown, a formed plan to enslave the orders by dividing them.' The Bretons and Robespierre's men from Artois wanted to ignore the King's command and a deputy from Picardy was wildly applauded when he said Louis was acting under orders from the bishops, who had already bribed many priests to stop them joining the Commons. There was immense enthusiasm when Mirabeau said they could not give the commissioners absolute power because the expression was no longer French and again when he refused to continue speaking because a sentry had entered the hall to eject a spectator who did not appear to be sufficiently respectably dressed. Because of the crucial nature of the debate the moderates wanted to exclude strangers but all they were able to obtain was a ruling that spectators should not make signs of approval or disapproval and should not sit among the deputies in the body of the hall. Both concessions were very revealing and they helped to explain why the debate was, in Dumont's words, 'long, violent and tumultuous'.[35]

It was inconceivable that any of this could have happened if Louis had sent such letters three weeks earlier. Then the great hall at Versailles had held the deputies of the third estate in serried ranks, each decorously garbed in the regulation black costume prescribed by the King. Now it was spilling over with men who dressed as they pleased and sat where they pleased, some proud to be members of 'the Commons' or 'the Assembly' and others self-confessed agitators from Paris come to cheer 'patriots' and hiss supporters of the old order of things. Three weeks ago debates had been about discovering the King's intentions so that they could be obeyed, but now obedience was itself the issue. After two days of argument and another lengthy nominal appeal the Commons finally agreed to let its commissioners attend on condition that proper minutes were kept and that the King received a Commons deputation as he had already received one from the nobility.

The conference ran into trouble as soon as it opened. When the clergy were asked if they had a conciliation plan to put forward the bishops said they had not and the lower clergy said they had. The nobles then blocked discussion of this plan by reading a long statement on their ancient rights, after which there was a fierce argument about minutes, the Commons saying they had to have them and the nobility saying they could not sign them. At last, when it was clear that nothing was being achieved. Necker asked in desperation: 'Gentlemen, you see all the dangers surrounding us, isn't there some way of reaching agreement?' 'It was you who kindled the fire,' replied the marquis de Bouthillier, one of the commissioners for the nobility. 'It's up to you to find a way of putting it out.' The conference was then adjourned for four days.[36]

Necker was normally home by ten or eleven o'clock but on the night of the conference he was said to have been late, so late that at two o'clock in the morning his wife went to the palace to see what had happened to him. The story went that she asked the valet outside the King's bedroom if he knew where her husband might be, whereupon the King woke up and called to ask what was going on. He then got up, assuring Mme Necker that he had not seen her husband, and insisted on going with her to the Queen's apartments, where he told the guard at the door not to announce him. On opening the door he found Necker deep in consultation with the Queen and with Artois, Condé and Conti, the three most reactionary of the royal princes, who were allegedly trying to get him to resign. 'It is not known what the King said,' concluded the teller of the tale, a lawyer's clerk in Paris who seems to have been well informed on other matters. If the story was a fabrication it is odd that the punch line should have been left out.[37]

What was certainly true, secret councils or no secret councils, was that the past few weeks had made the Court more reactionary just as surely as they had made the third estate more revolutionary. The days were gone when Marie Antoinette wanted to be 'Queen of the Third', nor was Bouthillier alone in thinking that a fire was raging and that Necker must either extinguish it or make way for someone who could. When the conference of the three orders met again on Wednesday 3 June and started arguing about the word 'Commons' the Keeper of the Seals said that he could not accept it because the King had not sanctioned it. The commissioners for the Commons said he had no right to say this because ministers were supposed to be impartial and for good measure they accused him of going back on his own earlier recommendation, made at the opening session, that verification should be in common. He hotly denied having said such a thing and once again the meeting broke up without agreement. The next evening Necker made his attempt at firefighting, putting before the conference a plan whereby the three orders would verify uncontested credentials separately and refer difficult cases to a commission of all three orders. Cases upon which this body could not agree would be decided by the King. The commissioners promised to refer the plan to their orders and the conference adjourned.[38]

It seemed that the Necker plan and the Necker ministry would stand or fall together. Clavière would have liked them both to fall because he had visions of being finance minister himself – as indeed he was three years later – but Dumont and Duroveray saw Necker's survival as the best guarantee of a balanced constitution as well as the best chance of help for the Genevese exiles. Dumont told Lansdowne on 3 June that they hoped to bring a motion about Geneva before the estates when the verification question was settled and the same day he wrote to Romilly saying that Mirabeau, once Necker's bitter critic, was now ready to support a vote of confidence in him: 'He will defend as a friend of the people the same minister he has attacked as a financier and as a politician.'[39]

This was also the day Jefferson took a hand in things. He had always been a firm supporter of the third estate and a fortnight earlier he had told friends in England and America that it would soon join with the liberal nobles and the lower clergy to form one all-powerful assembly. If the government did not do business with this assembly no taxes would be paid and there might be civil war. But now he was less sure and he wrote to Lafayette in the nobility and to Rabaut St-Etienne in the third estate suggesting that in order to break the deadlock the King and every member of the Estates General should sign a Charter of Rights which he had drawn up. It was an impressive document – he was after all one of the authors of the Declaration of Independence – but it offered no solution to the immediate problem of verification. 'I will endeavour to bring matters to the issue you point out,' replied Lafayette in some embarrassment and somewhat stilted English, 'but it is very hard to navigate in such a whirling.'[40]

The atmosphere in the great hall was not conducive to conciliation of any kind. 'The most extravagant and disrespectful language against government has been held,' wrote Dorset, 'the greatest approbation is expressed by the audience by clapping of hands and other demonstrations of satisfaction; in short the encouragement is such as to have led some of the speakers on to say things little short of treason.' The latest and most vehement complaint was that the King would not receive the deputation which the Commons had made the condition of their agreeing to the conference. For more than a year the King's eldest son the Dauphin, a boy of seven, had suffered from a mysterious illness that had crippled him and kept him in constant pain. His governor the duc d'Harcourt was said to have made him dislike his mother, so that when she tried to comfort him he turned away from her. It was because this long agony was now coming to its sad end that the King could not see the deputation. The Dauphin died early in the morning of 4 June, so that when Necker's plan was put before the assembly the following day it seemed that the reception of the deputation might be delayed indefinitely. There was resentment in the hall and an even steelier resentment at the palace, especially on the part of the Queen.[41]

The assembly's Dean had resigned, partly for health reasons but also because of rumours that he was in collusion with Necker, and the new Dean was Jean-Sylvain Bailly, one of the phalanx of Parisian deputies who had only recently arrived at Versailles because their election had been delayed. Early on Friday morning Bailly went to see the Keeper of the Seals and was told that the King had postponed not only the reception of the deputation but also the next session of the conference. This news made the assembly more truculent than ever and it refused to discuss the Necker plan until the deputation had been seen and the conference wound up. In Duquesnoy's eyes this was a fatal step. 'The present moment is decisive,' he wrote, 'if we accept the plan we can constitute ourselves and get somewhere; if we turn it down I don't know what will happen to us.' Three days later Pierre-Victor Malouet, another conservative who feared that they might be launching into the unknown, suggested that they should constitute themselves forthwith as 'the legitimate Assembly of the representatives of the Commons'.[42] This was rejected not only because it implied separate verification but also because it was premature. Nothing could be done until the conditions laid down had been met.

By this time one of them had already been met: the King had received the deputation on Saturday and after thanking the deputies for their condolences he had expressed the hope that the third estate would now help him in working for the good of his people. First there were obsequies to be performed and Bailly duly gave the assembly an account of the ceremony of sprinkling holy water on the Dauphin's body. 'Since the corpse was embalmed,' wrote Dorset, 'it has shrunk to less than the size of a new-born infant.' At last, on the morning of Wednesday 10 June, Bailly was able to inform the deputies that the conference had been brought to an end the previous evening. However, the minutes were not yet available and this provided a further excuse to put off the discussion of Necker's plan. Suddenly a deputy from Provence stood up. It was Mirabeau, the man whom Dumont thought he had brought to heel, the man who was supposed to be working with Necker in the way members of the House of Commons worked with ministers at Westminster. He made no reference to Necker's plan but said instead that the time had come to take a decisive step. He did not intend to propose it himself but he understood that one of the deputies from Paris would now do so. And the deputy from Paris was Sièyes, arch-enemy of all balanced constitutions and untiring advocate of one single National Assembly taking its authority from the people. His proposal was that the Commons should now start to turn itself into such an assembly. Having told the other orders to come to the great hall if they wanted to be part of the assembly it must then verify its powers, constitute the assembly and decide on its name. Two hundred and forty-seven deputies voted for Sièyes's motion as it stood and a further two hundred and forty-six wanted to add an amendment providing for the King to be informed of the reasons for it. Only fifty-one deputies had any alternative course of action to suggest. When Bailly put the amended motion to the vote in a resumed sitting after dinner it was carried with only three dissenting voices. The long delay was at an end.[43]

CHAPTER SIX

In the name of the people

'Nothing buzzing in my ears but the fête given last night by the Spanish ambassador,' wrote Arthur Young irritably as he left London for Paris early in June. 'The best fête of the present period is that which ten millions of people are giving to themselves, bosoms beating with gratitude for the escape of one common calamity'. British newspapers were fast losing interest in the stalemate at Versailles but instead of turning to the nationwide relief at George III's recovery, as Young would have wished, they concentrated on the lavish entertainments given by foreign embassies in London. At the French ambassador's ball the Prince of Wales refused to occupy a box prepared for him under two illuminated pictures, one showing France congratulating England on the King's restoration to health and the other depicting angels and graces crowning Queen Charlotte for having saved her sick husband from her undutiful son. Fearing a repetition of this embarrassing incident the Spanish ambassador provided no special seating for the Prince, thus giving rise to even more excited press comment.[1] Glittering occasions and nuances of royal behaviour were a lot more newsworthy than ten million beating bosoms.

The British press seemed to think the same was true of France. The Paris correspondent of *The Times* was no longer reporting on the Estates General but on what he called 'the procession of the blue ribands', the investiture of knights of the Order of the Holy Ghost, and he insisted that the whole of Paris had flocked to Versailles to see this ceremony. But when Young arrived in the

-103-

French capital on 8 June he found that 'Paris is at present in such a ferment about the States General, now holding at Versailles, that conversation is absolutely absorbed by them.' He was a guest of the Liancourt family, prominent among the liberal nobility and also high in favour at Court, and shortly after his arrival he dined with the duc de Liancourt in the palace of Versailles, meeting some twenty deputies. 'They all speak with equal confidence on the fall of despotism,' he wrote, 'the spirit of the people is too much excited at present to be crushed any more.' Again he reckoned up the numbers concerned – it was, he said, 'a crisis of the fate of four-and-twenty millions of people' – and Parisians seemed closer to these spirited and uncrushable millions than Londoners were to the ten million beating bosoms.[2] Excitement at reducing royal power forged stronger links than gratitude for royal recovery.

This did not mean that Young liked what Parisians were doing or accepted their claim to speak for the twenty-four millions. He was horrified when he visited the Palais Royal on his second day in the city. This was the town home of the duc d'Orléans, who had made it into the most extraordinary urban phenomenon of the age. 'It is unique,' wrote one enthusiast, 'nothing in London, Amsterdam, Vienna, Madrid, can compare with it. A man might be imprisoned within its precincts for a year or two and never miss his liberty. They call it the capital of Paris. Everything is to be found there.' The gardens had been dug up and the land let out for the building of brothels and gambling dens, cafés and theatres, shops and workshops of every kind. Young was appalled by the innumerable subversive tracts printed on the presses of this city within a city and offered for sale in its bookshops. 'Is it not wonderful,' he wrote indignantly, 'that while the press teems with the most levelling and even seditious principles, that if put into execution would overturn the monarchy, nothing in reply appears, and not the least step is taken by the Court to restrain this extreme licentiousness of publication?' Cafés in the Palais Royal were always crowded to hear the impromptu revolutionary sermons which demagogues preached from chairs and tables. 'The eagerness with which they are heard, and the thunder of applause they receive for every sentiment of more than common hardiness or violence against the present government, cannot easily be imagined. I am all amazement at the ministry permitting such nests and hotbeds of sedition and revolt.'[3]

Young was quick to see that the resolution of 10 June was a

turning point. He was not sure it was wise and he wanted to know what would happen if the other two orders declared it unconstitutional and demanded a dissolution. His doubts were brushed aside: 'I am always told that the first object must be for the people to get the power of doing good ... the common idea is that anything tending towards a separate order, like our House of Lords, is absolutely inconsistent with liberty; all of which seems perfectly wild and unfounded.' 'I find a general ignorance of the principles of government,' he added, 'no settled plan that shall give security to the people'. In 1783, after George III had used the Lords against the Commons, Pitt had claimed that royal power was 'part of the rights of the people'; so what rights or security could the French people expect if they allowed undisputed sovereignty to pass to a single and undivided body of men? 'All real power will be henceforward in the Commons,' Young concluded, 'having so much inflamed the people in the exercise of it they will find themselves unable to use it temperately.'[4]

Dorset reached much the same conclusion. 'They will consider themselves as representatives of the Nation and qualified to act as such independent of the other orders,' he told his government when he learned what the third estate had done, 'this determined and extraordinary resolution will be productive of infinite confusion and of insurmountable embarrassment to ministers'. Dumont and Duroverary, who had hoped to prevent ministerial embarrassment by holding Mirabeau in check, were alarmed to find him supporting Sièyes. 'I had assumed that this friend of liberty was bound to love the English,' Dumont said of Sièyes, 'and I was amazed to find that he viewed the English constitution as a piece of chicanery intended to fool the people.' The division of the legislative into Lords and Commons was part of that chicanery, as was the corruption which enabled the government to build up a party in Parliament. Sièyes wanted the total separation of powers, the breaking of all links between executive and legislative, as well as the supreme sovereignty of the people untrammelled by any theory of constitutional balance. And now it seemed Mirabeau wanted these things too. Something had to be done quickly. The Genevese contacted Malouet, who agreed to bring Mirabeau and Necker together. The meeting took place on the day after Sièyes's motion was carried. It was not a success. 'Monsieur Malouet has told me that you have certain propositions to put to me,' Necker said haughtily. 'What are they?' This was too much for Mirabeau's pride. 'My proposition is to bid you good morning,' he replied angrily and stormed out.[5]

It was a fateful moment. The Estates General did not meet that day because it was the feast of Corpus Christi but the next morning, just as the Commons began the verification of powers, a deputy from Villeneuve-de-Berg in the Rhône valley stood up and denounced Duroveray. He wanted to know why this foreign agent, this Swiss refugee paid from British secret service funds, had been allowed to sit for days on end in the body of the hall passing scribbled notes to deputies and apparently orchestrating their part in the debates. Mirabeau sprang to Duroveray's defence and was applauded when he described him as a martyr for liberty. Dumont managed to convince himself that the incident vindicated Mirabeau and his band of Genevese Anglophiles but more impartial observers noted sourly that there was 'a murmur of disapproval' when it was suggested that Duroveray should be assured that no offence had been intended. It was clear that offence had been intended and that suspicions had been aroused. At this critical juncture, as Sièyes strove to discredit everything that smacked of Westminster and of the influence government wielded there, Mirabeau played into his hands by admitting that his associates and advisers included men who were pensioners of King George III. This was to have an important impact on the events of the next few days. It was ironic, but not entirely coincidental, that the incident came hard on the heels of Mirabeau's unsuccessful attempt to make contact with Necker's ministry.[6]

The verification of powers was a tedious business. Constituencies were called out in alphabetical order and as each was called its deputies, clergy and nobility as well as third estate, were supposed to come forward and have their credentials checked. Constituencies from Agen to Hennebond were dealt with on Friday and in each case the response was depressingly similar: no clergy, no nobility, only deputies for the third estate. The process began again on Saturday morning at the letter L and continued uneventfully as far as P: Paris, Perche, Périgord, Péronne, Perpignan, Ploërmel. Then, with Poitou, came high drama. Three priests stepped forward and presented their credentials as deputies for the first estate. 'Preceded by reason's torch, led by love of the common good, we come to take our places alongside our brothers and fellow citizens,' they announced. 'They were received with immoderate transports of applause,' wrote Dumont. 'Several of the commons embraced them as saviours of their country'.[7] A few more appeared on Sunday and on Monday morning but the great majority of the clergy and the whole of the nobility still maintained that verification in common was unconstitutional.

Next came the problem of finding a name for the assembly. 'This vital question was exhaustively debated in our little society', claimed Dumont, meaning that he and the other Genevese tried to tell Mirabeau what to do about it. 'We took the English constitution as our model,' he added, 'and we thought that the division of the legislative into two branches would be far better than having one single assembly which could neither be controlled nor checked.' Young also thought that controlling and checking were essential – 'It now seems the opinion,' he noted, 'that the Commons in their late violent vote have gone too far' – and he decided to go to Versailles himself on Monday, 'a very important debate being expected on what in our House of Commons would be termed the state of the nation.'[8]

Sièyes opened the debate by proposing that they should call themselves 'Assembly of the known and verified representatives of the French nation'. Mounier, even more committed than Dumont to a British style constitution, suggested 'Legitimate assembly of the representatives of the majority of the French nation acting in the absence of the minority'. Mirabeau put forward a simpler title: 'Representatives of the French people'. 'Monsieur de Mirabeau was well heard,' reported Young, 'and his proposition much applauded.' The assembly adjourned for dinner at two o'clock* and when it reassembled at half past five Young was no longer in the gallery: he had been told that the debate would not be concluded that day and so he had gone back to Paris. If he had stayed he would have heard Mirabeau speak again, this time to considerably less applause. The theme of this second disquisition was the importance of a balanced constitution and in particular the need for the King to be able to veto the enactments of the assembly. Ministers were delighted and the Keeper of the Seals, the most reactionary member of the government, sent Louis an admiring account of the speech.[9]

The assembly was much less delighted and when the debate was resumed next morning it was clear that Mirabeau's stock had fallen considerably. His proposal was attacked on all sides as yet

*At this time it was fashionable to dine in the middle of the afternoon.

another Anglophile device, an attempt to turn the assembly into a lower house representing merely the common people. Just as he wanted Louis XVI to have the same powers as George III so he also wanted to leave a loophole for the first two orders to re-emerge as a House of Lords. Looking back on the debate some months later Dumont recalled that 'many deputies suggested that this title was intended as the foundation stone for a constitution modelled on that of Great Britain'; but at the time he was slow to read the danger signals. During the morning session he was sitting in the public gallery talking to Lord Elgin, a young Scottish peer who was later to distinguish himself by bringing the Parthenon friezes back to England. They were both appalled by the onslaught on Mirabeau. Dumont said the French should be made to realize that even if they were so stupid as to take offence at the word 'people' there were other and more sensible countries where it was properly valued. He jotted down some ideas along these lines and showed them to Elgin, who approved highly of them. When the assembly adjourned Dumont went to dine with Mirabeau and found him being taken to task by Duroveray for not answering his critics forcefully enough. The jottings were produced and Mirabeau agreed to use them in his closing speech.[10]

It was a mistake. Dumont's contribution was greeted with an unprecedented outburst of fury. 'These were not merely shouts,' he noted nervously, 'they were convulsions of rage.'[11] When the tumult lessened Mirabeau said that as the deputies had failed to understand what he was telling them he would deposit it with the President so that they could read it instead. Then he stalked out as angrily as he had stalked out of the interview with Necker five days earlier. Others had even more unpleasant experiences during this crucial debate. While Malouet was speaking in support of Mirabeau a man said to be 'well dressed but with the build and appearance of a hired thug' rushed from the public gallery and seized him by the throat, shouting 'Hold your tongue, enemy of the people!'* The guards were called but the man melted into the crowd and was never caught. Malouet averred that before this incident there were three hundred deputies prepared to vote against Sièyes; after it there were ninety. To the end of his life he maintained that it was this incident, not the setting up of the guillotine, that marked the beginning of the Reign of Terror.

*Tais-toi, mauvais citoyen!

'Those members who were known to be desirous of moderating the animosity that prevailed found it expedient to remove from their places to avoid the insults which seemed to threaten them,' reported Dorset.[12] Agents of the Palais Royal were said to be in the public galleries noting down the names of all who dared to oppose Sièyes. Towards midnight a deputy from Berry suggested that they should sweep aside the reservations about 'known and verified representatives' and simply call themselves 'the National Assembly'. Sièyes seconded this, delighted to find a title even more challenging than his own. There were calls for a division then and there but the moderates managed to get the vote put off until the next day.

'And so here we are transported to England,' wrote the Keeper of the Seals to Louis that night, 'and the Estates General convoked by Your Majesty transformed into the Commons.' This was the ultimate irony. British constitutional practice had been decisively rejected by the assembly yet those in government still thought it had triumphed. It seemed that the British constitution had become the thing everybody loved to hate. To those in authority it was an instrument of subversion and to those in revolt it was a symbol of tyranny. To make matters worse *The Times* chose that very morning to lecture the third estate deputies yet again on the proper use of terms like 'the Commons' and 'the people' and to tell them that their failure to copy the British constitution was losing them popular support.[13]

When the third estate assumed the title of the National Assembly by an overwhelming majority on the morning of 17 June there was great rejoicing in Paris but also some anxiety. 'These steps give great spirits to the violent partisans of a new constitution,' wrote Young, 'but amongst more sober minds I see evidently an apprehension that it will prove a precipitate measure.' Dorset told his government that Louis must crush the National Assembly straight away because if he did not 'it will be little short of laying his crown at their feet'. Jefferson told the American government that the King would have to give in to the Assembly because if he did not no taxes would be paid. The one thing upon which everyone was agreed was that Louis must make the next move. The Keeper of the Seals told him that 'he would not be able to remain silent any longer without taking the risk of seeing his crown's rights compromised and his authority destroyed'.[14] It was rumoured among the deputies that the King would summon all three orders and proclaim a charter of rights, rather like the one Jefferson had proposed two weeks earlier, but the constitutional debate was fast making the very phrase a contradiction in terms. Charters were things monarchs granted, in the way kings of England granted the privileges of Parliament, but rights were things which men and nations possessed irrespective of kings, in the way described in the American Declaration of Independence. Underlying the arguments about divided legislature and royal vetoes was a more profound question: was the National Assembly a body given by the nation to the king or by the king to the nation?

This was the parting of the ways. If the Estates General was to bring about the regeneration of France, the recovery of ancient liberties similar to those restored in England in 1688, then rights must be confirmed by royal charter and the Assembly must be sanctioned by royal decree. The alternative, a charter rehearsing natural and pre-existing rights and an Assembly deriving its authority from the people, would launch the French into the same dangerous void of uncertainty which the Americans already inhabited. The Genevese were determined that this should not happen. They had spent more than a month trying to make Mirabeau an effective mouthpiece for the traditional British view of revolution and they had failed. It seemed that any measure Mirabeau supported was sure to be defeated. There was a real possibility that the King might dissolve the Estates, putting paid to any political advantage that either the Genevese exiles or the marquis of Lansdowne might hope to gain from them. It was time to bypass Mirabeau and contact Necker. According to Dumont it was Duroveray who did this, drawing up a plan for a royal session at which the King would annul the decree creating the National Assembly and at the same time command the clergy and the nobility to join the third estate.[15] The reunion of the three orders would thus be brought about by constitutional means rather than by an illegal action on the part of the third estate.

It was vital that Mirabeau should be kept in the dark and this in turn meant that Duroveray must not be named. 'I have the honour to send Your Majesty a note from the person whom I mentioned to the King yesterday under the seal of secrecy,' wrote Necker to Louis.[16] By this time there was added need for decisive action because more than half the clergy had voted to join the National Assembly and were due to appear in the great hall on the morning of Saturday 20 June. Between a quarter and a third of the nobility had also signified their readiness to join. Louis summoned a meeting of the Royal Council at which it was decided that there would be a royal session on the following Monday and that in the meantime the great hall would be closed so that the necessary preparations could be made. When the deputies gathered outside the locked and guarded doors of the hall on Saturday morning it was raining steadily. They took shelter in a tennis court – tennis was played indoors at this time – and Sièyes, with support from the Bretons, proposed to transfer the Assembly to Paris and rally the people of the city in its defence. It was not a very practical suggestion – the roads were in poor condition after a lot of bad weather and there were relatively few carriages for hire – but as President of the Assembly Bailly saw its dangers and was taking no chances. In order to head it off he accepted instead Mounier's suggestion that they should stay where they were and take an oath never to separate until the constitution of the kingdom was established on firm foundations.[17]

The Tennis Court Oath began the French revolution. It also ended the prospect of an English-style revolution in France. In his anxiety to prevent power passing to the people of Paris – something which in fact he only managed to delay for three weeks – Mounier had shattered the dream of a balanced constitution by which he set such store. 'They have at one stroke converted themselves into the Long Parliament of Charles I,' commented Young. 'If it is not opposed all other powers will lie in ruins around that of the Commons.' The Genevese were furious. Dumont told his friends in London that the deputies had behaved like drunkards and that their foolish oath was an act of rebellion against the nation as well as against the King. They were quite wrong, he insisted, to think they were threatened with dissolution. The plan was to annul all decrees so far put out, both by the third estate and by the privileged orders, and to bring all three estates together to decide the question of vote *par ordre* or vote *par tête*. 'Even though I am an enemy of despotism,' he added, 'I confess that it seems to me wise to halt the progress of a division which is getting worse every day.'[18]

This letter, written on Sunday 21 June, made it clear that Dumont had inside knowledge of the royal session plan in its original form. What he did not know was that the plan was about to be radically altered. That day there was another meeting of the Royal Council at which it was decided to put off the royal session until Tuesday. It was further agreed that after annulling the decree establishing the National Assembly the King would command the three orders to go back to their separate chambers in order to debate a series of proposals which he would put before them. Not knowing of the postponement Young went out to Versailles early on the Monday morning to be present at the royal session and had to be content with witnessing instead an impromptu session of the Assembly in the church of St Louis at which the majority of the clergy were welcomed and sworn in. He then dined with Liancourt in the palace and was told that the reactionaries on the Council, led by the comte d'Artois, had drawn up a programme to be put before the three estates the following day. 'All is now anxiety to know what the plan is,' he concluded. Next morning he was horrified to find the streets of Versailles lined with troops. These precautions seemed to him very ominous: 'They pronounced, before the King left the château, that his plan was adverse to the people, from the military parade with which it was ushered in.'[19]

'The contrary, however, proved to be the fact,' wrote Young with some relief later in the day, 'the propositions are known to all the world; the plan was a good one; much was granted to the people in great and essential points'. But the people were not in the accepting vein. Already Young had been amazed to find that the whole population of Versailles supported the Assembly. 'As this town is absolutely fed by the palace, and if the cause of the Court is not popular here,' he reflected, 'it is easy to suppose what it must be in all the rest of the kingdom.' Mirabeau, unmuzzled and free of the Genevese, produced the gesture to match this reflection. When the session was over the nobility and some of the clergy left in accordance with the King's order but the members of the Assembly stayed where they were. It was Mirabeau who reminded them that the people expected them to oppose the forces of despotism and it was Mirabeau who defied the master of ceremonies when he tried to clear the hall. 'If they have ordered you to get us out of here,' he cried, 'you had better ask to be allowed to use force because we shall only leave at bayonet point.' Later, when Clavière blurted out the story behind the royal session plan, Mirabeau exploded in fury. 'Duroveray did not consider me fit to be consulted,' he told Dumont angrily. 'I know full well that he regards me as a madman who has occasional lucid intervals.

But I could have told him in advance what they would do with his plan. This is the sort of thing that leads kings to the scaffold.'[20]

Gouverneur Morris went to Versailles on 23 June, not to be present at the royal session but to make a round of social visits. At dinner he found himself sitting next to Lafayette, who accused him of being on the side of the Court instead of supporting the Assembly as good Americans should. 'I seize this opportunity,' wrote Morris, 'to tell him that I am opposed to democracy from regard to liberty. That I see they are going headlong to destruction and would fain stop them if I could.' 'Before we part,' he added, 'I take an opportunity to tell him that if the Tiers are now very moderate they will probably succeed, but if violent must inevitably fail.'[21]

If he had been at home in New York he would have seen no headlong rush to destruction, no agonized choice between a moderation that might succeed and a violence that must fail, but he would certainly have seen the beginnings of confrontation. As he talked to Lafayette that afternoon it was ten o'clock in the morning in New York and Senator Maclay of Pennsylvania had just arrived in the chamber to find himself alone with Vice President Adams, the man whom he suspected of trying to revive monarchy in the United States. Adams left his splendid chair of office and sat with Maclay, telling him half flatteringly and half mockingly what good republicans the Pennsylvanians were. Maclay replied coldly that they had 'a general abhorrence of the pomp and splendid expense of government, especially everything that bordered on royalty.' The President had been ill for some time, first with a fever and now with a dangerous abscess on his thigh, and it was widely rumoured that he would soon resign his office. 'And then,' observed Maclay grimly, 'Mr Adams will begin his reign.'[22] The tension between the two men carried faint but unmistakable echoes of the high drama which had just been played out in the great hall at Versailles.

Maclay had been sniping at federal authority ever since his arrival in New York. 'My mind revolts in many instances against the constitution of the United States,' he wrote. 'Indeed, I am afraid it will turn out the vilest of all traps that was ever set to ensnare the freedom of an unsuspecting people.' He railed against 'the high-toned manners of the pompous people of New York' and he was horrified when Washington announced that officials must be well paid because 'without large salaries proper persons could never be got to fill the offices of government with propriety'. Maclay read this as a declaration of intent to gather into presidential hands the sort of patronage which enabled George III to control Parliament. And now, as Adams and Maclay glared at each other in the empty senate chamber, the House of Representatives was discussing a Bill to give the President power to remove the Secretary of State for Foreign Affairs. If this went through, Maclay averred, there would be more legislation of the same sort and the President would finish up as a despot with arbitrary powers over both executive and legislative. 'Indeed, I entertain no doubt but that many people are aiming with all their force to establish a splendid court with all the pomp of majesty. Alas! poor Washington, if you are taken in this snare! How will the gold become dim!'[23]

The debate in the House on this issue was as rancorous as anything at Versailles. Opponents of the removability clause insisted that Congress had as much right to share executive power as the President had to share legislative power: 'It is in this way that the liberties of the people are secured'. Kings might have prerogatives because monarchies were based on the maxim that 'the King can do no wrong', but presidents could certainly do wrong and so must have their powers circumscribed: 'the chief magistrate under this constitution is a different character; there is a constitutional tribunal where he may be arraigned, condemned and punished if he does wrong.' In answer to this Madison argued that 'when we consider that the first magistrate is to be appointed at present by the suffrages of three millions of people, and in all human probability in a few years' time by double that number, it is not to be presumed that a vicious or bad character will be selected.' The President could do no wrong because the people could do no wrong. When the clause was finally approved by twenty-nine votes to twenty-two Thomas Sumter of South Carolina insisted on registering a formal protest: 'This bill appears to my mind so subversive of the constitution, and in its consequences so destructive to the liberties of the people, that I cannot let it pass without expressing my detestation of the principles it contains.'[24]

Meanwhile Madison had pushed his belief in the infallibility of the people still further by proposing a series of amendments to the constitution, the first of which declared that 'the people have an indubitable, unalienable and indefeasible right to reform or change their government, whenever it be found adverse or inadequate to the purposes of its institution'. If the removability clause could be seen as an invitation to despotism then this could be read as an invitation to revolution. It certainly alarmed conservatives like Fisher Ames of Massachusetts, who regarded Madison as the ablest man in the House but feared he was 'very Frenchified in his politics'. 'I am commonly opposed to those who modestly assume the rank of champions of liberty and make a very patriotic noise about the people,' Ames remarked. 'It is the stale artifice which has duped the world a thousand times and yet, though detected, is still successful.'[25]

It was to be another three months before New Yorkers learned of the success which a patriotic noise about the people had had in France. In the mean time American political life remained comparatively decorous. Senate debates, like those of the first two orders at Versailles, were closed to the public but the House admitted strangers and enhanced its reputation by so doing. 'The spectators who hear the debates of our national Representatives are unanimous in their applause of the candour and impartiality which appear in the deliberations,' reported the *Massachusetts Spy*.[26] Yet the issues under discussion in America were just as fundamental as those in France. Congress was trying to put flesh on a skeleton and turn it into a living and working constitution; the Estates General was trying to rescue and revive a constitution which had been smothered for centuries. Both were potentially hazardous exercises.

There were many in London who were confident that the Americans would be unable to steer a safe course between despotism and anarchy. When news came of the constitutional difficulties in New York *The Times* alleged that Washington in desperation 'has lately proposed to Congress a reunion with this country, a proposal which every Englishman must reject with contempt; for, as Shakespeare says, "What, wouldst thou have a serpent sting thee twice?".' Fears of French success were as potent as hopes of American failure. Three days after the royal session *The Times* declared that 'the Commons in France, when once firmly established in their situation, will become extremely formidable to this country. Taxes will fall less heavily on the people, making them readier to go to war. We well know the hostile inclinations of the French at all times.' 'This country trembles,' Jefferson's friends in London told him, 'when they even suppose that France will be as free as themselves; because should they put their funds on the same plan as those here this country will feel it very severely.' Opposition papers took a rather different view, declaring that the French would now force their government to tear up the Commercial Treaty and then 'old England will be in a pitiable state' because Pitt had proved 'so shallow a financier'.[27]

In fact Pitt was an extremely able financier and the smoothness with which his plans went through Parliament ensured that England's political and financial stability was far from pitiable. Nothing showed this more clearly than Parliament's own royal session, which took place just two weeks before the one at Versailles. The Commons stood dutifully at the bar of the House of Lords to hear the King's speech and then went back to their own chamber to hear Pitt's proposals for new taxes and government loans, all of which went through without a division. Ten days later, as the clergy in Versailles voted to join the Assembly, the Commons were busy with Beaufoy's Revolution Commemoration Bill. By hearing the Declaration of Rights read in church every year, Beaufoy said, 'the people would tend to the support of revolution principles and guard against the danger of any future attempts, if such should be made, to effect a change in the government and constitution of the country'.[28] This was pretty innocuous, considering that Beaufoy was supposed to be a radical out to 'sap the foundation and destroy the fabric of the British constitution'.* It was a far cry from Madison's declaration that the people had a right to change their government and an even farther cry from what the French were doing. In London, at least, revolution still had its comfortingly conservative meaning.

As for the people, it was their business to keep quiet and keep their hands off the property of the rich. On the day of the French royal session, as Mirabeau made his bayonet speech, the House of Commons was debating ways of protecting trees and shrubs. Sir James Johnstone, a sturdy independent and advocate of toleration for dissenters, said that 'he could not, as a man of humanity, vote that his fellow creatures should be transported for a trifling robbery of a garden'. The Commons nevertheless decided that transportation should be the penalty for the theft or uprooting of any plant valued at five shillings or more. After the loss of America, which had left the authorities with nowhere to

*See above, p.87.

send such desperate criminals, there had been a sharp increase in the number of hangings. Samuel Romilly, shocked by unprecedented mass executions in London, had written a tract which had convinced Lansdowne of the need for penal reform. Nine felons were executed outside Newgate prison in March 1789, eight men hanged and one woman burned after the hangman in his mercy had strangled her before the flames took hold. However, a week later it was learned that the first batch of convicts transported to Australia had arrived safely at Botany Bay. Once again it could be arranged for garden robbers to die slowly and at a distance, so that gentlemen could safeguard their trees without risking unpleasant scenes nearer home.[29]

The difficulties of protecting the lands of the few from the envy of the many transcended national boundaries. 'The peasants in the neighbourhood of the Court have committed great outrages in the King's forests in defiance of the gamekeepers,' wrote Dorset two days after the royal session, 'some of the keepers have already fallen victims to these depredators and one was shockingly butchered a few evenings since by three poachers not a league from Versailles.' 'I would destroy game rather than accept poaching,' wrote John Byng, who was touring the midland counties of England that June to seek confirmation of his own deeply conservative attitudes and prejudices. 'The poor must plunder because not provided for,' he continued, blaming both crime and poverty on absentee landlords who neglected their rural duties in order to dance attendance on political masters in London. He was sure, doggedly and pathetically sure, that honest country ways could flourish again if the corruption of capitalism and the capital city could be kept at bay. Propertied men should shun London and live on their estates, building their labourers decent cottages and setting up alms houses to shelter them in their old age. Then the rural idyll of merry England would be reborn and neither trees nor gamekeepers would be under threat.[30]

As Dorset wrote out his report on the anarchy in Louis XVI's forests Byng was just leaving Whittington, where he had been regaled with enthusiastic accounts of the 1688 centenary celebrations. He was impressed but anxious, fearing that such junketings might be used to cloak dangerous innovations and justify the irresponsible antics of opposition politicians. He had visions of a new revolution, not a return to ancient liberties but a descent into chaos as London both drained and infected the countryside:

'as that increasing wen the metropolis must be fed the body will gradually decay: all the canals, all the roads must be forced to supply it; and when they have brought all they can, and it should by oversize, or particular seasons, want more – why then there will come a distress, a famine and an insurrection; which the praetorian guards or the whole army cannot quell'.[31]

Across the Channel the nightmare was fast becoming reality. 'It is now said confidently,' wrote Arthur Young that evening, 'that if an order is given to the French Guards to fire on the people they will refuse obedience.' 'The *Gardes du Corps* are as warm adherents to the *Tiers* as anybody else,' Gouverneur Morris told the American Foreign Secretary. Louis would have to look beyond his praetorian guards to his whole army. 'I need to have someone at my side on whose loyalty I can rely and who is able to take command of the army,' he wrote secretly to the maréchal de Broglie. 'Please come directly to Versailles as soon as you can.' 'The disturbances which have continued in the capital ever since the *Séance Royale* have extended to almost all the neighbouring parts of the country,' reported Dorset. 'A famine in many parts of the kingdom is still apprehended, since every exertion has been made to avert that calamity from the capital, by which some of the provinces are nearly exhausted.'[32] It seemed that Byng had mapped out the path from famine to insurrection fairly accurately, even if he had done it for the wrong country.

Necker had stayed away from the royal session and it was assumed that he was opposed to the policies announced there. Within hours of the session an ugly mob had surrounded the palace at Versailles, shouting abuse and threatening to throw lighted torches through the windows. Only when the King sent for Necker and got him to make an appearance did the insults turn to cheers. Night after night excited crowds thronged the streets of Paris and Versailles and on 25 June they proposed to build a bonfire outside Necker's house and treat him to a firework display. With some difficulty he managed to persuade them that his wife was in delicate health and would be distressed by the celebration. 'While M. Necker's mob was heard through every apartment of the château,' noted Young, 'the King passed in his coach to Marly through a dead and mournful silence; and that just after having given to his people, and the cause of liberty, more perhaps than ever any monarch had done before.'[33]

That same day, 25 June, George III drove from Windsor to the

New Forest on his way to convalesce in Weymouth. The only thing he had done for his people and for the cause of liberty was to recover his health, but this was more than enough for the eager crowds that gathered to greet him in every town and village. On entering the forest he was presented, as custom required, with two milk-white greyhounds 'peculiarly decorated' and he was attended by foresters in cloth of green, some with longbows and others with bugle horns. When he dined he permitted the people to come to the window and watch. There were those in the crowd who were evidently hungry, one of the ladies of the Court reported, but nevertheless everyone manifested 'delight and rapture in seeing their monarch at table.' Government newspapers carried ecstatic reports of popular loyalty but one of the Prince's friends told Burke that the crowds saw full well that the King was being 'carried about in a state of idiocy'.[34]

Louis XVI was also in his royal forests that afternoon but he rode too fast to find out whether his subjects were hungry or loyal. 'While it was actually a question whether he should be a doge of Venice or a king of France, the King went hunting!' cried Arthur Young in exasperation. 'The power of the King of France is verging to a conclusion,' *The Times* pronounced solemnly.[35] While New York worried about the President's illness and the Vice President's allegedly kingly ambitions, while London buzzed with accusations that the Queen and her henchmen were concealing the King's real condition in order to usurp the Prince's rights, Paris waited to see who would inherit the throne which its King did so little to defend.

CHAPTER SEVEN

The four horsemen

B y now foreigners in Paris were speaking openly of a war of
succession, a struggle within the Royal Family to seize the
power that was slipping from the King's grasp. Jefferson
thought that while Louis himself feared confrontation with the
Assembly the Queen and her brother-in-law Artois were 'infatu-
ated enough to hazard it'. Young referred to ministerial measures
as 'the projects of the Queen and the comte d'Artois' and was
convinced that Orléans was planning an uprising in Paris in order
to dethrone his cousin: 'There is no doubt of it being the duc
d'Orléans's money; the people are thus kept in a continual
ferment, are for ever assembled and ready to be in the last degree
of commotion whenever called on by the men they have confidence
in.' Dorset spoke approvingly of Artois's defence of the nobility
and was alarmed by the growing popular support for Orléans.
Nevertheless he arranged for the duchess of Devonshire to be
received by the duchesse d'Orléans when she arrived in Paris
shortly after the royal session.[1]

While he was at the Palais Royal making these arrangements
he met Morris, who was so infuriated by his haughtiness that he
refused a supper invitation and went instead to his club, where
stories of mob violence instigated by Orléans were circulating
freely. Next day Jefferson told Morris that Artois had persuaded
Louis to send for the maréchal de Broglie and have Paris ringed
with troops to crush an insurrection. At first the duchess of
Devonshire gaily straddled the gap between reactionaries and
revolutionaries, borrowing Artois's box at the opera one night

and Orléans's the next, but when she heard the shouting at the Palais Royal she quickly made up her mind. These were not the reassuring revolution principles she was used to at home. 'I am *for* the Court,' she announced firmly, 'on Mme de Polignac's account'. Her old friend the duchesse de Polignac presented her to Artois and to the Queen. 'She is sadly altered,' remarked the duchess of Marie Antoinette, 'her belly quite big and no hair at all, but she still has great *éclat*.'[2]

Two days after the royal session Orléans forced the issue by joining the National Assembly at the head of forty-eight members of the order of nobles. 'It is impossible to foresee what measures the King will adopt in consequence of this event,' wrote Dorset. 'The people are now disposed to any desperate act of violence'. He predicted civil war if the King tried to enforce the commands he had given at the royal session but Morris pointed out that there could be no war without an army: 'perhaps the King will be prompted to attempt a resumption of his authority. All this is mighty well but under the existing ideas of this moment it is very doubtful whether he could prevail on his soldiery to act'. Louis decided to give in and on 27 June he wrote to the nobles asking them to join the National Assembly. 'This letter occasioned a very warm and interesting debate,' reported Dorset, 'and there is reason to think would not after all have produced the desired effect had it not been followed by one from the comte d'Artois.' 'The comte d'Artois wrote to tell them if they did not join the King's life was in danger,' the duchess of Devonshire told her mother. The King also wrote to the remainder of the clergy, who obeyed without demur. 'It was four o'clock in the afternoon,' said Dumont, 'when the two orders, each with its president at its head, walked out of their separate chambers into the common hall. A cold and solemn silence was observed, both in the assembly and in the galleries; there was no applause, for none was due to an act of necessity.'[3]

'The people are wild with joy,' commented the duchess of Devonshire, 'and all our friends miserable.' The marquis de Sillery, prominent among Orléanist nobles, recounted scornfully how Parisians turned the rest of the day into an orgy, 'demonstrating in drunkenness their patriotism and their love for their kings'.[4] The use of 'kings' in the plural, the suggestion of a future king as well as a present one, could not hide the fact that the people had made their masters dance to their tune. The mighty were trembling in their seats and those who had once been humble and meek were flexing their muscles. If Orléans sought to raise the people against his cousin in the way William III had raised the English against his uncle and father-in-law James II he might find himself the destroyed rather than the destroyer. Those he would be using were not sturdy seventeenth-century men of property and they were not interested in revolutions that came full circle. They were for a turning of the tables, an anticipation of divine retribution, a man-made apocalypse.

Unfortunately the comforting passage about filling the hungry with good things was not the only indication of how such an apocalypse might turn out. The Book of Revelation also foretold war and famine as four grim horsemen were given power to take peace from the earth and to kill with the sword and with hunger. If the humble and meek were impatient to be exalted, if the mighty sought to make use of them in order to hang on to their seats, then the result might be a hell on earth rather than a heaven. Arthur Young caught a first glimpse of this possibility during the last days of June. 'The whole business now seems over and the revolution complete,' he wrote after the privileged orders had joined the Assembly. Having found out from his host's collection of *cahiers* what the people's grievances were, what good things must be handed out, he set off to watch the distribution. 'These *cahiers* being instructions given to their deputies, I have gone through them all, pen in hand, to make extracts,' he wrote, 'and shall therefore leave Paris tomorrow.' But when he made his first stop at Nangis, some forty miles from the capital, he was told bluntly that 'everybody is determined to pay no taxes, should the National Assembly so ordain.' To the suggestion that taxes might be collected by force the reply was: 'French soldiers will never fire on the people, but if they should it is better to be shot than starved.'[5] It looked as though killing with the sword and with hunger was a lot closer than the filling of the hungry with good things.

Few doubted that when the killing started it would be the work of the great men who were fighting for the crown and of their sinister foreign backers. The British were said to be plotting with the duc d'Orléans to hold up American grain intended for re-export to France. The truth was that American wheat was so infested with insects that the British authorities were on the point of banning it. Louis XVI's ministers could not afford to be so fastidious and they had promised to pay bounties on wheat sent from America to France. Little had arrived and now they looked to emergency supplies from Britain. Rumour had it that although there were British and American grain convoys in the Channel waiting to enter French ports Necker had refused to admit them, making instead an official request to the British government for permission to import 20,000 sacks of flour. His enemies all agreed that he did this because he knew the request would be refused but they differed as to his motives. Some said he was creating a shortage in order to help Orléans seize the throne, others that he was secretly supporting the Queen's plans to crush the National Assembly.[6]

The one certain thing was that Paris was near to starvation. Morris said there were vast numbers of people in the capital 'whose only resource for bread is in the vigilance and attention of government, whose utmost exertion can but just keep pace with the necessity.'[7] But if the only available grain came from within France all that the vigilance and attention of government could do, as Dorset had already pointed out, was to feed Paris at the expense of the provinces. The question was not whether there would be food riots but merely where they would be. Only the 20,000 sacks of British flour could avert an uprising which might kill as many with the sword as with hunger.

Five days after the privileged orders joined the Assembly the French ambassador in London asked the British Prime Minister to allow the export of the flour. Pitt promised to help and government newspapers said it had been decided that 'this relief should be granted to the sufferers'. 'This ought to be a lesson for the Ministers of all countries,' they proclaimed, 'the illiberal considerations which govern narrow-minded politicians are beneath the descendant of the greatest statesman that ever existed.' But although Pitt's father might have been the greatest of statesmen he had still run into trouble when he had suspended the corn laws without consulting Parliament. His son took due heed and on 6 July the House of Commons debated the matter. Wilberforce was for granting the request because of 'the extreme scarcity of corn in France and the state of perturbation in which that kingdom was well known to be' but other members said it would be wrong to interfere with divine justice, since the French were so evidently being punished by God for their sinfulness in helping the American rebels. A select committee was set up and advised that permission for the export of the flour should not be given.[8]

Meanwhile *The Times*, splendidly and doggedly misinformed, declared that 'it reflects the highest honour on this nation to have complied so readily with the solicitation of the French Court for provisions. After such an instance of philanthropy, with their present congenial pursuit of freedom, we trust that we shall hear no more of the perverted phrase – natural enemies.' When these effusions were rendered nonsensical by the blank refusal to comply with the solicitation *The Times* showed commendable resilience, assuring its readers that bread was as cheap in Paris as it was in London. In any case, it added, it would do the French good to be kept short of flour because it would check their foppish tendency to use it as hair powder. The *Morning Post*, an opposition paper, reported that Parisians were crying out against Pitt, 'your cold unfeeling Minister', and that his niggardliness had made France look upon Britain as a tyranny to be distrusted rather than as a free country to be copied.[9] This newspaper confrontation was one of the first signs of the diverging attitudes to the French revolution which were later to dominate British politics.

On Monday 6 July, as the House of Commons chose its select committe, the National Assembly's committee on food supplies delivered its report. Mirabeau surprised the deputies by asking if the committee had taken into consideration offers of help from an anonymous donor in London and from Jefferson, who had promised supplies of grain in the name of the American people. 'I never made an offer to anybody,' Jefferson told Lafayette curtly. Necker had warned him that there was likely to be a shortage and he had arranged for merchants in American ports to be alerted. That was all there was to it and he asked that the Assembly be informed accordingly. The anonymous well-wisher in London also failed to materialize and Mirabeau had to abandon what now looked like a clumsy attempt to discredit the government. Lansdowne's tame intellectuals in London were already angry with him – they said he had published Bentham's ideas without acknowledgement – and this latest escapade widened still further the gulf between their airy idealism and the realities of French politics. Yet there had indeed been a plan to get American grain for France, put forward by two middlemen called Samuel Blackden and James Swan, and both Jefferson and Necker had been involved in it.[10] Mirabeau was paying the penalty of knowing too little rather than too much about international reactions to France's plight.

'The scarcity of bread grows every day more alarming, but hopes are given that there will be an ample supply of that article in the course of about ten days,' Dorset told his government on 6 July as Mirabeau asked about the British and American offers. The Orléanists were said to be working to a tighter schedule, issuing instructions to the bakers of Paris to keep the capital starving for another week in preparation for an uprising on the following Monday. Dumont and Duroveray suspected that Mirabeau was working for Orléans and they were alarmed to learn from Reybaz and Claviére, who reached Versailles from Paris at the end of June, that the capital was bound to erupt within a matter of days. Dumont thought things were being stirred up not by the Orléanists but by financiers who had lent heavily to the government and preferred a popular insurrection to the dissolution of the Assembly and the loss of their money. 'I am certain,' he wrote, 'that at that time the creditors of the state, a very numerous and active and powerful body in Paris, were all in open opposition to the Court.' Dorset provided unwitting corroboration for this theory when he reported with some surprise that 'the stocks, notwithstanding the complexion of the times, continue to rise.' French financial stability now depended not on buttressing the power of the government but on protecting the Assembly from the supposed designs of the King.[11]

Mirabeau was determined to find out what the designs were. In consultation with other leaders of the Assembly including Lafayette, Duport, Mounier and Bergasse he proposed to petition the King to remove all troops from around Paris and Versailles. He also put down a series of resolutions aimed at preserving law and order in the capital. Dumont wrote the speech on the address to the King and Duroveray drew up the resolutions. The only one which was rejected was a proposal to set up a militia along British lines. The Genevese were saddened by the Assembly's refusal to follow a British example but they still did not understand the ferocity of the backlash which their well-meaning advocacy of British ways was creating. While *The Times* in London commented rather wryly on Mirabeau's more extravagant remarks, including his assertion that George III would be guilty of treason if he allowed soldiers near Parliament, Dorset in Paris feared that if Louis continued to ring the Assembly with troops it would move to Paris, 'a step which I am persuaded would not fail of producing an open rupture which would make it necessary for His Majesty to call out his army for the protection of his person, as well as the only means of supporting the dignity of his crown.'[12]

The key question was not whether Louis would call out his army but whether his army would answer the call. The French Guards quartered in Paris had proved reliable at the time of the Réveillon riots but now groups of them were marching through the streets boasting that they would defy their officers. At the end of June, fourteen French Guards who had been imprisoned for a variety of offences ranging from theft to desertion were released by a mob of several thousands recruited at the Palais Royal. Dorset was shocked when the National Assembly petitioned the King on their behalf and he was glad to learn that 'the Regiment of Salis-Samande has been obliged to exert its discipline, for which it is so famed. Two of their men were hanged yesterday morning and several others received fifty *coups de sabre*, all of them for having aided and abetted the French Guards in their mutinous and disorderly behaviour.' But at Versailles non-commissioned officers of the King's bodyguard who had been reduced to the ranks for refusing to mount guard outside the Assembly had to be reinstated in order to avoid a mutiny. 'They said their job was to guard the King, not to threaten the people,' commented Creuzé-Latouche. A week later he was reporting 'bloody battles between the hussars and the Swiss and French Guards', battles which became bloodier when crowds in the streets around the palace came out in support of the French Guards and began stoning the hussars.[13]

Nevertheless the government seemed determined to resort to force and three regiments of cavalry and three of infantry, two of them German, were ordered to march on Paris. On 9 July Arthur Young met one of them at Châlons-sur Marne and an officer told him in English that 50,000 men were being drawn up around the capital under the maréchal de Broglie because 'the *tiers état* were running mad and wanted some wholesome correction; they want to establish a republic – absurd!' Since the man had learned his English while serving in America Young could not resist asking him why he had fought to set up a republic there if it was such an absurd thing for the French to want. 'Aye, damme! that is the way the English want to be revenged,' was the reply. 'It is, to be sure, no bad opportunity.' 'Almost every person I meet with has the same idea – *The English must be very well contented at our confusion*,' Young added. 'They feel pretty pointedly what they deserve.' In London it was felt that the French were indeed getting what they deserved. 'Had they not first secretly, and then openly, in the outset and progress of the American war, afforded assistance to the rebellion of our American Colonies against the mother country, the present day would not have related an annihilation of that monarchy,' declared *The Times* on 6 July. 'It will be a lesson for other nations to speculate on.' 'Almost every letter from America is full of the poverty, distress and misery of her citizens,' it added.[14] It was comforting to think that providence was punishing the rebels themselves as well as those who had helped them.

Americans knew otherwise. 'Providence is crowning the year with its bounty,' enthused the New York correspondent of the *Massachusetts Spy*. 'The vegetable world pours forth its treasures in luxuriant profusion – a more plentiful season was perhaps never known.' It seemed that the citizens whose poverty and distress and misery were most conspicuous were those in Rhode Island and North Carolina, the two states which had not yet ratified the constitution. Rhode Island was not the graveyard of living skeletons which Brissot had depicted* but it was still far from prosperous and its recovery was being hampered by the depreciation of its currency. North Carolina too had, according to one of Madison's friends there, 'a strong predilection for paper money'. It was also suffering from a plague of grasshoppers which ravaged the tobacco crop. Some growers had planted three or four times over without getting a satisfactory yield.[15]

In New York, as the vegetable world poured forth its treasures unchecked, the only danger from the animal world seemed to come from dogs and pigs. The *New York Journal* complained about the large numbers of rabid and unmuzzled dogs which roamed the city and also about the herds of swine in the streets between Powles Hook Ferry and Broadway. The owners of these animals claimed that they helped to keep the streets free of refuse but their critics said they made things worse by scattering it. As temperatures rose dogs and pigs and refuse all became more of a hazard and New Yorkers grew increasingly thirsty. After more than twenty people had died in a heatwave the newspapers warned that 'raw rum has been found exceedingly pernicious in this extreme heat', but it was by no means certain that other beverages were any safer. The city's drinking water was notoriously polluted

*See above, p.12.

and even the horses refused it. The Common Council had expressed interest in plans for an improved water supply put forward by the Rumsian Society of Philadelphia but so far these had come to nothing.[16]

'The day was hot, the walk was long, I was lame and the streets were ripped up a great part of the way,' grumbled Senator Maclay at the end of June after he had struggled across New York to visit the President. The people of Paris were soon to become accustomed to the ripping up of streets as barricades were thrown up to defend the city, but in the case of New York it reflected nothing more alarming than the Common Council's repaving policy. Maclay was suffering from an inflamed knee and he had hoped to relieve it by hiring a horse. 'Could not get a very indifferent one with saddle and bridle under two shillings an hour,' he noted angrily, 'thought this extravagant and would not pay it.' Congressmen felt they were being overcharged for everything. 'You have no conception at what extravagant rates everything is paid for in this place,' wrote Frederick Mühlenberg, also from Pennsylvania. 'There is not a place within the state of Pennsylvania where we could not live more comfortably on four dollars than here on six – it is vain at this place to talk of frugality.' He added that the locals knew their luck could not last – there were plans to move the seat of government to a site on the Susquehanna in Pennsylvania – and so were exploiting it while they could. Devoted radicals feared that New Yorkers were enemies to frugality because they were enemies to republicanism: luxury and ceremony went hand in hand and would lead to the betrayal of the revolution. 'It was a high day and celebrated with great festivity on that account,' wrote Maclay furiously when the city celebrated George III's birthday on 4 June. 'The old leaven anti-revolutionism has leavened the whole lump, nor can we keep the Congress free from it.' A month later good republicans were shocked when the Cincinatti of New York drank the health of the monarchs of Europe at their Independence Day banquet.[17]

New Yorkers were understandably resentful of these suspicions and accusations. They had laid out a lot of money to make Congress welcome and they were still paying for the alterations to the City Hall, now estimated to have cost over $65,000. They had already established the Society of Tammany to combat the monarchical and aristocratic tendencies of the Cincinatti and there was also the Society of Mechanics and Tradesmen, a staunchly revolutionary body. Its members were not planning apocalypse but they certainly had their own wry visions of symbolic horsemen. One of their favourite toasts was: 'A cobweb pair of breeches, a porcupine saddle and a hard trotting horse to all the enemies of freedom'. When the *New York Journal* heard stories about French noblemen fleeing to Spain while Louis XVI 'secreted himself from the vengeance of his people' it expressed the hope that 'every tyrant, oppressor and enemy to public liberty and the rights of freemen' might end up in the same way.[18] The Pennsylvanians did not have a monopoly of revolutionary fervour.

On 4 July a group of Americans living in Paris celebrated Independence Day by presenting a congratulatory address to Jefferson, not just as one of the authors of the Declaration of Independence but as a still active revolutionary who was helping Lafayette to draft a French Declaration of Rights. Morris took no part in the presentation, perhaps because he disapproved of Jefferson's support for the Assembly, and instead he marked the day by writing to tell the envoy in Madrid that 'our American example has done them good but, like all novelties, liberty runs away with their discretion, if they have any. They want an American constitution, with the exception of a king instead of a president, without reflecting that they have not American citizens to support that constitution.' He feared that the army would be unable to control Paris – 'The French troops, as far as can be ascertained, would not serve against their countrymen; and the foreign troops are not sufficiently numerous to make any serious impression' – and that the capital would lead the whole country in a slide into anarchy.[19]

Even Jefferson began to have his doubts and on 8 July he wrote to the French Foreign Secretary asking for a guard to be put on his house after it had been broken into three times. He was particularly annoyed by the theft of all his silver-plated candlesticks because there were none to be had in Paris and he was forced to send to London for replacements. Earlier in the year it had been the country areas that had gone in fear of robber bands* but now it was the capital's turn. Innumerable vagrants and thieves thronged the city and more were making their way towards it. Safety of life and property in Paris was threatened not by Parisians but by outsiders. Only a third of the Réveillon rioters

*See above, p.24.

had been born in Paris and the same was true of those who now attracted the attention of the police. The city was ringed round with customs barriers to enforce payment of dues – 'they are made of pine, occasionally of iron'; wrote Mercier, 'if the amount they earn had been employed in their building they might be wrought of pure gold' – and these also served to keep a check on people coming in. On Saturday night 11 July many customs posts were attacked and burned, leaving the way open for intruders. 'It is as if the rebels believed large numbers of comrades waited outside the city to aid them,' one historian has written. Lafayette reckoned there were now at least 30,000 intruders in Paris.[20]

Necker gave a small dinner party that Saturday afternoon. One of the guests was Bartholomew Huber, a Genevese who had taken British nationality and was a friend of William Eden, British ambassador in Madrid. Huber told Eden what happened: 'Before we sat down M. Necker was told M. de la Luzerne wished to speak to him. He returned, spoke a few words with his wife.... After dinner he said the weather was charming and having no council to attend that evening he would take an airing. He drove away to St Ouen with Madame Necker.' But at St Ouen the Neckers engaged horses to take them to the Swiss frontier: La Luzerne had brought a notice of dismissal from the King, coupled with an order to leave France immediately. Dumont later said that when Necker's exile became known 'Versailles was in the greatest consternation; it wore the appearance of a country which expected at every instant the invasion of a foreign army; the grief of the people was expressed without disguise at the very gates of the palace; no one entertained a doubt but that the most fatal designs were meditated by the Court.' Soldiers set up road blocks along the principal routes betweeen Versailles and Paris but somehow the news got through and it reached the capital on Sunday morning while the gutted customs posts still smouldered.[21]

Immediately an angry mob gathered at the Palais Royal. A bust of Necker was produced from somewhere – according to one account it came from a waxwork museum run by a man called Curtius – and it was carried through the streets decked in black. 'An immense crowd attended it,' wrote Dumont, 'it was contemplated with a kind of religious veneration and the praise of Necker was in every mouth.' As the processions became more numerous they also became more threatening, with mutinous French Guards taking the lead and drilling their civilian com-

panions into a semblance of military order. Huber told Eden how
'a party of these popular French Guards, at the head of many
thousand people, all armed as well as they could, carrying before
them pictures of their beloved minister and of the Duke of Orléans,
marched towards the Place Louis XV on their way to Versailles.'
There they met not the horsemen of the apocalypse but the
cavalry of the Royal Allemand regiment under the Prince de
Lambesc. 'The prince led,' Huber continued, 'and signalized
himself by cutting over the head an old inoffensive man.' At the
Palais Royal a young lawyer named Camille Desmoulins told a
vast crowd that the city was about to be put to the sword. They
must take up arms to save themselves and they must wear green
cockades, 'the colour of hope', to show they were good patriots
and not supporters of the Court. Even Gouverneur Morris thought
it wise to wear a green bow in his hat when at last he ventured
out. Soon it was realized that servants of the hated comte d'Artois
wore green livery, so the cockades became red and blue, the
colours of the city of Paris, or red and white in honour of the duc
d'Orléans.[22]

Orléans spent the day with his English mistress Grace Elliott
at Raincy, his country house a few miles to the east of Paris. They
returned to the city in the evening intending to go to the opera
but at the Porte St Martin they learned that all the theatres were
closed as a mark of respect for the exiled minister. The duc's
favourite club the Salon des Princes was also closed and he saw
street fighting on the boulevards. He thought it wise to go not to
the Palais Royal but to Monceau, his other house in Paris, and
there his servants said they had been told he had been beheaded
by order of the King. His friend the marquis de Sillery also
returned to Paris from the country that night and found fires
blazing in many parts of the city. 'The constant noise of muskets
being discharged told me that the revolution had begun,' he noted.
The gullible quickly assumed that this was the Orléanist uprising
allegedly planned for the following day. 'I have seen a six-franc
crown piece which certainly served to pay some wretch on the
night of July 12th,' wrote one of the Queen's ladies-in-waiting,
'the words *Midnight, 12th of July, three pistols*, were rather deeply
engraved on it. They no doubt communicated a signal for the
first insurrection.' As Grace Elliott went from group to group of
bystanders that night she was told over and over again that the
whole thing was an Orléanist plot. Finally, at two o'clock in the

morning, she went down on her knees and begged Orléans to go to Versailles and tell the King that the mob had made use of his name without his permission. Next day she learned that he had done so.[23]

'The night was terrible,' wrote Dumont. 'Sleep was banished from all but the cradles of children and about them their restless parents watched in the most anxious alarm, not knowing whether the armed men whom they observed passing under their windows were friends or foes.'[24] In fact the baron de Besenval, commander of the royal troops, had given up the attempt to regain control of the city and had pulled his forces back across the Seine to the Champ de Mars. Most of the armed men who passed in the night were now under the orders of the emergency city government. This provisional authority, later to be reorganized as the Commune, had been set up by the four hundred electors originally chosen by the city's sixty districts to elect the deputies to the Estates General. Sitting in continuous session at the Hôtel de Ville they ordered the firing of cannon and the ringing of church bells to convene district meetings and then, with remarkable efficiency, they co-ordinated measures to bring order out of chaos. Anyone in possession of arms was required to hand them over to the district authorities for distribution to the *milice parisienne*. Two hundred men in each of the sixty districts were to register for militia service on the first day and the same number on each of the next three days. There would thus be a total force of 48,000 men of which 12,000 would be available at any one time.[25]

'Twenty-four hours have made a total change,' wrote Huber on Tuesday morning, 'a mixture of *Gardes françaises* and Gardes bourgeoises have patrolled and guarded Paris; last night not a gun, not a noise heard. This excellent conduct will strengthen and facilitate that of the States General, who behave like Romans'.[26] At first there had been alarm at Versailles at the prospect of a breakdown of law and order in the capital but now the deputies decided that 'the people of Paris, pushed to the point of despair, have taken up arms in order to repel the foreign troops' and that the people of Paris must therefore be given support. The Assembly declared its confidence in Necker and asked the King once more to withdraw the forces stationed between Versailles and the capital. When he refused to do so it was assumed that the Queen and Artois were pressing him to dissolve the assembly and arrest its leading members.

In Paris the municipal authorities prepared to defend the city. On Monday morning large quantities of corn and firearms were discovered in the convent of St Lazare and taken to public dépôts for distribution. Next day two of Dorset's servants were swept up in a crowd which attacked the hospital of Les Invalides and found a store of arms and ammunition. When these were handed out the men from the embassy took their turn – luckily Dorset had told them not to wear his livery that day – and they received 'two very good muskets which they brought away with them'.[27] Meanwhile the electors had turned their attention to the fortress prison of the Bastille. They knew that gunpowder and arms had been moved there from the Arsenal and they also knew that the governor, the marquis de Launay, was fiercely loyal to the King and might give support to any attack launched by the royal troops drawn up on the Champ de Mars. During the morning of Tuesday 14 July deputations were sent to de Launay, first asking for guarantees that he would not open fire and later demanding the surrender of the fortress. He gave the guarantees but would not surrender. Early in the afternoon the garrison opened fire in spite of the governor's promise and the French Guards led the infuriated crowd in a full-scale attack on the fortress, which fell within a matter of hours.

It was soon to become clear that by taking the Bastille the people of Paris had inflicted a crushing defeat on the forces of counter-revolution. At the time it was not so obvious. In spite of all that the municipal authorities had done Paris still lay open to attack from the Champ de Mars and it was widely assumed that Besenval would now order his men to close in. Barricades were thrown up and the city remained on alert throughout the night, with militiamen and guardsmen patrolling the streets and citizens making ready to defend their homes and their families against the King's soldiers. The King himself went to bed knowing of the trouble at the Bastille but unsure of its outcome. According to some accounts the duc de Liancourt brought him the news of the fortress's fall at midnight, assuring him that this was 'not a revolt but a revolution.'[28] According to others he did not know until he woke the next morning. A number of deputies remained in the hall all night ready to go into emergency session if any news came through. Now that the King had turned down two more appeals to withdraw the troops many felt that civil war was inevitable. 'The night was long and painful,' wrote Dumont, 'in the midst of the anxiety which everyone felt about the present state of affairs and his apprehension of what might follow. Our only consolation was a doubtful belief that the Bastille was taken.'[29]

Early in the morning Mirabeau got back to Versailles after attending his father's funeral. When the Assembly went into session he proposed another and more strongly worded address to the King:

Tell him that the hordes of foreigners with which we are encompassed yesterday received visits from the princes of the blood, and the princesses, and the favourites, and the minions of the Court; that they are loaded with caresses, exhortations and presents. Tell him that during the whole night those foreign mercenaries, enriched with gold and gorged with wine, predicted in their impious songs the servitude of France and vomited forth brutal prayers for the destruction of the National Assembly. Tell him that in his very palace his courtiers mingled in dances to the sound of that savage music; and tell him that similar orgies were the prelude to the massacre of St Bartholomew.[30]

This grandiloquence was wasted because Louis had already decided on surrender. He entered the great hall without guards and without ceremony, accompanied only by his brothers, and announced that he would withdraw the troops and co-operate with the Assembly in bringing back peace and tranquility to Paris. Two days later he went to the capital to make his act of submission. He was escorted not by his bodyguard but by the newly formed Versailles militia. Outside the city he was met by the Paris militia under Lafayette – 'one who had fought in the cause of liberty,' commented Dumont, 'and who had studied under Franklin and Washington how the yoke of kings was to be broken' – and as the procession made its way to the Hôtel de Ville there were cries of *'Vive la Nation!'* and *'Vive Necker!'* but none of *'Vive le Roi!'*. At the Hôtel de Ville Louis agreed to the appointment of Lafayette as commander of the militia and of Bailly, the man who had defied him in the name of the Assembly, as mayor of Paris. The President of the Commune told the King that whereas he had previously ruled by right of birth he now reigned by the consent of his people. Then and only then did the crowds begin to shout *Vive le Roi!* '[31]

'Whoever advised the King to take this step was a brave man,' said Mirabeau, 'for without it Paris would have been lost to him.' Because Dumont suspected Mirabeau of being an Orléanist he took this to mean that Louis's visit had forestalled an Orléanist takeover in Paris. After a week in command of the Paris militia Lafayette said darkly that 'the populace is guided by an invisible hand', but it was in London that allegations about Orléans were made most freely. 'Thus has this great Revolution been effected, which has been conducted throughout the whole with wonderful system,' wrote the *St James's Chronicle*. 'The Duke of Orleans is adored as the life and soul of those proceedings.' *The Times* announced first that Orléans was to be arrested and then that the people of Paris would make him Lieutenant-General of the kingdom, 'which would place him at the head of public affairs'. It then ran an extraordinary story to the effect that Louis had sent for the Prince of Wales 'to confer with him on what was most prudent to be done'. Earlier in the year Orléans had been an enthusiastic supporter of the Prince's claim to be Regent and now the parallel between the two aspirants to power was underlined by George Selwyn, a borough monger and government supporter in the Commons. 'I am assured that if the King had not gone as he did to the Hôtel de Ville the duke of Orléans would immediately have been declared Regent,' he wrote. 'There seems some sort of fatality in the scheme of forming a Regent who, in neither of these two kingdoms, is *destiné à ne pas arriver à bon port*.' Orléans ordered his London house to be got ready and the rumour spread that he was coming to consult with the Prince. *The Times* was able to assure its readers that it was not Orléans himself but the Princesse de Lamballe who was expected.[32]

On 22 July William Windham, prominent in the Prince's party and a friend of Edmund Burke, urged the Commons to 'show their kindness, their goodness and the sincerity of their friendly professions towards France' by allowing the export of flour after all. He was met with thinly veiled suggestions that he wanted to send London down the road Paris had travelled. 'Great tumults had arisen in Paris from the scarcity of bread,' said Sir James Johnstone, 'and tumults might arise from the same account in the city of London.' An opposition member replied indignantly that 'the lower orders of the people here were actuated by the same spirit of liberty that had been lately manifested in France and would willingly suffer a small temporary inconvenience rather than not afford the relief of which their neighbours on the Continent stood in such extreme need.'[33]

Opposition newspapers like the *Morning Post* played safe, declaring that 'an Englishman not filled with esteem and admir-

ation at the *sublime* manner in which one of the most IMPORT-
ANT REVOLUTIONS the world has ever seen is now effecting
must be dead to every sense of virtue and freedom' but at the
same time attacking Pitt for underestimating the threat from
the Paris mob, 'who are now LORDS PARAMOUNT of that
kingdom.' 'Several families in England are in consternation about
Paris,' it added on 21 July, 'trembling for the safety of great
numbers of females sent there for education.'[34] The following day
the importance of playing safe was dramatically illustrated. While
in London the Commons turned down for the second time the
French request for flour Joseph-François Foullon and his son-in-
law Berthier de Sauvigny were dragged from hiding and lynched
in the streets of Paris. Some said they were murdered by order of
the Orléanists – Foullon was supposed to have advised Louis to
arrest Orléans and put him on trial – and others said it was because
they had plotted to starve the capital into submission and had
suggested contemptuously that if Parisians had no bread they
should eat grass. The baron de Besenval had already decided that
the insurrection he had so conspicuously failed to control had
been the work of 'brigands paid by the duc d'Orléans and by
the English' and now it was being whispered that Orléans was
deliberately getting the British to hold up grain supplies in order
to prolong the discontent in Paris for his own purposes.[35] It was
certainly not a propitious moment for any sympathy that might
exist between the Orléanists and the Prince's party to be made
public knowledge.

At the end of July Charles Fox sent his compliments privately
to Orléans, telling him that his conduct throughout the crisis had
been exemplary and that he could depend on traditional Whig
hostility to the French monarchy being replaced by a more
friendly attitude. In public the *Morning Post* had been taking a
very different line, declaring that if Fox were in power he would
control the situation in France by offering British help to which-
ever side would pay the highest price for it. Louis XVI did not
want to become a mere cypher and his people did not want to be
reduced to slavery again, so both would be anxious for British
intervention. In the previous century Cromwell had used French
civil strife in order to get Dunkirk and now Britain should demand
the return of that port along with La Rochelle, Rochefort, Brest
and St Malo. A few days later the same newspaper widened
its plans, suggesting that Britain should seek to bring about a

revolution in Madrid in order to break the long-standing alliance between the French and Spanish kings. And then, on the day before Fox sent his message to Orléans, it published a ferocious diatribe against mob rule in Paris, saying that 'tyranny is not less tyranny because it is exercised by the people than if it was exercised by a king' and condemning Orléans as a dissolute and unprincipled intriguer.[36] Opposition attitudes to France seemed to show more hostility than consistency.

Government newspapers were not much better. On the morning of the attack on the Bastille *The Times* announced that Louis XVI would seek foreign help, probably from Spain, in order to put down the revolution. Next day it pointed out sourly that in spite of everything he was still building ships at a great rate in order to threaten Britain. A week later it said he would soon regain his power and become internationally dangerous again. By the beginning of August it was openly advocating war against him because he had aided the American revolutionaries: 'It will be a false delicacy if England does not, at the first opportunity, improve upon these principles to do herself justice for what she has suffered.' As well as providing future opportunities for hostile intervention the troubles in France also provided irresistible present opportunities to blacken opposition politicians. *The Times* linked the revolutionaries in Paris with Burke's notorious speech against George III by pretending that Pitt had received a request from France for 'some person capable at this moment of *smiting* the FRENCH KING upon the head, *hurling* him from his Throne and reducing him to a condition with the meanest member of the *Tiers Etat*'. Later in the month, when reports came in of disturbances in the Paris area as seigneurial hunting rights were swept away, it took occasion to attack Orléans – 'This comes of your LIBERTY HUNTING, Monsieur!' – and also to predict that similar scenes would take place in London 'if *Runnymede Oliverians* under the banners of Black Charley got possession of the helm of government.' The supposed Foxite revolutionary pedigree was later extended to include Jack Cade and Wat Tyler as well as Oliver Cromwell and the barons at Runnymede.[37]

The war of words in London was beginning to have its effect in France. *The Times* was quick to point out that by denouncing mob rule in Paris the opposition newspapers were putting English visitors there at risk, but it conveniently forgot that its own reporting was doing much the same thing. Particularly damaging was its gibe about the duke of Devonshire forgetting his Whig revolution principles and 'wrapping them up in an occasional napkin at Madame de Polignac's.' By the time this was published the Devonshires had fled from Paris and the *Morning Post* was asserting that the duke of Dorset, the other notorious English ally of the duchesse de Polignac and the Queen's party, had also left because of strained relations between the British and French governments. In fact Dorset was still at his post and growing increasingly worried. He told the Foreign Secretary that 'insinuations which might prove essentially injurious to the English now resident in Paris have been industriously propagated here for some days past and instilled into the minds of the populace'. These were allegations that English agents were fomenting revolution and that he was himself 'distributing great sums of money for the purpose of cherishing and augmenting the discontents that prevail here.' He had written to the French Foreign Secretary refuting these charges. While he had been composing this letter Huber had come to warn him of quite different allegations, to the effect that he was plotting with Artois and the Queen.[38]

Dorset's letter was read out in the National Assembly on 27 July. A week later he sent another to say that his government approved of what he had done and had nothing but friendly intentions towards France. The Assembly communicated both letters to the municipal authorities in Paris and arranged for them to be published throughout the kingdom, for belief in criminals and secret agents was not only persisting but widening. 'The Paris militia has driven out a horde of brigands who will take refuge in the provinces,' wrote the marquis de Ferrières on the day of the King's visit. In his first letter Dorset pointed out that some months earlier the British government had been asked to support a plot to seize Brest and had very properly revealed it to the French authorities. *The Times*, which had already been very scathing about Dorset's dealings with Artois, now suggested that he had been naïve not to realize that the supposed plot had been an attempt by the French to smoke the British secret service into the open.[39]

Meanwhile those opposition newspapers in London which had advocated armed intervention in order to take over Brest and other ports now announced that there was a British fleet waiting in the Channel 'to aid the French aristocratic party'. On the other side of France at Besançon Arthur Young heard lurid tales of peasant uprisings and marvelled that the propertied classes did so little to defend themselves: 'That universal circulation of intelligence which in England unites in bands of connection men of similar interests and situations has no existence in France.' A few days later at Dijon he was assured that it did exist, that the National Assembly's attack on property would lead to 'general and confirmed civil war, or dismemberment of the kingdom'. At Avignon he was told that the English would join in but would be stoutly resisted: 'The only political idea here is that if the English should attack France they have a million of men in arms to receive them.' 'I assured them,' Young wrote loftily, 'that should the English attack them at present they would probably make the weakest figure they had done from the foundation of their monarchy; but, gentlemen, the English, in spite of the example you set them in the American war, will disdain such a conduct.'[40]

But the French had little faith in British disdain. By the time Dorset went home on leave on 8 August, leaving his secretary Lord Robert Fitzgerald in charge of the embassy, the allegations against the British were no longer about fomenting trouble in Paris but about plunging the whole country into civil war. Mention of the Brest affair had led to suspected British agents being arrested in Brittany and Fitzgerald was being asked to provide further information. 'We have great reason to believe that the duke of Dorset will not again return to his embassy in France,' wrote *The Times* after he had held urgent consultations with Pitt in Downing Street. And so it proved: in due course Fitzgerald was appointed as his successor. A friend once remarked that Dorset was 'soft, quiet, ingratiating and formed for a court.... He displayed, indeed, neither shining parts nor superior abilities.' He was certainly not formed to be ambassador to a country in the throes of the greatest revolution of the century.[41]

News travelled slowly from Europe to America in the face of the prevailing winds. At the time of the fall of the Bastille New Yorkers were still reading about the Paris elections and the opening sessions of the Estates General. But they were also reading about wars and rumours of wars. 'The American revolution has originated two factions,' wrote the *New York Journal* on 16 July. 'On the one side France and Spain, on the other side England. England has also drawn Holland and Prussia into her party ... is it to be supposed that England would not seize an opportunity of avenging the injuries that were rendered here in America?' In

Paris Jefferson refused at first to believe that such vengeance was being contemplated. 'It is rumoured and believed in Paris that the English have fomented with money the tumults of this place and that they are aiming to attack France,' he wrote early in August. 'I have never seen any reason to believe either of these rumours.'[42] But by the end of the month he had changed his mind and he sent his government an account of the Orléanist and British threat which was more explicit than any rumour:

Another faction too, of the most desperate views, has acquired strength in the assembly as well as out of it. These wish to dethrone the reigning branch and transfer the crown to the Duke of Orléans. The members of this faction are mostly persons of wicked and desperate fortune who have nothing at heart but to pillage from the wreck of their country. The Duke himself is as unprincipled as his followers.... He is certainly borrowing money on a large scale. He is in understanding with the court of London, where he has been long in habits of intimacy. The ministry here even apprehend that that court will support his designs by war. I have no idea of this, but no doubt at the same time that they will furnish him money liberally to aliment a civil war and prevent the regeneration of this country.[43]

Particularly worrying was the suggestion that Orléans might sell the French West Indian sugar islands to Britain in order to raise money for his nefarious enterprises. When Jefferson went to see the French Foreign Secretary about this, pointing out that the monopoly of the Caribbean by any one power would be against American interests, he was told that in any case the French government doubted its ability to hang on to its West Indian possessions. They were said to be in open rebellion and might well have declared their independence already.[44] This was even more disturbing. Jefferson and his fellow Virginians might find revolution exhilarating in France but they would find it less so if it erupted among slave populations dangerously close to their own. Suddenly the visions of apocalypse seemed more immediate and more relevant. Good Americans, or at any rate those from the southern states, could hardly believe that when the Bible had talked about exalting the humble and meek it had meant that they should be black.

Jefferson's imaginings were no wilder than those which gripped the greater part of the population of France during late July and into August. As the fantasies rippled outwards, breeding reality as they went, they spoke continually of brigands. Whatever the unknown terrors – Orléanists or foreign invaders, apocalyptic horsemen or hungry seekers after good things – the popular imagination dressed them as brigands. 'Much has been reported of brigands but nothing proved,' wrote Arthur Young at the beginning of August. 'At Besancon I heard of 800; but how could a troop of banditti march through a country and leave their existence the least questionable?' 'The rumours of brigands here had got to 1600 strong,' he recorded at Autun three days later. 'They were much surprised to find I gave no credit to the existence of brigands, as I was well persuaded that all the outrages were the work of peasants only, for the sake of plundering.'[45]

Nor was it just a matter of imagined brigands being driven out to ravage the countryside around Paris. All over France, spontaneously and simultaneously, wild currents of irrational fear ran from place to place. At Autun Arthur Young was close to the epicentre of one which spread from the Bourbonnais into Burgundy. Others began in Champagne and Normandy and Poitou. From village to village warning was sent that desperate men were on their way, burning and pillaging as they came. They were sometimes said to be robbers but more often they had a political complexion: they were foreign troops called in by Marie Antoinette or they were evil noblemen seeking to claw back feudal rights. In Franche Comté Young was threatened with hanging because he was said to be 'a seigneur, perhaps in disguise, and without doubt a great rogue' and in Auvergne he was accused of being 'an agent of the Queen's, who intended to blow the town up with a mine and send all that escaped to the galleys.'[46]

It is not easy to gauge the nature and extent of the outrages committed under cover of these fears. Young met a nobleman and his family who had escaped from their flaming château half-naked in the night but when he made further inquiries he found that the number of châteaux burned was in fact 'not considerable'. Even the pillaging seemed to have objectives other than theft, as the comte de Germigny made clear when he told the National Assembly of an attack on his château in Normandy. 'Not content with burning my papers,' he complained, 'they have killed all my pigeons.' Cupboards had been wrenched open and their contents – title deeds, registers of feudal obligations, records of debts – had been systematically destroyed along with the birds whose right to ravage crops had been a long-standing grievance. And that was all. This was not indiscriminate robbery but a carefully planned

destruction of legal documents coupled with an attack on seigneurial game rights. Before the attack the church bells had been
rung so that all those who wanted to destroy evidence of
obligations or indebtedness could know what was to happen and
could play their part. At Versailles the agrarian revolt was
described as 'a war of the poor against the rich', but this was only
part of the truth.[47] Those who are abjectly poor do not attack the
houses of the rich in order to go away empty-handed and leave
behind a pile of charred paper and a scattering of dead pigeons.
This was the work not of the hungry but of the moderately well
fed, of men who saw that they could increase the value of their land
by freeing it from further payments and stopping the depredations
upon it. It was the revolt not of the have-nots but of the want-
mores, not apocalypse but appropriation. As such it was to test
the political skill and nerve of the deputies at Versailles to the
limit and beyond.

CHAPTER EIGHT

Making a constitution

On the day after the Bastille fell Charles Fox told members of the Commons that they had betrayed their revolutionary heritage. 'When they talked in that House day after day of the birthright of Englishmen, for which they had shed their blood and were ready to shed it again,' he cried, 'did they mean nothing but empty words?' In his opinion they did, for they were allowing the government to push taxes through late in the session when most members had left town. The previous day the debate on Beaufoy's Revolution Commemoration Bill had been adjourned because there were less than forty members present. It finally got its third reading the following Monday by twenty-three votes to fourteen, which with two tellers on each side made up the required minimum with one to spare. Fox was not present on that occasion but Sir Joseph Mawbey, a crusty supporter of Pitt, attacked the Bill because it gave an excuse for the sort of bombast they had heard the previous week. In his eyes it was all just 'a race for popularity' in which opposition members vied with one another to make brave speeches about constitutional principles for which they had no real respect. When Fox had first entered politics he had been a fawning courtier: 'being just arrived from France his clothes were of the newest fashion. To him, I believe, we were indebted for the introduction of the *d'Artois* buckle'. Fox's new-found enthusiasm for the popular cause was only skin-deep, Mawbey insisted.[1]

Lansdowne's dissenter friend Richard Price agreed. 'Our Patriots are vicious men and their opposition in general is nothing but a vile struggle for power and its emoluments,' he told Jefferson early in August. 'I scarcely believe we are capable of making such an exertion as the French nation is now making with a spirit and unanimity altogether wonderful. We are duped by the form of liberty.' Beaufoy's Bill, the nearest thing to a revolutionary exertion at Westminster that summer, was now dead. After its laborious passage through the Commons it had been killed in a few minutes in the House of Lords by Dr John Warren, Bishop of Bangor and brother of the Dr Richard Warren who had tried to help the Prince's party to power by denying that the King had recovered. Earl Stanhope, the Bill's only effective friend in the Lords, said that if the bishop thought the existing form of commemoration was satisfactory he must be viewing the Glorious Revolution as the triumph of an invading foreign army rather than as a restoration of liberties. Stanhope was sternly called to order for this suggestion and the Bill was thrown out, whereupon its sponsors in the London Revolution Society turned from Westminster to Versailles. 'The French, Sir, are not only asserting their own rights but they are also asserting and advancing the general liberties of mankind,' they told the president of the National Assembly's constitutional committee. 'France herself takes the constitution of England for her model; in doing so she acts with much wisdom.... But, in the sacred names of freedom and virtue, let her, Sir, be warned to shun those deplorable errors through means of which that admirable constitution has fallen a victim to corruption.'[2]

Arthur Young thought the French had already shunned all the errors they needed to shun. 'My argument was an appeal to the English constitution,' he wrote, 'take it at once, which is the business of a single vote; by your possession of a real and equal representation of the people you have freed it from its only great objection'. The pity was that Louis had already lost the chance of a Parliament like the one at Westminster: 'when the Court found that the states could not be assembled on the old plan ... they ought to have taken the constitution of England for their model; in the mode of assembling they should have thrown the clergy and nobles into one chamber, with a throne for the King, when present.' At the end of July, when he heard that Necker was on his way back to Versailles from exile, Young commented bitterly that 'he had the greatest opportunity of political architecture that ever was in the power of man; in my opinion he missed it completely.' This was because Necker had failed to take advantage of events in such a way as to transform the Estates General into a House of Lords and a House of Commons.[3]

There was more to it than political architecture. In the summer of 1789, as the National Assembly settled down to decide whether and to what extent it should copy the constitutions of other countries, the most obvious difference between Britain and France lay in the prestige of the monarchy and in the degree of stability which that prestige might be expected to ensure. In the spring, after his recovery, George III had endangered his popularity in Britain by planning a visit to Hanover. Jefferson in Paris had been delighted. 'He is going with his queen to Germany,' he wrote. 'England chained to rest, the other parts of Europe may recover or regain tranquillity.' George was clearly 'in an imbecility which may possibly be of long continuance' and this meant that Britain was of no account. But in fact the Hanoverian visit had been cancelled within days of being leaked to the press and the monarchy was immensely popular. *The Times* recounted ecstatically how the King and his family 'return the civilities of the meanest subject. Such condescension at once commands respect and love.' 'The KING is not more popular at this day in England than he is Ireland,' it added some weeks later. 'The delusion of having an Irish sovereign independent of Great Britain is gone by, the people returned to their senses.' In July the mayor of Weymouth gave great offence by not kneeling in the presence of royalty. He was forgiven when it was discovered that he had a wooden leg but, as one scandalized lady-in-waiting exclaimed, 'the absurdity of the matter followed – all the rest did the same; taking the same privilege, by example, without the same or any cause!'[4] In Paris on 17 July the mayor and municipality had not a wooden leg between them but none of them knelt to Louis XVI.

In New York the *Gazette of the United States* was more amused than offended by the fact that the President addressed the monarchs of Europe by elaborate titles while being himself plain Mr Washington. 'If titular distinctions have any influence at all upon human ears,' it remarked, 'methinks these are somewhat humiliating to the brave, daring and intrepid sons of American liberty.' Other newspapers still spoke of the President as 'His Excellency' and 'His Highness', in spite of the rejection of these titles in Congress, and a framework of semi-monarchical protocol was being built up around him. He consulted John Jay and James

Madison on this matter, as well as Alexander Hamilton and Vice-President Adams, and they all said that there should be rigid presidential etiquette and that 'the dignity of the office should be supported'. The President, like George III and Louis XVI, would hold *levées* at which he would appear for a limited period – Hamilton suggested half an hour – to selected visitors assembled in advance. Like George III, he won great popularity and public sympathy as a result of his illness, during which 'a chain was extended across the street to prevent the passing of carriages before his door'. 'His death at the present moment would have brought on another crisis in our affairs,' wrote Madison on 24 June after the abscess had been lanced and the worst seemed to be over.[5]

Washington was still weak and it was another month before he was able to sit in a chair. Congress continued to argue not only about his constitutional position but also about the details of his household. On 13 July in the House of Representatives, when John Vining of Delaware asked why they were prepared to provide the President with silver plate and fine furniture but not with a secretarial staff, he was told that secretaries were dangerous because they represented the corrupting influence of patronage. The next day, the day the Bastille fell, Senator Elsworth of Maryland shocked William Maclay and other good republicans by condemning the power of impeachment and declaring that it would be sacrilege for Congress to touch a hair of the President's head. When Maclay got leave of absence to go home on health grounds other Senators 'seemed to think that my going was owing to disaffection to public measures as much as to indisposition'. He replied sourly that the slide towards monarchy had no doubt exacerbated his illness. But while he was away the presidency suffered further reverses. When the Senate struck out a clause in the Tonnage Bill, which would have made British goods pay higher duties than French, Washington declared stiffly that it was 'adverse to my ideas of justice and policy'. At the beginning of August his recommendation of Colonel Benjamin Fishbourne as naval officer for the port of Savannah was turned down by the Senate. The President put up an alternative candidate but he also sent the Senate a very cold letter indicating that he saw the rejection of Fishbourne as a personal insult.[6]

The esteem in which the three heads of state were held reflected the nature of the constitutions they adorned. For most of his subjects George III's recovery seemed in some strange way to have demonstrated not just his own resilience but the resilience of the constitution which his illness had put in jeopardy. George Washington's personal prestige as the man who had saved his country was enormous, but his public image as President of the United States was just as much in the making, just as subject to political accident, as the constitution which was still ripening from a paper document into a system of government. And in France the change from absolute to limited monarchy went hand in hand with changing attitudes to Louis XVI and Marie Antoinette. On the day Necker was dismissed the Assembly was discussing Lafayette's plan for a Declaration of Rights and Jefferson, who had helped to draft it, was writing to tell Tom Paine that the deputies had the government and the aristocracy at their feet and were about to construct 'a superb edifice'.[7] But five days later, when business was resumed after the Paris insurrection and the King's surrender, it was necessary to put aside the future edifice and consider what was to be done there and then to consolidate the victory that had been won. Mirabeau proposed asking for the recall of Necker and it was suggested that this demand should be put to the King as the unanimous wish of the Assembly.

This suggestion gave rise to a rather curious exchange between Mounier and Mirabeau. Mounier warned against making the demand too peremptory and said that Parliament's readiness to express confidence or lack of confidence in ministers was a defect of the British constitution because it encouraged members of the government to corrupt the legislative in their attempts to build up support there. 'That is what has sunk England!' somebody shouted. According to Dumont this was a favourite phrase of Brissot's and Mounier certainly denied using it. But whoever used it Mirabeau latched on to it in order to make one of his least successful speeches. First he pretended to be appalled by the news, asking anxiously in what latitude this disastrous shipwreck had taken place, and then he gasped with relief when he was assured that it was only a metaphor. 'England flourishes still,' he cried, 'for the eternal instruction of the world'. He then gave the Assembly an account of the British constitutional crisis of 1783, asserting that George III had on that occasion saved his country from 'a greedy and factious coalition'.[8]

Mirabeau had hoped to save the monarchy from the monarch, to ensure the future strength of the crown in spite of current suspicions of royal intentions. Instead he ensured that from now on his Anglophilia was ridiculous as well as unpopular. It was also inconsistent, for he was in favour of part of what had happened in 1783 while being opposed to the rest. On the one hand he wanted France to have a monarchy strong enough to veto the decrees of the legislative and appoint ministers without consulting it but on the other he was determined that the legislative should consist of one chamber only. He had been deeply impressed by a book published earlier in the year by the marquis de Casaux entitled *The simplicity of the idea of a Constitution*, in which Casaux had praised the British constitution but had condemned the power of the Lords as 'an infernal poison which might well lead to civil war'. Dumont later pretended that he opposed Mirabeau on this point but he seems to have been converted easily enough at the time. 'I fully accept the arguments of the marquis de Casaux,' he told Lansdowne at the beginning of July, 'there is only one national interest and so there should be only one Assembly.'[9] It was silly of Mirabeau to tell the deputies that England flourished for the eternal instruction of the world and it was even sillier to recommend what had been done in 1783 if he and his helpers thought that the means by which it had been done, the power of the Lords, was a poison and a recipe for civil war.

The links between Mirabeau and his Genevese helpers were now closer than ever. On 15 July he wrote to ask Lansdowne to let Dumont stay in France. 'I must tell you, my Lord,' he added, 'that he has been profoundly useful to me.' Lansdowne gave the necessary permission and authorized Dumont to draw on his bank account in Paris. 'The comte de Mirabeau begs me to assure you,' Dumont told Lansdowne when he wrote to thank him, 'that the wish and the hope that he may have support as precious as yours is one of the things that sustain him in his public career.' 'He was kept carefully informed of everything that passed in Paris,' wrote Lansdowne's biographer, 'not only by his old correspondent Morellet but by his eldest son Lord Wycombe, by Benjamin Vaughan, who made more than one journey at this period to the French capital, and by Dumont, who had gone there to be by the side of his friend Mirabeau and to assist him with his own invaluable political knowledge'. Dumont continued to insist that the revolution in France was going exactly as Lansdowne would have wished and in August, when he heard the news of Lady Lansdowne's death, he suggested that his patron should try to forget his grief by coming to Paris. 'If anything can bring solace to your spirit,' he wrote, 'it is the revolution which is taking place in France and the knowledge of the influence which your wisdom and your counsel will exercise over the leading participants.'[10]

It was as well Lansdowne turned down the suggestion, for the Assembly was in no mood to listen to the wisdom and counsel of Englishmen. The French translation of Samuel Romilly's book on House of Commons procedure had now been published and Mirabeau presented copies of it to the Assembly's committee on procedure. It was greeted with angry cries of 'We want nothing English, we don't want to copy anyone!' Romilly himself, unaware of this storm of abuse, told Dumont on 28 July that Mirabeau was acting a noble part but had been too generous in the things he had said about the book's author.[11] Even as he wrote the Assembly was adopting rules of procedure as different as possible from those he had recommeneded. Almost as marked as the rejection of all things English was the enthusiasm for all things American. 'It is impossible to desire better dispositions towards us than prevail in this Assembly,' Jefferson told Madison. 'Our proceedings have been viewed as a model for them on every occasion ... our authority has been treated like that of the Bible, open to explanation but not to question.' The Assembly's constitutional committee asked for Jefferson's help in preparing its initial draft but he pleaded pressure of work and would not attend its meetings. Even Gouverneur Morris, though under suspicion as a friend to aristocracy, was asked to 'throw together some thoughts respecting the constitution of this country'.[12]

Nevertheless when constitution-making began in earnest at the end of July London still cast its shadow over Versailles. After receiving two reports from its constitutional committee, followed by a predictably Anglophile draft constitution from Mounier, the Assembly found that one of the few things it could agree upon was the way of setting up a regency if the King should go mad. 'The States General of France, in adopting many of its leading features, have given the most unequivocal testimony of approbation to the conduct of the British Parliament and Ministry in the affair of the Regency,' declared *The Times*. And it was this regency debate that was interrupted by the reading of the first of Dorset's letters to the Assembly. The second was read out in the morning session on 4 August, as deputies were preparing to discuss the Declaration of Rights which they had decided should precede the constitution. In the evening session, when the vicomte de Noailles announced that he had an important motion to bring forward, it was assumed that he wanted an emergency debate on Dorset's assertions about the Brest affair.[13]

Noailles had quite different intentions. The accounts of disturbances throughout France had now become so alarming that even Target, deputy for the Paris third estate and a staunch opponent of the nobility, was asking the Assembly to promulgate a decree requiring payment in full of all taxes and dues. Whether or not the peasant revolution was filling the hungry with good things it certainly seemed likely to send the rich empty away. And the rich were not all noble: just as earlier in the year many *cahiers* had complained of feudal exactions by middle-class landowners who had bought seigneurial rights, so now it was the representatives of such landowners who reacted most fiercely to what was going on in the countryside. Property rights must be defended even if it meant propping up feudalism. But the Breton deputies and their radical allies had other ideas. They saw all privilege, feudal or otherwise, as a denial of that equality which the Declaration of Rights was supposed to be about. For them the consideration of the agrarian revolt was not an interruption of the Assembly's work on the Declaration but an essential prelude to it. They had decided in advance to block Target's demand and they had prevailed upon the duc d'Aiguillon, one of the greatest landowners in France, to make an opening speech suggesting the renunciation of feudal rights in return for compensation. It was this speech that Noailles – a man with little land – now managed to forestall by proposing that Target's decree should be prefaced by the immediate abolition of the most hated feudal rights without compensation and the redemption of others over a period of years.[14]

When Noailles sat down d'Aiguillon made the speech he had prepared. Dupont de Nemours made a fierce demand for the restoration of order by force of arms, after which the Bretons seized the initiative again. Their man Leguen de Kérangal declared that 'the people, impatient to obtain justice and tired of oppression, is eager to destroy these title deeds, monuments to the barbarism of our ancestors.' 'Who among us, gentlemen, in this century of enlightenment, would not make a funeral pyre in expiation of these infamous parchments?' he cried. Enthusiasm mounted and turned to hysteria. Soon it was not just infamous

parchments that were being thrown upon the bonfire. By the time
the Assembly adjourned at two o'clock in the morning it had
abolished not only feudal privileges but also provincial privileges,
municipal privileges, ecclesiastical privileges, judicial privileges
and privileged entitlement to offices and pensions. It had made
all citizens eligible for all offices and it had proclaimed equality
of taxation back-dated to the beginning of the year. To mark its
achievements it decreed that a medal should be struck and a
solemn *Te Deum* sung. A deputation was sent to tell Louis what
had been done and to greet him as 'Restorer of French Liberty'.[15]

The title summed up very neatly the traditional view of revolution as something which came full circle. The assumption was
that the Assembly in its wisdom and in the King's name had
swept away the accumulated injustices of many centuries in order
to reveal and restore the ancient liberties of all Frenchmen that
lay beneath. Unfortunately there were no such liberties. France
was a corporate state, an agglomeration of feudal units and
municipal units acquired by the Bourbon monarchy at different
times and in different ways. The rights and customs and franchises
which these units had brought with them had been stitched
together into something which passed for a national legal and
administrative system. But it was at best a patchwork and when
the patches were torn out on the night of 4 August it fell apart.
The deputies had already announced that in framing the constitution they would not be bound by the instructions of their
constituents as set down in the *cahiers*, but this was the first time
they had deliberately flouted those instructions. Many of them
destroyed the very rights their constituents had sent them to
Versailles to defend and they also destroyed the only existing
framework for the liberties they were claiming to restore. While
they argued about the superstructure, about the constitution with
which they were going to endow the newly liberated France, the
substructure upon which it was supposed to rest crumbled into
nothing. They went on to ordain what France should do but they
had already taken away her ability to do it.

Observers in London were predictably pleased. They had hoped
the French would accept their conservative idea of revolution and
now it seemed that the French had done just that. 'It is expected
that the GENERAL ASSEMBLY of FRANCE will copy after the
constitution of Great Britain,' declared *The Times* on 11 August.
'The deity to whom France kneels and whose presence her people

worship is LIBERTY,' it wrote later, 'that very God whose standard has so long flourished in the Empire of Great Britain.'[16] And liberty could flourish precisely because privilege was dead. Ordinary propertied Frenchmen, the equivalents of English county freeholders and city freemen, had cut their haughty clergy and nobility down to size and could now enjoy their ancient and undoubted liberties in peace. What the British still did not understand was that French privilege and British freedom were much the same thing. It was as if Parliament had swept away the rights of freeholders and freemen in the name of some supposed communal claims of the remote and probably non-existent past.

There were a few who saw that if feudal property in France was under threat freehold property in Britain might be also. 'He is very much of the opinion the spirit of the times will come round to this island,' wrote Fanny Burney after discussing the French revolution with Lord Mountmorres. 'In what, I asked, could be the pretence? – The game-laws, he answered, and the tithes.'[17] But Mountmorres was in a minority: most of George III's subjects could see no parallel between the ill-gotten gains of the superstitious French clergy and the tithes gathered in by honest parsons. Nor could they equate archaic French seigneurial rights with current British game laws. *The Times* was indignant to hear that when Parisians were let loose on seigneurial game reserves they destroyed 'twenty shillings worth of corn for every shilling's worth of game killed', but there was no indignation when it was learned a few days later that one of Lord Berkeley's gamekeepers had been shot dead while fixing a spring gun to kill poachers. The same gun had been responsible for the deaths of three keepers in four years but nobody suggested that its use should be discontinued.[18] Byng had argued that it was better to destroy game than accept poaching* and now it seemed it was better to destroy gamekeepers as well. The British were able to applaud the French for restoring imaginary ancient liberties while at the same time applauding themselves for retaining ancient tyrannies which were not imaginary at all.

It took the deputies a week to turn their original ecstatic resolutions into detailed decrees. In doing so they took away most of the concessions they had appeared to make. 'It can hardly be denied,' one historian has commented, 'that the defrauding of the

*See above, p.117.

peasants had become one of the traditions of the revolution.'[19] The decrees of 11 August did away with serfdom and game rights and feudal jurisdiction but all other rights and dues and services were to continue until arrangements had been made for them to be redeemed in cash. When redemption terms were announced the peasants found that they would have to pay between twenty and twenty-five times their annual dues if they were to buy themselves out of their feudal obligations. Very few had this sort of money and so the demolition of feudalism, which should have been the positive achievement of the night of 4 August, only made the rich richer and the poor poorer. But the negative effects, the dislocation of law and administration, remained to dog the Assembly in the confident constitution-making to which it now returned on 12 August.

'I remember that long discussion, which lasted for weeks, as a time of deadly boredom,' Dumont wrote later. He took the British view, that rights could not exist in society unless and until there were laws to define and protect them. The idea of declaring the rights first was 'an American idea, a puerile fiction'. In London even the *Analytical Review*, a radical journal which consistently supported the French revolution, thought that it was 'ludicrous to see a multitude of scribblers sallying forth from their garrets for the purpose of new-modelling the French government'.[20] But the Assembly, snowed under with proposals for draft constitutions and fundamental charters and declarations of rights, including a rhapsody by Mounier on the British House of Lords as being 'the most perfect of peerages', decided once more that the declaration must come first. A committee was set up to draw up a definitive draft declaration. Mirabeau served on the committee and presented its report but he also said, speaking for himself rather than as a member of the committee, that a declaration coming before the constitution and separated from it would be an absurdity. The Assembly nevertheless set itself to work through the draft, arguing about every article and almost about every word, and on 27 August the *Declaration of the Rights of Man and of the Citizen* was promulgated. It was yet another defeat for Mirabeau and for all those who wanted France to copy the British rather than the Americans.[21]

The next day Jefferson wrote to Madison repeating what he had already told his government about the Orléanists. 'That faction is caballing with the populace and intriguing at London, the

Hague and Berlin,' he wrote. 'Mirabeau is their chief.' The United States must oppose British influence at all levels and its customs tariff must discriminate against British goods and in favour of French. If the House allowed the Senate to block this policy of discrimination it would imperil the enormous respect which the French now had for America and make things easier for Mirabeau and his faction at all levels, from the importing of British constitutional principles to the caballing and the intriguing. One thing that did cheer Jefferson, however, was Madison's proposal to bring a Declaration of Rights'before Congress. 'I like it as far as it goes,' he said of the draft Declaration Madison had sent him, 'but I should have been for going further.'[22] He considered that the original Declaration of Independence was no longer sufficient and that the Americans, like the French, needed a clear statement of fundamental human rights as a preface to their constitution. They must join with the French in rejecting the British idea that laws came before rights.

'Madison is charged with having laboured for the whole business of discrimination in order to pay court to the French nation through Mr Jefferson, our Minister in Paris,' wrote Senator Maclay on 1 July, the day after Madison sent Jefferson his draft Declaration. Next day Madison finally lost his battle to get the House to defy the Senate over discrimination. Fisher Ames of Massachusetts, who thought Madison was far too enamoured of French ideas, wrote that he was 'struggling to disentangle himself from his own web.' There were those who thought that his proposed Declaration and other alterations to the constitution were 'ardently desired by many of the states', but others accused him of 'sowing seeds of discontent from New Hampshire to Georgia'. 'Paper declarations of rights are trifling things and no real security to liberty,' wrote the *New York Daily Advertiser*. Madison's phrase about the people having 'an indubitable, unalienable and indefeasible right to reform or change their government' was attacked as being liable to 'risk the tumults that must grow out of another debate upon the constitution in every one of the United States'. On 13 August, the day after the French National Assembly returned to its discussion of a Declaration of Rights, the House at last decided to discuss Madison's proposals but it insisted that even if they were passed they must be added to the constitution as amendments and not written into it as a preface. 'We ought not to interweave our propositions into the work itself,' declared

Roger Sherman of Connecticut. Some amendments were subsequently accepted but the Declaration itself was thrown out on 19 August.[23] Whatever the French might do the Americans were not prepared to imitate their imitators.

The French still looked to the Americans for help. At the end of August Lafayette begged Jefferson to break all his engagements in order to give a dinner party for eight leading members of the Assembly. It was the only way, he wrote anxiously, of breaking the deadlock over whether or not the constitution should give the King the right to veto the decrees of the Assembly. But the dinner party does not seem to have been given and certainly the deadlock was not broken. Whereas the Declaration had raised the question of copying the Americans the veto turned the spotlight once again on the British. On 1 September Mirabeau gave the deputies another history lesson, telling them that the Long Parliament had overturned liberty by cutting off Charles I's head rather than by getting rid of the House of Lords. In a properly balanced constitution it was the King who was 'the perpetual representative of the people' and would guard them against any attempt by an Assembly to make itself permanent. A second chamber would provide no such safeguard. This rather partial view of the British constitution led inevitably to accusations that Mirabeau sought only to increase the power of the crown in readiness for his master to seize it. 'It was not for Louis he pleaded,' wrote Montjoie, 'it was for Orléans'. Three days later the abbé Grégoire told the Assembly roundly that it had no right to give the King an absolute veto and that it was not in his interest to have one. It was absurd to suggest that the British had the best possible constitution, he wrote later, and this would be even more obvious when the French had finished theirs. Even Mounier said that the Assembly now had it in its power to produce a constitution superior to that of Great Britain.[24]

Surprisingly enough *The Times* agreed. On 9 September, when both the royal veto and the division into two chambers still hung in the balance, it declared that 'if the French persevere in forming their system of a new government it ought to be the most perfect in Europe, not like England whose government has been formed at different periods from necessity but a regular system by mature reason and deliberation.' The following day Robert Jenkinson, son of Pitt's cabinet colleague Lord Hawkesbury, wrote home telling of uproar in the Assembly when Mirabeau's party tried to force a vote on the issue of the second chamber. Pruned of its more lurid passages his letter was made the basis for an official statement in the *London Gazette* to the effect that one of the great questions in France had been settled – the Assembly had decided that the new legislative would be permanent, not periodic as in Britain and America – and that the votes on the other two were imminent. Dorset's successor Lord Robert Fitzgerald assured Jenkinson that Mirabeau would carry the proposal for an absolute veto by a handsome majority. 'I persisted in the contrary opinion,' claimed Jenkinson, 'though at that time few would believe me.'[25] He was proved right: a proposal that the King should have only a suspensive veto was carried by 673 votes to 325 on 11 September. Meanwhile the plan for a second chamber had been rejected by 849 votes to 89 and Mounier had resigned in despair from the constitutional committee. 'I learn that the *Assemblée Nationale* have agreed to single chamber legislature and a suspensive veto in the King,' wrote Gouverneur Morris. 'This is travelling the high road to anarchy and that worst of all tyrannies, the despotism of faction in a popular assembly.'[26]

He wrote these words as he travelled the high road back to Paris after spending a month in London. In the forest of Chantilly, once the hunting preserve of the prince de Condé, he watched delighted citizen sportsmen beating hares and partridges to death with clubs. 'I suppose there will be this evening a grand fête at which all the world will agree *que la liberté vaut quelque chose*,' he noted coldly. 'One would think that every rusty gun in Provence is at work killing all sorts of birds,' complained Arthur Young five hundred miles away on the high road from Avignon to Marseilles, 'the shot has fallen five or six times in my chaise and about my ears. The National Assembly has declared that every man has a right to kill game on his own land.'[27] He was convinced that the British took a more intelligent interest in all this than the French themselves:

The abolition of tithes, the destruction of the *gabelle*, game-made property and feudal rights destroyed are French topics, that are translated into English within six days after they happen, and their consequences, combinations, results and modifications become the disquisition and entertainment of the grocers, chandlers, drapers and shoemakers of all the towns of England; yet the same people in France do not think them worth their conversation, except in private. Why? because conversation in private wants little knowledge; but in public it demands more and therefore I suppose – for I confess there are a thousand difficulties attending the solution – they are silent.[28]

As far as the British were concerned it was an idealized view of things. Romilly assured Dumont that the French revolution had produced 'a very sincere and very general joy' and that it was 'the subject of all conversations', but Morris only found, even among the shrewd businessmen of the City of London, 'a world of talk upon French politics, which they know nothing about'. Although Young spoke both of disquisition and of entertainment most Londoners were more interested in the latter. Within three weeks of the fall of the Bastille the Royal Circus in St George's Fields was advertising 'an entirely new and splendid entertainment, founded on the subject of the French Revolution, called The Triumph of Liberty or The Destruction of the Bastille.' Astley's amphitheatre at Westminster Bridge countered with 'Paris in an Uproar or The Destruction of the Bastille', with a model of Paris as an added attraction. 'Astley must have been at great expense in procuring such exact drawings of the Bastille,' commented *The Times*, 'for his representation of that place, both internal and external, is done with the most scrupulous exactness possible.' The reactions of the spectators were all that could be wished: 'the appearance of the skeleton of a man starved to death in the iron cage was finely felt by the audience and had that effect which barbarism always has on the breast of an Englishman.' Sadler's Wells presented a double bill: 'Britannia's Relief or The Gift of Hygeia', a celebration of George III's recovery, was followed by 'Gallic Freedom or *Vive la Liberté*', featuring 'that ever memorable event the attacking, storming and demolition of The Bastille.'[29]

'Three mighty Bastilles are nightly besieged in London,' recorded *The Times* at the beginning of September. By then Astley had already netted more money than in the whole of any previous season. Displays of horsemanship, for which his establishment had always been famous, were now said to be 'second to interludes and scenery'. Paris had come to London and French liberty was all the rage. Even government newspapers announced that France was now a free country and that the old jokes about French slavery and wooden shoes and the tyranny of the *Grand Monarque*, 'that were wont to set honest John Bull in a roar', had lost their point. Tom Paine told Jefferson that the death of these jokes had brought with it the rise of discontent: 'While the multitude could be terrified with the cry and apprehension of arbitrary power, wooden shoes, popery and such like stuff, they thought themselves by comparison an extraordinary free people, but this bugbear now loses its force'. There were 'very considerable remains of the feudal system which people did not see till the revolution in France placed it before their eyes.' Londoners were now 'turning their eyes towards the aristocrats of their own nation, a new mode of conquering'.[30]

Ordinary Londoners showed few signs of wanting to rise against their masters but those that were manifested were taken seriously by the authorities. In mid September an anonymous letter was found in the garden of a Clerkenwell churchwarden, warning that 'if you dont do justice to the poor woman that was murdered at the workhouse your Life shall pay the forfit for it and if you interfear to stop the publick houses in Turnmill Street as you have done your Life shall be stopped. If you dont take this warning you shall soon be dead a going home.' The Home Secretary had the letter printed in the *London Gazette*, together with the promise of a reward and a pardon for anyone who would inform on the writer. It was left to the journalists and caricaturists of the opposition press to depict London as a city of despotism and discontent while Parisians rejoiced in their new-found liberty. James Gillray's *France freedom, British slavery* showed Lafayette and Orléans holding Necker aloft with the crown of France in his hands while Pitt trampled upon the British crown and held his countrymen in chains.[31]

George III was among the fettered in Gillray's print but the King of France was nowhere to be seen. Although *The Times* still suggested occasionally that Louis might be biding his time and preparing a counter-revolution the general view was that the French revolution was over and that the monarch had ceased to have any political importance. 'Louis is a good creature,' remarked the *St James's Chronicle* disparagingly. 'They have destroyed all his partridges and so he has nothing now to lose worth preserving.' *Les Sacrifices Forcés*, a caricature version of the night of 4 August, showed French noblemen and dignitaries bewailing the loss of their privileges while Louis merely begged to be allowed to keep his hunting and 'a few pieces of iron for rainy days' – a reference to his interest in metalwork. At the beginning of October, when westerly gales in the Channel held up the mails from France, it was assumed in London that no news was good news. *The Times* reported that after the constitutional decisions of mid September there was 'calm in the hemisphere of politics' and 'utmost tranquillity' in Paris and Versailles.[32] In fact the calm and the tranquillity had already been shattered as Louis put his hunting and his metalwork behind him and prepared to defy the Assembly once more. This time his challenge to its authority was to lose him his freedom of action for ever and give the city of Paris undisputed control of the French revolution.

CHAPTER NINE

The year's end

In Paris Jefferson became increasingly apprehensive. On 13 September, two days after the Assembly made its constitutional decisions, he assured Tom Paine that 'there is no possibility now of anything's hindering their final establishment of a good constitution, which will in its principles and merits be about a middle term between that of England and the United States.' On the same day he told other radical friends in London that the French nation was now so solidly united that neither the machinations of the Orléanists nor the threat of foreign intervention could shake it. But less than a week later he feared that 'we are in danger of hourly insurrection from want of bread' and on 23 September, in his final dispatch to his government before leaving for home, he discussed at length the possibility of France being plunged into civil war. 'Without doubt England will give money to produce and to feed the fire which should consume this country,' he added. 'But it is not probable she will engage in open war for that.' On the other hand he was convinced that Prussia was ready to intervene – *The Times* reported 50,000 Prussian troops advancing to the French frontiers – and so there was a third possible cause for civil war, as well as food shortages and the prospect of government bankruptcy. It was 'the absconding of the King from Versailles', which Jefferson said 'has for some time been apprehended as possible.' If Louis could escape from his palace and join the Prussians he might yet rally the old France against the new.[1]

At Versailles the Assembly interrupted its debates on the constitution in order to discuss means of averting starvation and bankruptcy, but there was little it could do about Louis's supposed intention to flee. Having established a constitutional monarchy the deputies had to have a constitutional monarch. If Louis XVI did not want to be one they could either force him into it or they could look for a successor. The idea of forcing the King to play his part had been mooted at the beginning of the month when the marquis de St Huruge, one of the most notorious agitators at the Palais Royal, had tried to lead a march on Versailles to bring the King back to Paris as a prisoner. A week after this attempt *The Times* was still talking of 'deep laid schemes of Parisians to declare the King and the Dauphin not safe at Versailles',[2] but the deputies had been outraged and St Huruge had been arrested. Nothing could be said in public about the alleged plan for the King to leave Versailles but if the Assembly was not prepared to stop him going it would need to think what to do if he went. And so in the middle of September, when discussion of the constitution turned to the question of the succession, it led to some of the ugliest scenes the Assembly had yet witnessed. Deputies were supposedly debating a remote contingency but many feared they were talking about imminent events.

The full extent of the problem was explained later by the *Maryland Gazette* after the news had crossed the Atlantic. The Dauphin and the two sons of the comte d'Artois held out 'a slender hope of exemption from a contest that must plunge Europe into a war.' The hope was slender because the new Dauphin was said to be as sickly as his elder brother had been and because Artois had fled from France, taking his sons with him. Therefore 'the pretensions of the house of Orléans, maintained by an able and popular prince, will be opposed to the prejudices of a great body of the French nation, in favour of their fundamental laws, and to the whole force of the Spanish monarchy'. After Louis XVI and his brothers and their children it was the Spanish Bourbons who had the best claim to the French throne but they had been excluded by the treaty of Utrecht, imposed upon France and Spain in 1713 by those nations who wanted to prevent the upset in the balance of power which would result from a union of the two crowns. And so now, as the Bishop of Langres pointed out in the Assembly on 15 September, the French would incur the enmity of Spain if they upheld the exclusion and the enmity of almost every other country if they did not.[3]

These diplomatic considerations were linked to domestic suspicions. It was the British who had been the architects of the
treaty of Utrecht and it was the British who were now thought
to be financing the Orléanists so as to 'produce and feed the fire
which should consume this country'. Since it was Orléans who
stood to gain by the Utrecht exclusion being upheld the debate
soon turned into an open confrontation between his supporters,
led by Mirabeau and Sillery, and their opponents under Duval
d'Eprémesnil. At first the Orléanists agreed that it would be wiser
not to debate the exclusion but later, when the duc de Mortemart
asserted that it was only about the union of the crowns and
not about the succession itself, Mirabeau accused him angrily of
insulting the whole French nation. Then Sillery produced details
of the Utrecht settlement from his pocket and Duval d'Eprémesnil
started talking about an Orléanist attempt to change the
succession. According to official accounts the debate became more
and more embarrassing and had to be adjourned because of the
appalling noise and because it was impossible to reach any
decision. Next day things were said to be 'more tumultuous than
ever' and Mirabeau and Duval came near to blows.[4]

At the British embassy on 17 September Robert Jenkinson
noted in exasperation that 'for the last two or three days the
Assemblée have been wasting their time in useless discussions on
the succession to the throne. This unnecessary delay creates great
discontent at Paris.' But Parisian discontent was more closely
linked to the seemingly useless discussions than he realized. Those
discussions had convinced many deputies that the real danger
came not from any intention the King might have to leave Versailles but from the plans of others to force him into leaving so
that Orléans could be proclaimed as his successor. And these plans
were thought to be based upon an uprising in Paris. As mayor of
the city Bailly spent September worrying about bread supplies
and by the end of the month he was sure the bakers were about
to bring production to a halt in accordance with secret instructions
from the plotters. 'In Paris not to bake was to give the signal for
insurrection,' he wrote, 'an insurrection which had been planned
for more than a fortnight.'[5]

Meanwhile Louis had instructed the Flanders infantry regiment
to leave its quarters in Douai and march on Versailles. Two days
after he gave these orders his refusal to sanction the August
decrees produced an outburst of fury in the Assembly. 'Does

the nation stand in need of any will other than its own?' cried Robespierre. In Paris the fury was even greater. The refusal to sanction the decrees was a call to civil war, declared the radical journal *L'Ami du Peuple*, the signal for the reduction of the capital by starvation and by force of arms. In fact many of the men of the Flanders regiment were from areas around Paris and when they arrived in Versailles on 23 September they were soon on friendly terms with the local National Guard, the new name for the town militia set up in July. They took the civic oath and handed their artillery over to the municipal authorities. But on 1 October, at a banquet given by officers of the royal bodyguard for those of the Flanders regiment, the King and the Queen and the Dauphin made an appearance and were wildly cheered. Guests were said to have torn off tricolour cockades, trampling them underfoot and replacing them with white ones in honour of the Bourbons and black ones in honour of Marie Antoinette. Next day the Assembly increased the pressure on the King by requiring him to sanction not just the August decrees but the Declaration of Rights and the preliminary articles of the constitution.[6]

When accounts of the Versailles banquet appeared in the Paris newspapers on Saturday 3 October Lord Fitzgerald reported that 'the Palais Royal was much disturbed and it became unsafe to walk in the streets with black cockades, as several strangers experienced, from whose hats they were torn with much violence and abusive language.' All day long on Sunday the orators at the Palais Royal made their denunciations and their exhortations while district assemblies met to decide what action to take. The demand for a concerted march on the royal palace was now irresistible and an enormous and determined crowd, made up largely of women from the Paris markets, broke into the Hôtel de Ville and seized money and arms. 'On Monday morning, My Lord,' Fitzgerald told the British Foreign Secretary, 'we were much surprised and at first much entertained with the ludicrous sight of a female army proceeding very clamorously but in order and determined step towards Versailles.'[7] This army, between 5000 and 6000 strong, left Paris at noon and reached Versailles four hours later.

Meanwhile at the Hôtel de Ville Lafayette was threatened with impeachment in the name of the people if he did not lead the Paris National Guard to join the women. At four o'clock in the afternoon, just as the women were surrounding the royal palace and pouring into the public galleries of the Assembly, he gave in and set off for Versailles at the head of more than 25,000 men, half of them National Guards and the rest irregular volunteers. He got to Versailles towards midnight to learn that the men of the Flanders regiment had refused to fire on the crowd and the King had made a total submission, telling the Assembly that he accepted the Declaration and the constitution without reservations. When Lafayette delivered a formal request from the authorities in Paris, to the effect that the King should leave Versailles and take up residence in the capital, Louis countered with a declaration to the members of the Assembly saying that he would never desert them.[8] By two o'clock in the morning the King and the Queen and most of the deputies had gone to their beds.

The first to be woken was Marie Antoinette. The market women had declared that they would make cockades out of her bowels and shortly before five o'clock a group of them fought their way past her bodyguard and into her bedroom. 'Many have asserted that they recognized the duke of Orleans at half past four in the morning, in a greatcoat and slouched hat,' declared one of the ladies-in-waiting, 'at the top of the marble staircase pointing out with his hand the guard-room which preceded the Queen's apartments.'[9] The Queen fled to the King's bedroom and later in the morning, after continued fighting between the rioters and the bodyguard, she and Louis were greeted with a mixture of cheers and threats when they came out on the palace balcony. Lafayette helped to win over the crowd, bowing to the Queen and kissing her hand, and Louis announced that he and his family would now leave for Paris. They arrived there soon after seven o'clock in the evening, accompanied by most of those who had marched to Versailles the previous day. Advance parties had returned earlier, carrying the heads of slaughtered bodyguards on pikes, so Parisians already knew of the victory. The King and the Queen and the Dauphin were escorted to the Tuileries palace, where they were to remain captive until their abortive attempt to escape twenty months later. 'The blind and headlong will of the populace directs all,' concluded Fitzgerald, 'and all submit with fear and trembling to their government as the dangerous maxims that all men are equal, and that numbers can overcome a few, are in the mouths of every vagabond at present'.[10]

Two days later London got wind of trouble in Paris and the *St*

James's Chronicle announced that 'the capital of France as well as Versailles are plunged in all the horrors of a civil war'. By 12 October *The Times* was able to give a full account of the affair under the headline FRANCE, CONFINEMENT OF THE KING, QUEEN AND ROYAL FAMILY AND *The Attempt to Murder the Queen*. 'Independent of the awful crisis of his MAJESTY's late illness,' it observed, 'there never was a moment which excited the anxiety and attention of all ranks of people so much as the present revolution in France.' The fate of all Europe was in the hands of 'a BARBAROUS AND UNRESTRAINED MOB'. The *Morning Post* reported that Marie Antoinette had been paraded around the place of public execution with a noose round her neck. Other and more dangerous stories were also given credence. 'It is confidently said that an offer has been made to Great Britain in the course of the summer of one of the French and Austrian provinces,' asserted the *St James's Chronicle*, 'under no other stipulation than that of protection, which was peremptorily refused on our part.' *The Times* declared that the uprising had been intended to force the King into flight so that Orléans could be proclaimed Lieutenant-General of the kingdom. 'Perhaps a more iniquitous plot was never contrived,' it commented. The *St James's Chronicle* assured its readers that Orléans would be put on trial within days.[11]

In fact Orléans was on his way to London. In Paris Fitzgerald had been amazed to learn of his departure, which he thought was 'the summit of imprudence at a moment when numberless accusations appear against him as the chief promoter of all the troubles and misfortunes of this country'. The French ambassador in London insisted that the journey was 'by no means in consequence of any danger arising to the duke's person from the unsettled situation of affairs in France', but George III refused to believe it. 'I confess I attribute it to his finding his views not likely to succeed or some personal uneasiness for his own safety,' he growled. It was then learned that Orléans was indeed suffering some uneasiness, having been 'seized by the populace' in Boulogne and prevented from leaving France. Urgent instructions from Paris secured his release and on 20 October he finally arrived in England – 'the land of *true* liberty', remarked the *St James's Chronicle* archly as it reported his arrival.[12]

The following day an anonymous pamphlet was published in Paris entitled *Domine Salvum Fac Regem*. This Latinizing of the British national anthem was heavily ironic, since the pamphlet purported to tell how the British had plotted not to save the King of France but to dethrone him and get their puppet the duc d'Orléans made Lieutenant-General. Mirabeau was said to have been their chief agent, assisted by a motley crew of conspirators including Duroveray, Clavière, Dumont and Richard Price. Fitzgerald sent a copy of the pamphlet to his government, which had been bombarding him with questions about what Orléans was supposed to have done and how his visit to London should be handled. 'The general idea is that that Prince was chief promoter of all the disturbances here,' Fitzgerald replied, 'of the expedition on Monday the 5th of this month to Versailles, that his designs against the King were of a very criminal nature, that he aimed at the regency of the kingdom for himself and proposed to bring his own party into power.'[13]

George III granted Orléans an audience at the end of October but left it to the Foreign Secretary to make clear the attitude of his government. Orléans was advised 'not to look to foreign countries either with hope or apprehension', but to lend his authority to the restoration of order in France, without which neither he nor his country could expect 'any favourable estimation on the part of other nations'. Orléans brought up the problem of the Austrian Netherlands, where Marie Antoinette's brother the Emperor was meeting continued resistance. It seemed as though Brussels might soon rival Paris as a city of revolution – 'The moment of the GRAND REVOLUTION approaches fast, and perhaps it will take place in a few hours,' a newspaper correspondent there wrote in mid October – and *The Times* had already suggested that the Triple Alliance of Britain and Prussia and the Dutch should use the revolt in order to weaken France and Austria. Louis XVI was said to have entrusted his cousin with a confidential mission to the British government and if there was such a mission it almost certainly concerned the Austrian Netherlands. Orléans did his best to sound out British intentions and he even hinted at the possibility of joint Franco-British action, only to be told sternly that the Emperor had a perfect right to put down the revolt and that Great Britain had no intention of giving aid to revolutionaries. The Foreign Secretary brought the interview to an end by saying that George III and 'every person in his dominions possessed of common humanity' deplored Louis XVI's predicament and trusted it would not be of long duration.[14]

It seems he was right. The march on Versailles had totally changed British attitudes to the French revolution. Romilly, back in London after a visit to Paris, reported that 'I find the favour with which the popular cause in France is considered here much less than it was when I quitted England.' Orléans was hissed in the London streets and the press accused him of trying in vain to incite Billingsgate fishwives to riot in the way he had raised the market women of Paris. He had long been a personal and political associate of the Prince of Wales and now government newspapers did their best to discredit the Prince's party by suggesting that they were in continual conference with the suspect from France. 'The duke of Orléans is feasting with the Prince of Wales in ignominious safety,' Romilly told Dumont. A satirical print entitled *Who kills first for a Crown* showed the Prince hunting down a stag with the features of his father while Orléans chased one resembling his cousin Louis XVI. From Lille, where she had gone to take refuge from the revolution in Brussels, the duchess of Devonshire wrote urgently to warn the Prince to be on his guard against Orléans because 'he has heavy accusations and I fear proof against him.' Even Charles Fox forgot his earlier remarks about Orléans's conduct having been perfect and warned the Prince that he must on no account allow himself to be used as a figurehead for Orléanist schemes to take control of the Brussels revolution.[15]

A few weeks earlier the opposition had been making useful political capital out of Orléans and his revolution. *The Offering to Liberty*, a print showing him bringing the supporters of the Queen and the comte d'Artois in chains to make their submission to the goddess of liberty, had labelled the chained figures 'Pests of France and Britain, German toadeaters and German counsellors.' While the Queen of France had plotted with one set of evil-minded German courtiers to crush liberty the Queen of England had plotted with another to subvert the constitution and stop the Prince becoming Regent. But now the only concern of opposition newspapers was to distance themselves from Orléans and from all he stood for. The *Morning Post* protested angrily against the habit of dubbing as Tories 'those who look with horror on the lamentable consequences of insurrection in France' and even more angrily against calling the French revolutionaries Whigs. 'We would not wish so honourable a name to be disgraced,' it thundered, 'by being bestowed on savages who debase the Majesty of the People, miscreants in rebellion against the King and the People.'[16]

The opposition politician who was most mercilessly pilloried in the press for his supposed revolutionary sympathies was Burke. 'Mr Burke is shortly to visit France,' alleged *The Times* on the day the women marched out to Versailles, 'he has wrote out a new constitution for them, formed partly from Messrs Cade and Tyler and partly from Mr Oliver Cromwell'. Burke had indeed told his friend William Windham that the new French constitution was 'more truly democratical than that of North America', but it was by no means certain that he meant this as a compliment. 'The spirit it is impossible not to admire,' he had written after the fall of the Bastille, 'but the old Parisian ferocity has broken out in a shocking manner.' When news of the attack on the palace came through he spoke of 'the portentous state of France, where the elements which compose human society seem all to be dissolved and a world of monsters to be produced in the place of it, where Mirabeau presides as the Grand Anarch.'[17]

Some months later, when Burke found out about the links between the Grand Anarch and the marquis of Lansdowne, he made effective political use of them. What he did not know – and what Lansdowne did not know either, fortunately for his peace of mind – was that Mirabeau had already come close to turning the fantasies of *The Times* into reality. Without telling Dumont or Duroveray he had got together a selection of English seventeenth-century republican writings under the title *Theory of Kingship according to the doctrines of Milton, translated from the English by the comte de Mirabeau*. Milton had been Cromwell's secretary and the extracts included arguments justifying the killing of kings. Intended for publication in September, the pamphlet was held up at the printers and copies did not arrive until the middle of October. Mirabeau was already suspected of plotting to dethrone the King and the publication of such a pamphlet with his name on it would clearly be an act of supreme folly. Madame Le Jay, the money-grubbing wife of Mirabeau's publisher, wanted to go ahead with it but Dumont and Duroveray insisted that the whole edition must be destroyed. Since they came from a republican city and were far more familiar than Mirabeau with the English language suspicion would clearly fall on them – and perhaps, through them, on their dissenter friends in London who were known to regard 1688 as insufficiently radical. Duroveray personally supervised the burning of the pamphlets but Le Jay managed to save a few copies, one of which is now in the *Bibliothèque Nationale* in Paris.[18]

'The verdict of the Assembly is not the verdict of history,' Dumont remarked coldly after the National Assembly had cleared Mirabeau of involvement in the events of 5 and 6 October. He remembered that Camille Desmoulins, one of the chief instigators of the troubles in Paris, had stayed with Mirabeau in Versailles for a fortnight before the uprising and had subsequently denounced both Dumont and Duroveray as Pitt's secret agents. He also remembered that throughout September Mirabeau had seen a great deal of Choderlos de Laclos, who had been Orléans's secretary. Although he assured Lansdowne that there was no truth in the allegations made in *Domine Salvum Fac Regem* (Lansdowne, fearing that he might be compromised, had sent three anxious letters to Paris within a week), Dumont clearly had suspicions of his own which the business of the Milton pamphlet did nothing to allay. The day after it had been burned he told Romilly that he was determined to break with Mirabeau and return to London by the end of November.[19] In the event it took him another four months to get away, unhappy months during which he became increasingly disgusted with Mirabeau's shady political manoeuvring. The wider hope, the prospect of an exchange of ideas leading to moderate and constructive reform on both sides of the Channel, was to all intents and purposes dead. It was only a few short weeks since Mirabeau had spoken of Lansdowne's support as the mainstay of his career, yet in that time he had turned from an investment into a liability. Instead of buttressing and strengthening Lansdowne's political position he looked like making it infinitely more precarious.

The radical intellectuals associated with Lansdowne refused to accept that their hopes were dead. Bentham continued to pester Dumont about his work on political tactics, convinced that the Assembly could somehow be made to see its importance, and shortly after the march to Versailles he wrote to tell Mirabeau that he was prepared to write a series of articles on France's financial problems. When this came to nothing he settled down instead to write his *Draught of a new plan for the organization of the Judicial Establishment in France*, a hundred copies of which were in due course sent to the National Assembly and ignored.[20] In the middle of October, when Mirabeau wanted to propose laws to curb riots, Duroveray asked his English friends in Paris about the British Riot Act. They in their turn applied to Romilly in London, who sent the required details but said the French should be thinking about improving on the Act rather than copying it.[21] Having hoped that revolution in Paris would be the spur to reform at Westminster he now found that the only things the French wanted to imitate were the very things he most wanted to change.

Necker had now made it clear that he would not advocate any change in French policy towards Geneva. The only hope for Dumont and Duroveray and their friends lay in a change of ministry and so, in spite of their own reservations and in spite of Lansdowne's anxieties, they still backed Mirabeau's bid for power. On 19 October, in the Assembly's first session after it had followed the King from Versailles to Paris, a speech by Mirabeau praising Lafayette instead of attacking him seemed to open the way to an alliance between the two men against Necker. Dumont, who had written the speech, was much flattered to be invited to a dinner given by Lafayette for Mirabeau and other would-be ministers. 'I was delighted with a reconciliation which I had brought about without anyone suspecting that I was responsible for it,' he wrote. A few days later Mirabeau told the comte de la Marck, his go-between in the negotiations with Lafayette, that he had three first-class assistants and needed money urgently in order to pay them and stop them going back to England.[22] Clearly he still needed the Genevese, just as they still needed him, even though earlier idealism had given way to distrust and disillusionment.

It had also given way to deceit of a particularly dangerous kind. Unknown to his first-class assistants Mirabeau had sketched out a plan for counter-revolution, whereby Louis would leave Paris and raise an army in Normandy to challenge the Assembly. Gouverneur Morris, whose mistress the comtesse de Flahaut kept him in touch with most of what was going on, heard that Mirabeau was to have a secret meeting with the King. In fact the interview was with Louis's brother the comte de Provence, to whom Mirabeau gave written details of the plan. Morris saw that 'the great question is how to get rid of Necker, who unfortunately possesses the popular opinion but has not talents equal to the situation of affairs', but he warned Lafayette against Mirabeau, saying that he would disgrace any government he joined. The man he thought should succeed Necker was the Bishop of Autun, Charles-Maurice de Talleyrand-Périgord, who had a formidable reputation in the Assembly as a speaker on financial matters. After some initial reluctance Mirabeau accepted this, proposing an administration with Talleyrand as finance minister and himself as minister without portfolio. Lafayette and Mirabeau got as far as planning a joint attack on Necker in the Assembly and then, on 26 October, their alliance fell apart when Mirabeau received what he called 'a monstrous proposition' that he should be an ambassador rather than a member of the government. On the same day the Paris correspondent of *The Times* reported that Necker and his whole cabinet had offered to resign because 'the anarchy in France is complete'. It seemed that Mirabeau had undermined the ministry without being able to put anything in its place.[23]

Duroveray returned to London at the end of October to report to Lansdowne. While he was away Mirabeau patched up his quarrel with Lafayette and received renewed assurances of his support, together with urgent warnings that Necker was preparing to strike back. These were followed by further warnings from Lamarck and his friends to the effect that there was 'a terrible cabal' against Mirabeau in the Assembly. Its aim was to push through a clause forbidding members of the Assembly to accept ministerial office, thus scotching not only Mirabeau's bid for power but also the last chance of French political life conforming to the Westminster pattern. Although the Assembly had turned down the idea of a second chamber and an effective royal veto it could still ensure a reasonable working relationship between government and legislative as long as it did not insist on the total separation of powers, as long as it did not stop deputies being ministers. On Thursday 5 November Mirabeau told Lamarck that anyone with any sense must realize that ministers could not do their job properly unless they sat in the Assembly. He knew all about the terrible cabal, he added scornfully, and he would be ready to deal with it when it introduced its ridiculous clause on the following Monday. By then he might already be a minister.[24]

His enemies were well aware of this possibility and they brought in their proposal not on the Monday but on the Saturday when he least expected it. He made a desperate and bitterly ironic speech, suggesting that the prohibition should extend only to himself, but it was to no avail. His ambitions were resented, his British connections were suspect, his friends were divided and unprepared. The clause was passed and the principle of the separation of powers, one of the great shibboleths of eighteenth-century theorists, was established as the basis of the new French constitution.[25] It was already written into the constitution of the United States and it had once been part of the British constitution, having been enshrined in the Act of Settlement of 1701 and then dropped shortly afterwards as being unworkable. Successive opposition groups at Westminster had been trying for more than eighty years to get it put back but successive administrations had blocked it because it would have made the management of Parliament impossible. Radicals regarded such management as corrupt when they were out of office but if they ever got into power they tended to find it essential. The British system of cabinet government, whereby the executive was formed by members of the party dominant in the legislative, necessarily depended on powers not being separated. Even though the Assembly's decree of 7 November was welcomed by some British reformers and idealists it nevertheless marked the parting of the ways as far as London and Paris were concerned. Mirabeau knew this as well as anyone: later that month he finally wound up his *Analysis of English Newspapers*, a weekly journal he had been running for the past two years.

The basic reason for Necker's weakness and for Mirabeau's and Talleyrand's determination to replace him had been the simple fact that the initiative in matters financial had to come from deputies rather than from the government. Having used the threat of non-payment of taxes as a weapon against the King, having turned a blind eye to current tax evasion, having swept away in the August decrees much of the administrative framework that made collection of taxes possible, the Assembly now had to find some way of saving France from bankruptcy. It had been pretty evident for the past three months what way it would choose. On 8 August, the day after Necker outlined the desperate state of government finances to the deputies, the marquis de Lacoste proposed a decree declaring that all ecclesiastical property belonged to the nation. 'The clergy in France, it seems, are to pay for all,' observed *The Times*. 'The FRENCH CLERGY are in a most deplorable state,' it added six weeks later, 'their sins lie heavy on their heads and even repentance cannot save them from the plundering hand of new-born Liberty.' By that time Talleyrand had become the chief advocate of the policy and was being tipped to succeed Necker. Significantly enough, when Mirabeau was warned at the end of October of another contender, it was Lacoste's name that was mentioned. It seemed that no one could be considered fit to govern France unless he was prepared to seize the wealth of the church.[26]

Five days before the Assembly excluded them from office Talleyrand and Mirabeau established their claim to it by collaborating to push through a decree declaring all ecclesiastical property to be at the disposal of the nation. In return the nation would undertake to pay the clergy and would guarantee them a minimum wage. Six weeks later the Assembly decided to begin selling off church lands and other confiscated property. Four hundred million livres' worth would be put on the market and the government would issue four hundred thousand interest-bearing certificates known as *assignats*, each to the value of a thousand livres, which would be taken in payment. In this way the government would be sure of getting its money in advance and in full, whatever happened to land values later. The Assembly took care not to make the *assignats* legal tender because of its traditional French distrust of paper money as an evil and dangerous instrument of London's bubble economy. Nor was Brissot alone in seeing the depreciation of paper currencies as the cause of many of America's ills.* French finances would be based, as they always had been, on the solid realities of landed wealth.[27]

On Christmas Day Arthur Young re-entered France after spending three months in Italy. The following day he started to note down his impressions of the country again, just a week after the decree authorizing the issue of *assignats*. He was told that 'the country is perfectly quiet everywhere' and he drew grim satisfaction from the sight of a peasant who had been hanged for taking part in the burning of a château. On the last day of the year he found himself back in the Bourbonnais at Riaux, where the marquis Desgouttes had an estate for sale – 'a good house, a fine garden, ready markets for every sort of produce; and, above all the rest, 3000 acres of enclosed land capable in a very little time of being, without expense, quadrupled in its produce'. Early in August, when he had last been at Riaux, Young had been deterred from making an offer for the property because 'in buying an estate I might be purchasing my share in a civil war'. Now things were very different. 'Never have I been so tempted,' he mused. 'God grant that, should he be pleased to protract my life, I may not in a sad old age repent of not closing at once with an

*See above, p.II.

offer to which prudence calls and prejudice only forbids!' He got the marquis to promise him first refusal and he went on his way, apparently convinced that the Assembly had made France once again a country fit for landowners to live in.[28]

He was much mistaken. The year ended in comparative tranquillity, with high hopes of that restoration of ancient liberties which was supposed to be the proper object of revolution, but the seeds of future trouble were germinating fast. Within less than four months the Assembly was to find itself making the *assignats* legal tender, thus opening the way to currency depreciation and runaway inflation. Three weeks after that disastrous decision Mirabeau would be writing secretly to the King and setting him on the counter-revolutionary road which led to his execution. Another two months and the Assembly would be turning the nationalization of church property and the payment of priests into the Civil Constitution of the Clergy, an enactment which alienated not only the papacy but also many hundreds of thousands of devout Frenchmen and Frenchwomen. All these developments, which between them were to destroy the moderate revolution of 1789 and plunge France into two decades of political turmoil and civil strife and foreign war, were the direct and inescapable results of the decisions which now seemed so sensible and solid and reassuring.

CHAPTER TEN

Revolution reconsidered

After breakfast on his first day back in Paris Arthur Young went to see what he called 'the most extraordinary sight that either French or English eyes could ever behold'. First he watched from a distance as the King took the air in the Tuileries gardens with an escort of National Guards and then, when Louis went indoors, the gates were thrown open and the crowd poured in to gape at Marie Antoinette, who was still walking in the gardens. 'A mob followed her, talking very loud and paying no other apparent respect than that of taking off their hats whenever she passed, which was indeed more than I expected.' Overlooking the terraces to the north of the gardens was the Manège, the royal riding school which had been converted into a hall for the Assembly, and beyond that again, on the other side of the Rue St Honoré, the former Dominican convent of St Jacques which now housed and gave its name to the Jacobin club. A fortnight later Young's Parisian friends got him elected a member of this club, which had grown out of Le Chapelier's phalanx of Breton extremists, and he was told he could take part in its proceedings whenever he pleased. It was no mean honour, for the Jacobins held the National Assembly in their grip as firmly as the Assembly held the captive King. 'Such is the majority of numbers,' wrote Young, 'that whatever passes in this club is almost sure to pass in the Assembly.'[1]

Young saw that the ascending levels of power represented by the Tuileries and the Manège and the convent of St Jacques were French and not merely Parisian. Whereas before the move to

Paris the deputies had only been concerned with planning the future, with giving France a constitution, they were now 'equally answerable for the whole conduct of the government of the state, executive as well as legislative.' Other centres of power and authority, the Hôtel de Ville and the sixty district assemblies, were supposedly concerned only with the running of the city; but the Palais Royal, further down the Rue St Honoré on the way from the Jacobins to the Hôtel de Ville, was still a powerhouse of revolution and a bridge between municipal and national affairs. It had already galvanized Paris into saving France twice and it might need to do so again. When Young pointed out the dangers of allowing the capital to give the law to the whole country he was told that 'the predominancy which Paris assumed at present was absolutely necessary, for the safety of the whole nation; for if nothing were done but by procuring a previous common consent all great opportunities would be lost and the National Assembly left constantly exposed to the danger of a counter-revolution.'[2] Paris was the revolution's only guarantor and custodian. Whoever and whatever the politicians held captive, they were themselves the captives of the city.

It was a city changed beyond recognition. 'Paris is strangely altered from what it was,' commented Dumont. 'Once the theatre of luxury and pleasure, it is now perpetually harassed with supposed plots and real insurrections.' 'How times are changed!' observed Young as he sat down to dinner with men who had not bothered to powder their hair or change their muddy boots. 'When they had nothing better to attend to, the fashionable Parisians were correctness itself, in all that pertained to the *toilette*, and were therefore thought a frivolous people; but now they have something of more importance than dress to occupy them'. Paris had long been a centre of conspicuous expenditure, a city whose prosperity depended on the readiness of the rich to live extravagantly and ostentatiously. Now a good many of the rich had fled – Dumont put the number at a hundred thousand[3] – and those who remained were not disposed to flaunt their wealth. The district assemblies and the National Guard were in the seats of the mighty, wielding more power than the grandest nobleman had ever had, and so it was not wise to appear too noble or too grand. Long before nobility was officially abolished in June 1790 many of its outward trappings had been quietly discarded.

The result was widespread unemployment. 'Judge, from this

circumstance,' wrote Dumont, 'what an army of servants out of place, labourers out of work, men wholly dependent upon the luxuries of the great and now stripped of all resources, must have been turned loose upon the public.'[4] With more time on their hands than food in their bellies the unemployed gravitated to the district assemblies or to the Palais Royal, there to discuss the wicked plots being hatched by aristocrats and rich men. This made aristocrats and rich men all the more reluctant to be conspicuous or ostentatious, so that still more people found themselves out of work. Informed outsiders, brought up to believe that only the wealth of the few could give employment to the many, considered that the authorities simply could not allow the vicious spiral to continue. At the end of July, in his last dispatch before he retreated to London, Dorset had predicted that Parisians would soon be seeking the return of those 'august personages' whom they had driven into exile, 'when it is considered what immense sums of money will be thrown into the hands of foreigners during their absence from the kingdom.'[5]

Instead Parisians made sure that the Assembly seized as much as it could of the wealth the august personages had left behind. Rather than bow to economic reality, as its enemies had hoped, the revolutionary city bent reality to its will and moved inexorably from political to social revolution, from the dream of regeneration to a vision of apocalypse. American observers, themselves among the first to equate plain living with revolutionary fervour, were quick to glimpse what might lie ahead. 'The abolition of the noblesse, clergy, parliament, pensions etc. reducing so many persons to absolute distress on the one side, and the total stagnation of commerce and the consequent want of money on the other, keep us in constant fear of some disastrous event,' declared the Paris correspondent of the *Maryland Gazette*.[6]

At first it seemed that the other and more traditionalist revolutionary city across the Channel might reap the advantages Paris was neglecting. On the day Dorset reflected on the immense sums the French were throwing into the hands of foreigners *The Times* announced that there were more Frenchmen in London than ever before. Londoners who had spent more than a century as custodians of their own very profitable revolution principles could now minister equally profitably to refugees from a revolution of a different kind. Even the American newspapers listed 'the most distinguished French families in London' and told how

Calonne at his villa in Wimbledon entertained the exiles so beguilingly that they came for breakfast and stayed until five o'clock in the afternoon. The duc de Luxembourg, who had presided over the doomed order of nobility at Versailles, took a large furnished house in Soho Square and paid respectful visits to the rather more resilient House of Lords at Westminster.[7]

But by the end of August the French emigrés were already beginning to leave England, even though they were still promising 'a great entertainment at the Pantheon this coming winter in gratitude for the protection this country afforded them'. Luxembourg let it be known that he was displeased with his reception in London and would be going to Milan. Some of the aristocratic refugees were said to be travelling to Venice in September for the carnival and then to Turin for the winter while others, more militant, were gathering in Brussels: 'a kind of congress is to be held there on what measures it will be proper to pursue.' If those measures included the use of force, as the London correspondent of the *Gazette of the United States* hinted, then support from the aristocratic insurgents in the Austrian Netherlands, close to the frontiers of France, would be more appropriate and more useful than anything that might be hoped from London. The Brussels revolutionaries were defending the catholic clergy against a secularizing Emperor, just as any attempt at counter-revolution in France would presumably be concerned to defend the French church against a secularizing Assembly. In mid October Mirabeau secretly suggested using the troubles in the Austrian Netherlands as a means of raising an army in northern France to support the King. From the middle of December onwards the comte de Lamarck, Mirabeau's agent in his secret dealings with the Court, was in Brussels ready to make contact with insurgents or emigrés.[8]

Nevertheless it was from London that the most impassioned and most influential summons to a counter-revolutionary crusade was to come. The call was sounded by Edmund Burke, the man whom *The Times* had accused of leading the French in the footsteps of Wat Tyler and Jack Cade and Oliver Cromwell.* Born in Dublin, of a catholic mother and a father who had conformed to exported Anglicanism, Burke had soon learned that he too must conform and accept the rape of Irish catholicism if he was to make his way in the world. That rape had begun two and a half centuries

*See above, p.168.

earlier, when Parliament at Westminster had anticipated the French National Assembly by taking over the lands of the catholic church. Although many of the estates seized had since passed into private hands the Church of England was still a great landowner as well as a powerful and privileged religious establishment. Nowhere were its powers and privileges greater than in Ireland. Yet it was an adopted Irish Englishman who now summoned the Church of England to denounce the despoiling by the French of the church it had once itself despoiled.

Burke's book was published in November 1790 and it was called *Reflections on the Revolution in France and on the Proceedings in certain Societies in London relative to that event; in a Letter intended to have been sent to a gentleman in Paris.* It was a tediously but necessarily lengthy title, because the purpose of the work could not be and still cannot be understood without knowing what London societies had taken what proceedings and why the letter to the gentleman in Paris had not been sent. Charles-Jacques-François Depont, known to the Burke family as Picky Poky, had written a flattering letter on 4 November 1789 asking Burke to 'deign to assure him that the French were worthy to be free.' Burke had passed the letter on to his son Richard, remarking that the French did indeed seem to be more united in pursuit of liberty than he would have thought possible. He had then written to Depont to say that all who desired liberty were worthy of it. He had warned against excesses but he had also said that the French were right to struggle for a new form of government.[9]

In late December, before receiving this reply, Depont had written again to say that the approval and support given by the London Revolution Society had encouraged him to think that he and his countrymen were indeed following in the footsteps of English revolutionaries and proving themselves fit to be free. By the time Burke got this second letter he had read not only the sermon preached by Lansdowne's dissenter friend Richard Price to the London Revolution Society on 4 November but also Mirabeau's speech of 16 July, in which he had maintained that George III's ability to defeat the 'greedy and factious coalition' of 1783 was one of the glories of the British constitution.* Between them these two utterances totally changed Burke's attitude to the French revolution and more especially to Lansdowne's con-

*See above, p.147.

nections with it. Lansdowne had been the enemy in 1783 and he was the enemy still, using Mirabeau to further his foul schemes in Paris and Price to further them in London. If he had his way he would replace true revolution principles with his own far more radical ones, in the hope that the success and example of the French would change the British political climate and make his tiny following more acceptable than the Whigs as an alternative to Pitt's government. And so Lansdowne must not have his way. The revolution and its British advocates must be condemned, not in a further letter to Picky Poky – he had in any case forfeited his claim to sympathy by looking to Price and the Revolution Society – but in a major published work.

Little had changed in France. The humiliation of the Royal Family and the pillage of the church, the things upon which Burke was to wax most eloquent, were no more egregious when he settled down to compose the *Reflections* than they had been at the time of his first friendly and moderate letter to Picky Poky. But much had changed in Burke's mind as it came under increasing pressure. On 21 January 1790 John Frith, a crazed half-pay lieutenant with an imagined grievance, threw a stone at George III's carriage. Ten days later a satirical print entitled *Frith the Madman* was published, in which a demented Burke tried to hurl missiles at his sovereign as ferociously as he had hurled accusations of divine retribution a year before. Early in February, when the House of Commons debated the army estimates, Fox and Sheridan from the opposition benches argued that less money was needed for defence now that the French had curbed Bourbon despotism, always the major threat to the peace of Europe and the security of Great Britain. Burke rose to say that by opposing an anointed King and putting power into the hands of 'an irrational, unprincipled, proscribing, confiscating, plundering, ferocious, bloody and tyrannical democracy' the revolution had made France not less but more dangerous, whereupon the delighted caricaturists portrayed him not just as a lunatic but as a hypocrite and a turncoat. There could be neither consistency nor integrity, it was suggested, in a man who held George III and Queen Charlotte in contempt while venerating Louis XVI and Marie Antoinette.[10]

In the face of such attacks Burke's determination to demonstrate his consistency and integrity became all the more obsessive. 'I must have something terrible in me which intimidates all

- 180 -

the others,' he told Philip Francis, the only one of his friends who was prepared to read the first draft of the *Reflections*. Francis got little but abuse for his pains and when he pointed out the absurdity of adulating the Austrian Queen of France so soon after vilifying Queen Charlotte's German connections he was told curtly that it was necessary in order to expose the 'wicked principles and black hearts' of Lansdowne and his set. And the wickedest principle of all was Price's contention that the French revolution was in line of descent from the Glorious Revolution. 'After sharing in the benefits of one revolution I have been spared to be a witness to two other revolutions, both glorious,' Price had cried, 'the light you have struck out, after setting America free, reflected to France, and there kindled into a blaze that lays despotism in ashes, and warms and illuminates Europe!' He had then gone on to suggest that the things which 1688 had left undone, such as the granting of civil rights to dissenters and the reform of parliament, would now be brought about by the irresistible force of French example. Bills to achieve both aims were brought into the Commons at the beginning of March and Burke was greatly relieved when they were decisively defeated. His friend William Windham, once reckoned a supporter of the French revolution, was now so won over to Burke's views that he implored the Commons not to repair its house in a hurricane, not to meddle with any kind of reform for fear of catching the terrible infection from France.[11]

Other friends feared for Burke's sanity. 'Burke continues quite implacable,' James Hare told the duchess of Devonshire, 'and as his son, Dr Lawrence and every Irishman that has access to him encourages him to persist in his madness, I despair of a cure.'[12] Hare was one of Charles Fox's most trusted parliamentary followers, as well as his gambling companion, and he could see that Burke would end up by splitting the Whig party over the issue of reform. But for Burke it was no longer a matter of parties or issues, or even of his own reputation. It was a matter of principle, revolutionary principle. The Whigs and all the world must be made to realize that what was happening in France represented the total negation, not the continuation or fulfilment, of the Glorious Revolution of 1688.

Burke was to make this diametric opposition between 1688 and 1789 into an article of faith, almost an axiom, among the educated and propertied classes in Britain. He had already outlined it in the speeches he had made during the army estimates debate and now, in the *Reflections*, he put it before a wider audience. In 1688 James II, in alliance with catholics and dissenters, had challenged the rights and freedoms which men of property and substance enjoyed as members of the Church of England. He had been quite legitimately stopped in his tracks by the nobility and gentry, by the freeholders and the freemen of England. William III, 'a prince of the blood royal called in by the flower of the aristocracy to defend the ancient constitution', had restored the prestige of the monarchy and retained its prerogatives. And this most respectable of revolutions had restored the church as well as the monarchy: 'Her estates, her majesty, her splendour, her orders and gradations remained the same.'[13] But in France in 1789 the envious and the unpropertied, men as justifiably excluded from the political nation as the English catholics and dissenters of 1688, had attacked religion and property and the whole fabric of society in the name of a reluctant and captive king. If there was a parallel to be drawn at all it was with what James II had been prevented from doing rather than with the revolution that had prevented him.

'If God did not exist,' remarked Voltaire, 'it would be necessary to invent him.' One is tempted to think that if the French revolution had not existed it would have been necessary for Burke to invent it. It was a heaven-sent chance for him to assert the consistency and continuity of his political life: even the Whig tussle with the crown in 1783 could be fitted into the pattern, since the dissenters and the other envious excluded had supported the upstart Pitt then just as their forebears had supported James II in 1688. It also transformed Burke from a discredited figure of fun into a prophet and philosopher respected throughout Europe. To an extent his prophecies were self-fulfilling. When Dumont returned to Paris shortly after the publication of the *Reflections* he found that its ferocious denunciations had made the extremists in the Assembly more extreme than ever.[14] Now that Burke had warned the world against their wildness they would have to be wilder yet in order to repel whatever the warned world might do. He was like a man who predicts that a dog will turn vicious and then kicks it until it does. He did not invent the French revolution but he certainly helped to fuel its later excesses and to draw a clearer line between revolutionaries and counter-revolutionaries.

He also helped to draw new lines in British politics and society. The Whigs were already heading for schism, as traditionalists and reformers came more and more into conflict, but Burke hastened the division and made it irreparable. In due course differing attitudes to the French revolution led one wing of the party to come into government under the duke of Portland while the other continued in opposition under Charles Fox. Equally important but more difficult to assess were the effects outside Parliament. If the *Reflections* had not been published moderate radicalism within the propertied classes might have become an effective political force. Burke made sure that it shrivelled and died, leaving the field open for more extreme movements springing from the labouring classes. If the wars against the French revolution saw the birth of modern class barriers in Britain, as has sometimes been argued, Burke may well have been one of the midwives.

The one line Burke did not draw was the one which his views seemed to necessitate either between New York and London or between New York and Paris. Price's sermon had been about the three successive revolutions of 1688 and 1776 and 1789, each burgeoning from the one before it in a majestic progression, but the *Reflections* was only about two of these and it made no attempt to set them in historical sequence. It simply asserted that they were completely different, the one wholly excellent and the other wholly disastrous. Where did this leave the revolution which was being brought to fruition in New York even as Burke wrote? Had the switch from good˙ to bad come between 1688 and 1776 or between 1776 and 1789? Had the Americans been fulfilling and consummating 1688 or had they been anticipating 1789? The question was academic if Burke was wrong but vital if he was right. If lines of battle were to be drawn between the angels of London and the devils of Paris then New York could not be left in limbo.

First attempts to find a new answer to the question had been made more than a year before the publication of Burke's book. Jefferson quitted Paris on 26 September 1789, leaving his secretary William Short as United States *chargé d'affaires*, and a week later General William Dalrymple sounded out Gouverneur Morris about a possible change in America's policy now that her notoriously anti-British ambassador had gone. Morris was by this time the most respected and best informed American in the capital and it was he, not Short, who was later to be appointed as Jefferson's successor. Dalrymple, who was spending the summer in Paris, had served in America during and after the War of

Independence and now sat in the Commons with links both with government and with opposition. His argument was that since Morris was so bitterly opposed to what was happening in France he ought to persuade his government to exchange the French alliance for a British one. It was no longer a question of siding with supposed progressives in France against alleged British hostility but of upholding the traditional British view of revolution against dangerous French extremism. Morris was not to be tempted. 'An answer of perfect good nature joined to perfect integrity shows him all the impropriety of his proposition without wounding his feelings,' he wrote. But when the same suggestion was made again after the march to Versailles his reaction was different. 'I swallow all their arguments and observations,' he noted in his diary, 'in such a way as to induce the belief that I am convinced or at least in the way of conviction.'[15]

Meanwhile Alexander Hamilton, newly appointed United States Treasury Secretary, was having exploratory conversations with George Beckwith, British resident in New York. 'We wish to form a Commercial Treaty with you to every extent to which you may think it for your interest to go,' he told him. 'The French revolution made the substitution of an Anglo-American alliance for the Franco-American alliance a long-term objective for Hamilton,' one historian has written. Hamilton, who had already written to Lafayette deploring 'the vehement character of the French people and the effects of the reveries of speculative philosophers', was convinced he was not alone in his views. 'These are the sentiments of the most enlightened men in this country,' he told Beckwith, 'they are those of General Washington, I can confidently assure you, as well as of a great majority in the Senate.'[16] Washington for his part wrote to Morris on 13 October expressing fears about the licentiousness of Paris and asking him to open negotiations in London with a view to settling outstanding differences between Great Britain and the United States. Later, when news of the October uprising came through, Washington found it necessary to express doubts about the French revolution even to Catherine Macaulay Graham, one of its staunchest supporters in London. 'My greatest fear has been,' he told her, 'that the nation would not be sufficiently cool and moderate in making arrangements for the security of that liberty of which it seems to be fully possessed.'[17]

By the time Morris received Washington's instructions and

went to London to see the British Foreign Secretary in March
1790 Pitt's government knew it might have a war on its hands in
America because Spain was contesting British control of Van-
couver Island. It was a prospect that alarmed Americans – the
Pennsylvania Packet feared that American sailors would be at risk,
'the Spaniards not being able to distinguish an American from a
Briton' – and Hamilton warned Washington to beware of 'a desire
of shielding Spain from the arms of Britain.'[18] Even Jefferson,
now Secretary of State for Foreign Affairs and as anti-British as
ever, had to admit that if British troops marched from Canada
through American territory to attack the Spaniards the United
States would be unable to stop them. In the event the war did
not take place, largely because the National Assembly refused to
let Louis XVI honour his treaty obligations to Spain, but its
shadow made the British and American governments realize the
need for better relations between them.

The apprehensions of men in government had little effect on
public opinion. Most Americans continued to think of the French
as carrying on the great work they had themselves begun. When
news of the fall of the Bastille reached New York in September
1789 Senator Maclay was predictably delighted and he rejoiced
that 'royalty, nobility and vile pageantry, by which a few of the
human race lord it on the necks of their fellow-mortals, seem likely
to be demolished'. 'O France! I love thee and thy sons!' cried the
American Mercury. 'When my nightly supplications forget to ask
a blessing on thy great exertions and on thy councils, I shall lose
my claim of being a Christian.'[19] When Congress adjourned at the
end of September, having set up all the main departments of
government and sanctioned a small federal army, the New York
correspondent of the *Massachusetts Spy* linked French and American achievements and looked forward to the next stage in the
unfolding of the divine plan:

The present year is the most remarkable that the annals of time have
produced. No other period of equal extent is marked with such efforts
of the human mind to increase and perpetuate human happiness. Look
at and compare the situation of the United States now and twelve
months past! How much has been accomplished and with what wisdom
and patriotism have our affairs progressed! Many a patriot doubted
whether the new government would have so readily assumed an oper-
ative appearance. Great were our fears that prejudice and discord would
have infused themselves into our early attempts to put our system in
motion. All has terminated well. The government is organized and the

people are happy. The spark from the altar of liberty in America, which has communicated its fire to France, has not yet expended its animating fervour. Look to your Inquisition – to your racks – to your tortures – and to your religious tyranny, O Spain! for the day of your emancipation cannot be far off – the right hand of your tyranny is cut off and freedom approaches to place her standard on the walls of your Inquisition.[20]

At the end of the year, after details of the October uprising had been received, the same writer again predicted the downfall of the Inquisition and declared that 'the Bastille has been a paradise to that place of torments'. Even the London press agreed that the French revolution had sounded the death knell of popery: 'Spain is ripe for revolt, the Portuguese Inquisition begins to shake, the present Pope will probably be the last.' Good protestants had always known that the catholic church was 'the mother of harlots and abominations', whose final overthrow had been predicted in the Book of Revelation. Now the moment of destruction had arrived. 'The prophecies of the New Testament are accomplishing very fast', announced *The Times*, pointing out that 'the rabble of the people' was God's natural chosen instrument now that the time had come to put down the mighty from their seats in France.[21]

This did not of course mean that readers of *The Times* approved of what the rabble was doing. Most Anglican freeholders knew just how much they had to lose and joined wholeheartedly in Burke's condemnation of 'the pillage of the church'. But in the United States, where established religion was expressly forbidden, the French campaign against priestcraft and superstition was seen not as pillage but as a process of liberation in which clerics were themselves willing participants. The Philadelphia *Freeman's Journal* proclaimed that 'the army of the church militant in France is undoubtedly the most numerous in Europe, not only upon paper but in palaces, castles, convents, cells, cloisters, etc' and rejoiced that this great army was now taking the first steps towards the collapse of papal power and the end of the Inquisition's torments: 'The petitions from the religious bodies to the National Assembly for the suppression of their institutions have been very numerous. Half the nuns in France are willing to recant their vows and return to society.' Even the *Maryland Gazette*, which counted many catholics among its readers, did not hesitate to show approval when the barefoot Carmelites of Marseilles, 'one of the severest disciplinarian bodies in France', announced their intention of dissolving their order and giving their property to the nation.[22]

Even though Americans did not have ecclesiastical vested interests they had other forms of property which might be threatened by what the French were doing. Throughout the War of Independence the British had made effective propaganda out of the fact that the Americans were claiming liberty for themselves while denying it to their slaves. Runaway slaves had enlisted in the British forces and when the fighting was over Britain had failed to observe the clause in the peace terms requiring them to be returned to their masters. Now the threat to the slave owners came not from British reneging but from French idealism. Within a week of the promulgation of the Declaration of Rights *The Times* was speculating as to whether it meant that 'negroes are become a free people'. 'As the colonists rise on you,' Burke warned the National Assembly in the *Reflections*, 'the negroes rise on them. Troops again – massacre, torture, hanging! These are your rights of men! These are the fruits of metaphysic declarations wantonly made and shamefully retracted!'[23]

It was more than a flight of fancy. As early as November 1789 the British press had welcomed a declaration of independence by French colonists in Martinique while condemning an abortive negro insurrection there as 'the most diabolical design that ever was formed'. By 1793 successful slave uprisings in the neighbouring French island of St Domingue were beginning to pose a threat to the United States. Slaves owned by French refugees from the island were said to have 'sown the seeds of revolt' in Virginia and in South Carolina. Jefferson warned the governor of South Carolina that two Frenchmen from St Domingue called Castaing and La Chaise were leaving Philadelphia for Charleston 'with a design to excite an insurrection among the negroes'.[24]

If Castaing and La Chaise existed they were doomed to disappointment. There was to be no slave insurrection. The humble and meek in the southern states of America, like the French peasants who were being so ingeniously cheated by the National Assembly, were to remain for many generations at a great distance from the seats of the mighty. Nor was there to be a sudden collapse of the papacy or a dramatic end to the torments of the Inquisition. Apocalypse did not take place but apocalyptic language remained in vogue. Jefferson said he would rather see half the earth desolated than see the French fail. 'The liberty of the whole earth is depending on the issue of the contest,' he told William Short. As late as 1795, well after France had become an officially anti-christian state, American preachers were still prepared to tell their congregations that Washington was betraying Christianity as well as republicanism when he exchanged the French alliance for a British one. Three years later, when President Adams stood poised for war with an increasingly belligerent revolutionary government in Paris, the tune remained the same even though the words had changed their meaning.[25] Preachers still saw apocalypse approaching but now it was the French who were the servants of antichrist while the established governments of the world stood firm and waited for the Last Judgement.

The conviction that the year 1789 was the beginning of the end of the world proved remarkably resilient. On both sides of the Atlantic the learned and the devout delved into biblical prophecies in order to prove that the French revolution represented the first of the seven vials of wrath which God would pour out upon the earth as the end of all things drew near. These expositions of apocalypse were still selling well in the 1840s, when one went through three editions in as many years. But by that time Karl Marx was minting another apocalyptic coin which was to devalue most of the biblical prophecies and most of the easy assumptions of the world the French revolution had destroyed. If there was an inscription running round its rim it did not run full circle. The days of the three hundred and sixty degree revolution were over.

References

Unless otherwise stated, place of publication is London in the case of printed sources in English and Paris in the case of those in French. The following abbreviations are used:

MANUSCRIPT COLLECTIONS
Add Additional Manuscripts, British Library, London.
AN Archives Nationales, Paris.
BN MSS Francais, Bibliothèque Nationale, Paris.
MD MSS Dumont, Bibliothèque Publique et Universitaire, Geneva.

NEWSPAPERS AND MAGAZINES
AR Annual Register.
GM Gentleman's Magazine.
GUSA Gazette of the United States.
MG Maryland Gazette.
MP Morning Post.
MS Massachusetts Spy.
NYJ New York Journal.
SJC St James's Chronicle.
T The Times.

OTHER PRINTED SOURCES
AP   *Archives Parlementaires, Première série 1787 à 1799*, 2nd edn. (1879–1914).
Browning *Despatches from Paris 1784–90*, ed. O. Browning, 2 vols. (1909–10).
Egret   J. Egret, *The French prerevolution 1787–89*, tr. W.D. Camp (Chicago, 1977).
Groenvelt E. Dumont and S. Romilly, *Letters containing an account of the late Revolution in France and observations on the Constitution, Laws, Manners and Institutions of the English, Translated from the German of Henry Frederic Groenvelt* (1792).

Jefferson *The Papers of Thomas Jefferson*, ed. J.P. Boyd, 21 vols. (Princeton, 1950–83).
Maclay *Journals of William Maclay*, ed. E.S. Maclay, (New York, 1890).
Morris Gouverneur Morris, *A Diary of the French Revolution*, ed. B.C. Davenport, 2 vols. (Westport, 1939).
PH *Cobbett's Parliamentary History.*
PPS *Catalogue of Political and Personal Satires in the British Museum Vol. VI, 1784–92*, ed. M.D.George, 1978.
PR *Debrett's Parliamentary Register.*
Roberts *French Revolution Documents Vol. I*, ed. J.M. Roberts (Oxford, 1966).
Souvenirs E. Dumont, *Souvenirs sur Mirabeau et sur les deux premières Assemblées Législatives*, ed. J. Bénétruy (1951).
Washington *Writings of George Washington*, ed. J.C. Fitzpatrick, 39 vols. (Washington, 1931–44).
Young Arthur Young, *Travels in France 1787–89*, ed. C. Maxwell (Cambridge, 1929).

Chapter 1

1 V.F. Snow, 'The Concept of Revolution in seventeenth-century England', *Historical Journal* (1962) pp.167–74.
2 *Ibid.*
3 *The Grenville Papers*, ed. W.T. Smith, 4 vols. (1852–3), ii, 199.
4 *Washington*, xxix, 51.
5 J.P. Brissot, *New Travels in America*, ed. D. Echeverria (Harvard, 1964), pp.128–30.
6 Cited Louise B. Dunbar, *A Study of Monarchical Tendencies in the United States 1776–1801* (University of Illinois, 1922), pp.71, 57, 58.
7 *Maclay*, p.12.
8 *NYJ*, 23 Oct 1788, p.3.
9 *Abstract of History and Proceedings of the Revolution Society*, 1789, p.9.
10 Young, p.85.
11 *Ibid.*
12 *AR*, 1787, p.185.
13 *Ibid*, p.176.
14 *Ibid*, pp.174–5.
15 *The Papers of James Madison Volume XI*, eds. R.A. Rutland *et al.* (Charlottesville, 1977), pp.331–2.
16 *Jefferson*, xii, 356.
17 *Ibid*, xii, 424.
18 P. Clément and A. Le Moine, *M. de Silhouette, Bouret et les derniers fermiers généraux*, (1872), p.25.
19 Cited W.J. Stankiewicz, *Politics and Religion in Seventeenth-century France* (Berkeley, 1960), p.206.
20 H. Doniol, *Histoire de la participation de la France à l'établissement des Etats-Unis d'Amérique*, 5 vols. (1886–99), i, 81–2.
21 B.F. Stevens, *Facsimiles of Manuscripts in European Archives relating to America 1773–83*, 25 vols. (1889–98), ix, no.861.
22 Accarias de Serionne, *La Richesse d'Angleterre* (Vienna, 1771), pp.1, 170.

23 Accarias de Serionne, *Les Intérêts des Nations de l'Europe*, 2 vols. (1766), i, 200.
24 C.C.F. d'Albon, *Discours sur l'histoire de plusieurs nations de l'Europe* (Geneva and Paris, 1782) pp.7, 12; *Discours politiques, historiques et critiques sur quelques gouvernements de l'Europe Neuchâtel* (1779), p.40.
25 *Remontrances du Parlement de Paris au xviiie siècle*, ed. J. Flammermont, 3 vols. (1888–98), iii, 319; Voltaire, *Oeuvres complètes*, 52 vols. (1877–85), xv, 367; G. Bonno, *La constitution britannique devant l'opinion français* (1932), p.97; J. Andrews, *A Comparative View of the English and French Nations* (1785), p.264.
26 D. Echeverria, *Mirage in the West: a History of the French Image of American Society to 1815* (Princeton, 1957), p.77; E.S. Corwin, *French Policy and the American Alliance of 1778* (Princeton, 1916), p.264.
27 *Jefferson*, xii, 438–43.
28 M.S. Anderson, *Europe in the Eighteenth Century* (1961), p.167.

Chapter 2

1 *NYJ*, 31 July 1788, p.2; *GUSA*, 28 Oct 1789, p.225; 9/13 May 1789, p.34.
2 *NYJ*, 18 Sept 1788, p.3; 25 Sept, p.2; *AR*, 1789, pp.29, 31.
3 G. Lefebvre, *The Great Fear of 1789*, tr. J. White (New York, 1973), p.17.
4 *Georgiana: extracts from the correspondence of Georgiana, Duchess of Devonshire*, ed. the Earl of Bessborough (1955), p.127.
5 *Souvenirs*, p.51.
6 Egret, p.102; Add, 33 121 ff.7, 9.
7 *Mémoires du Baron de Besenval*, 2 vols. (1821), ii. 341.
8 Young, p.102.
9 Browning, i, 264; ii, 4.
10 *Ibid*, ii, 4.
11 F.L. Nussbaum, 'Vergennes and Lafayette versus the Farmers General', *Journal of Modern History* (1931), pp.592–613; *NYJ*, 25 Dec 1788, p.2; Brissot, *New Travels*, pp.29–51.
12 Egret, pp.86, 114–15; Brissot, *New Travels*, pp.148–9.
13 *Souvenirs*, p.114; C.F.L. de Montjoie, *Histoire de la Conjuration de Louis-Philippe-Joseph d'Orléans surnommé Egalité*, 3 vols. (1796) *passim*.
14 Egret, pp.57, 86.
15 Browning, i, 231–2.
16 Browning, ii, 28–34.
17 Roberts, p.27; *Mémoires de Weber*, 2 vols. (1822) i, 218; *NYJ*, 31 July 1788, p.2.
18 Browning, ii, 44, 54; Bessborough, *Georgiana*, p.130; Browning, ii, 72.
19 *Ibid*, ii, 74.
20 *Washington*, xxx, 131; Rutland, *Papers of Madison XI*, p.330.
21 Egret, p.89; R.R. Palmer, *The Age of the Democratic Revolution*, 2 vols. (Princeton, 1959, 1964) i, 222.
22 Browning, ii, 60; Young, p.108.
23 Browning, ii, 81.
24 *Ibid*, ii, 83, 91–2.
25 Egret, pp.127, 188, 71.

26 J. Egret, *La Révolution des Notables: Mounier et les Monarchiens* (1950), p.17.
27 Browning, ii, 98–9.
28 Egret, pp.153, 183; Roberts, p.32.
29 Browning, ii, 90–1.
30 Montjoie, *Conjuration*, i, 67.
31 Browning, ii, 100; Egret, p.190.
32 Browning, ii, 108.

Chapter 3

1 *Abstract of the History and Proceedings of the Revolution Society* (1789), pp.6–9; Sir Lewis Namier & John Brooke, *The House of Commons 1754–90*, 3 vols. (1964), iii, 452–3; *GM* 1788, p.1024.
2 *AR*, 1788, pp.249–50.
3 *Ibid*, pp.250–1.
4 Namier & Brooke, *Commons*, ii, 354.
5 J.A. Cannon, *The Fox–North Coalition* (Cambridge, 1969), p.163; Bessborough, *Georgiana*, p.72.
6 *MP*, 2 Jan 1789, p.3.
7 W.S. Sichel, *Sheridan ... including a manuscript diary by Georgiana, duchess of Devonshire*, 2 vols. (1909), ii, 402; *Diary and Letters of Madame d'Arblay*, 6 vols. (1904–5), iv, 134; Sichel, *Sheridan*, p.406.
8 Browning, ii, 112; J.W. Derry, *The Regency Crisis and the Whigs 1788–89* (Cambridge, 1963), pp.38–9.
9 *PH*, xxvii, 757.
10 *Letters to Members of the Continental Congress*, ed. E.C. Burnett, 8 vols. (Washington, 1921–36), viii, 743.
11 *Jefferson*, xiv, 303.
12 *Ibid*, 293–5, 399–400, 446.
13 *Ibid*, 399; Burnett, *Letters to Members*, viii, 732.
14 Brissot, *New Travels*, pp.237–8, 9.
15 *Washington*, xxx, 131; Rutland, *Papers of Madison XI*, p.356; Dunbar, *Monarchical Tendencies*, p.99.
16 Rutland, *Papers of Madison XI*, p.340.
17 *Washington*, xxx, 149.
18 *Ibid*, 168–70, 170–1, 281.
19 *Ibid*, 88; Brissot, *New Travels*, pp.32, 103; *NYJ*, 9 July 1789, p.3.
20 *Letters of Benjamin Rush* ed. L.H. Butterfield, 2 vols. (Princeton, 1951), i, 487; Burnett, *Letters to Members*, viii, 743; *NYJ*, 27 Nov 1788, p.3.
21 *Works of Benjamin Franklin*, ed. J. Bigelow, 10 vols. (New York, 1887–8), x, 41; *MS*, 1 Jan 1789, p.3; *Jefferson*, xii, 378; xiv, 47, 188.
22 *Ibid*; Palmer, *Democratic Revolution*, i, 144, 267–8; Brissot, *New Travels*, pp.102, xx.
23 Browning, ii, 117, 119.
24 *Ibid*, ii, 131.
25 Montjoie, *Conjuration*, i, 205; Egret, p.212.
26 Rutland, *Papers of Madison XI*, p.307.
27 Derry, *Regency Crisis*, pp.40–1, 55; Bessborough, *Georgiana*, p.139; Namier and Brooke, *Commons*, iii, 301.

28 Derry, *Regency Crisis*, pp.115–16; Sichel, *Sheridan*, ii, 405, 409, 410; *D'Arblay Diary*, iv, 205.
29 Sir N. Wraxall, *Historical Memoirs*, 5 vols. (1884), v, 203; *PR*, xxv, 24, 28–9.
30 L. Dutens, *An History of the late Important Period from the beginning of His Majesty's Illness ... to the period of His Majesty's Re-appearance in the House of Lords* (1789), pp.151–2.
31 Derry, *Regency Crisis*, pp.81–2; Wraxall, *Memoirs*, v, 208; *SJC*, 3/6 Jan p.1; L. Reid, *Charles James Fox* (1969), p.244.
32 *PR*, xxv, 30.
33 Derry, Regency Crisis, p.160.
34 *AR*, 1789, p.310.
35 *T*, 1 Jan 1789, p.3, 2 Jan, p.3, 15 Jan, p.2.
36 *Ibid*, 14 Jan 1789, p.3, 13 Jan, p.3, 6 Jan, p.2; Browning, ii, 133; Montjoie, *Conjuration*, i, 202.
37 *SJC*, 1/3 Jan 1789, p.3; *T*, 3 Jan, p.2.
38 *PH*, xxvii, 1213, 1248.
39 Sir N. Wraxall, *Historical Memoirs*, 2nd ed. 2 vols. (1815), i, preface p.iii; *T*, 15 Jan 1789, p.2.
40 Browning, ii, 23, 110.
41 *Ibid*, 151; *T*, 17 Feb 1789, p.2, 26 Feb, p.2, 7 Mar, p.2.
42 *Ibid*, 7 Mar 1789, p.2; *Jefferson*, xiv, 431.

Chapter 4

1 *Correspondence of Jeremy Bentham Volume 4*, ed. A.T. Milne (1981), p.21.
2 *PH*, xxvii, 878–9.
3 *Memoirs, Correspondence and Miscellaneous Papers of Jefferson*, 4 vols. (Charlottesville, 1829), ii, 465; H. Doniol, 'Le ministère des affaires étrangères de France sous le comte de Vergennes', *Revue d'histoire diplomatique*, vii (1893), pp.528–60.
4 *D'Arblay Diary*, iv, 289–90; *T*, 9 Mar 1789, p.2; *Life and Letters of Sir Gilbert Elliot*, 3 vols. (1874) i, 281; *Analytical Review*, Mar 1789, p.359.
5 *Life and Correspondence of Priestley*, ed. J.T. Rutt, 2 vols. (1831–2), i, 197; Lord E. Fitzmaurice, *Life of William, Earl of Shelburne*, 2 vols. (1912), i, 424–30; C. Blount, 'Bentham, Dumont and Mirabeau', *University of Birmingham Historical Journal*, iii (1952), pp.153–67; J.H. Burns, 'Bentham and the French Revolution', *Transactions of the Royal Historical Society*, xvi (1966), pp.95–114; Bigelow, *Works of Franklin*, x, 83.
6 *NYJ*, 12 Feb 1789, p.3, 19 Feb, p.2; D.M. Ellis, *New York, State and City*, (Cornell, 1979), *passim*.
7 A.F. Young, *The Democratic Republicans of New York: the Origins 1763–97*, (Chapel Hill, 1967), pp.138–40.
8 H. Methivier, *L'Ancien Régime* (1961), p.72.
9 Sir L. Namier, *The Structure of Politics at the accession of George III*, 2nd edn. (1961), p.1.
10 Browning, ii, 167.
11 *Ibid*, ii, 174.
12 *T*, 28 Mar 1789, p.3.

13 E.-J. Sièyes, *What is the Third Estate?*, tr. & ed. M. Blondel, S.E. Finer, P. Campbell (1963), p.113.
14 *Ibid*, p.110n.
15 J.L. Delolme, *The Constitution of England*, 1st ed. 1775, 4th ed. 1784.
16 *Mercure de France*, Jan 1789, pp.109–28, 150–66.
17 J.L. Delolme, *The Present National Embarrassment considered* (1789), p.66; Anon, *Answer to M. de Lolme's Observations* (1789) p.9.
18 J.J. Mounier, *Nouvelles Observations* (1789), pp.245, 274; *Lettre de M. Bergasse sur les Etats Généraux* (1789), pp.30–1, 51.
19 *T*, 2 Apr 1789, p.3; Browning, ii, 176.
20 *Ibid*, ii, 147–8.
21 W.R. Fryer, 'Mirabeau in England 1784–85', *Renaissance and Modern Studies* (1966), pp.34–87; Milne, *Correspondence of Bentham*, pp.39–42.
22 Browning, ii, 153.
23 Milne, *Correspondence of Bentham*, p.44.
24 *Souvenirs*, p.43.
25 E.J. Ferguson, *The Power of the Purse*, (Chapel Hill, 1961), pp.256–64.
26 *Ibid*, pp.260, 265–7; Morris, i, xxxv.
27 *Ibid*, 20, 43, xxix, xliii–xliv.
28 *Ibid*, xxxvi; *Washington*, xxx, 237–41; *NYJ*, 2 Apr 1789, p.3.
29 J.T. Flexner, *George Washington and the New Nation* (Boston, 1969), pp.178–81; *GUSA*, 22/25 Apr 1789, p.15.
30 *PR*, xxvi, 1–2; *T*, 11 Apr 1789, p.2, 20 Apr, p.1.
31 *GM*, 1789, pp.366–70.
32 Browning, ii, 155; Morris, i, 42; BN, 6687, vol.viii, f.301.
33 Roberts, pp.40–1; *T*, 23 Apr, p.3; BN, 6687, vol.viii, f.306.

Chapter 5

1 *Correspondance entre le comte de Mirabeau et le comte de la Marck 1789–91*, ed. A. de Bacourt, 3 vols. (1851), i, 342.
2 Egret, p.161; *Mémoires de Mirabeau*, ed. L. de Montigny, 8 vols. (1834–5), v, 200; Egret, p.197.
3 MD, 35, f.2; *Groenvelt*, p.6; *Souvenirs*, p.43; MD, 17, f.22.
4 *Souvenirs, p.43; MD, 17, ff.21–4.*
5 Ch.-L. Chassin, *Les élections et les cahiers de Paris en 1789*, 4 vols. (1888–9), iii, 58; J. Droz, *Histoire du règne de Louis XVI*, 3 vols. (1839), ii, 170; *Mémoires de Besenval*, ii, 348.
6 N. Hampson, *A Social History of the French Revolution* (1963), p.55; Montjoie, *Conjuration*, i, 294.
7 *AR*, 1789, p.216; *GM*, 1789, p.437; Morris, i, 64.
8 Browning, ii, 192.
9 *Groenvelt*, p.17; Roberts, pp.100–1; *T*, 19 May 1789, p.3.
10 *T*, 12 May 1789, p.2; 19 May, p.3; 27 May, p.3.
11 *PR*, xxvi, 106–28.
12 *Correspondence of Edmund Burke*, eds. T.W. Copeland *et al.*, 10 vols. (Cambridge and Chicago, 1958–78), v, 470–2; *PR*, xxvi, 8, 40–2, 85.
13 *PPS*, No.7529.
14 *PR*, xxvi, 210–4, 232–6.

15 In the 1789 session, as Rhode Island and North Carolina had not ratified the constitution, there were 59 members of the House of Representatives and 22 senators, of whom the two for New York did not take their seats until July.

16 *Washington*, xxx, 226; *Jefferson*, xv, 22, 224.

17 *Debates and Proceedings of the Congress of the United States Volume I* (Washington, 1834), pp.28, 32, 247.

18 *Maclay*, pp.7–25.

19 *Proceedings of Congress*, pp.319–22; *MS*, 6 May 1789, p.2; 11 June, p.2.

20 *Jefferson*, xv, 115, 153–4, 170.

21 Browning, ii, 195; *Jefferson*, xv, 146, 182.

22 *Souvenirs*, p.47.

23 *Groenvelt*, pp.23–4.

24 Browning, ii, 196; *Lettres et Bulletins de Barentin à Louis XVI*, ed. A. Aulard (1915), pp.4–5; *Groenvelt*, p.68; J.D. Jarrett, *The Bowood Circle 1780–93*, unpublished Oxford B.Litt thesis (1955), p.101; Roberts, pp.101–2.

25 *Groenvelt*, pp.26, 28–9.

26 *Mirabeau: Discours*, ed. F. Furet (1973), p.32.

27 *Procès-verbal des séances de la chambre de l'ordre de la noblesse*, 2nd edn. (1792), p.61; M.G. Hutt, 'The Rôle of the Curés in the Estates General of 1789', *Journal of Ecclesiastical History*, vi (1955), pp.190–220.

28 *Life of Sir Samuel Romilly*, 3rd edn. 2 vols. (1842), i, 267; Jarrett, *Bowood Circle*, pp.117–20.

29 *Journal d'Adrien Duquesnoy*, ed. R. de Crèvecoeur, 2 vols. (1894), i, 21–23, 25.

30 *Groenvelt*, p.27; *Correspondance de Maximilien et Augustin Robespierre* ed. G. Michon, 2 vols. (1926, 1941), i, 40; Browning, ii, 195; *Groenvelt*, pp.68–9.

31 *Souvenirs*, p.60.

32 *Groenvelt*, pp.34–5.

33 *Lettres de l'abbé Barbotin*, ed. A. Aulard (1910), p.8.

34 Browning, ii, 203, 206.

35 *Groenvelt*, pp.37, 38, 41–2; *Récit des Séances des députés des communes*, ed. A. Aulard (1895), p.43.

36 A. Brette, 'Rélations des évènemens depuis le 6 mai jusqu'au 15 juillet 1789: Documents inédits', *Révolution Française*, xiii (1892), p.461; *Groenvelt*, pp.43–44.

37 BN, 31713, f.6.

38 *Procès-verbal des conférences sur la vérification des pouvoirs tenues par MM. les Commissaires du Clergé, de la Noblesse et des Communes*, 1789.

39 *Souvenirs*, pp.264–5; *Lettre inédite d'Etienne Dumont sur quelques séances du Tiers Etat, mai 1789, publiée avec introduction et notes par J.M. Paris* (Geneva, 1877) p.23.

40 *Jefferson*, xv, 136, 138, 165–6.

41 Browning, ii, 207; J.L.H. Campan, *Memoirs of Marie Antoinette*, ed. A.R. Waller n.d. p.200.

42 Crèvecoeur, *Duquesnoy*, i, 73; Aulard, *Récit des Séances*, p.96.

43 Browning, ii, 213; *AP*, viii, 84–7.

Chapter 6

1 Young, p.131; *T*, 30 May 1789, p.2, 3 June, p.2.
2 *T*, 13 June 1789, p.3; Young, pp.132, 144–5.
3 *The Waiting City: Paris 1782–88, Being an Abridgement of L.S. Mercier's 'Le Tableau de Paris'*, ed. H. Simpson (1933), p.273; Young, p.134.
4 *Ibid*, pp.136–7, 160.
5 Browning, ii, 210; *Souvenirs*, pp.61, 64; *Mémoires de Malouet*, 2 vols. (1874), i, 274–82.
6 *Souvenirs*, p.62.
7 *Groenvelt*, p.57; *AP*, viii, 97.
8 *Souvenirs*, pp.70–1; Young, p.138, 142.
9 Young, pp.143–5; Aulard, *Lettres et Bulletins de Barentin*, pp.32–3.
10 MD, 35, f.22; *Souvenirs* p.72.
11 *Ibid*.
12 *Mémoires de Malouet*, ii, 9–10; Browning, ii, 215.
13 *The French Revolution: Selected Documents*, ed. R.H. Beik (1970), p.66; *T*, 16 June 1789, p.2.
14 Young, p.147; Browning, ii, 217; *Jefferson*, xv, 187–91; Beik, *Selected Documents*, p.65.
15 *Souvenirs*, p.74.
16 Roberts, p.109.
17 *Mercure Britannique*, 25 July 1800, p.19.
18 Young, p.149–50; MD, 17, f.30.
19 Young, pp.150–2.
20 *Ibid*, pp.151, 152–3; Furet, *Mirabeau: Discours*, p.65; *Souvenirs*, p.79.
21 Morris, i, 121.
22 *Maclay*, pp.85–6.
23 *Ibid*, pp.74–5, 82.
24 *Proceedings of Congress*, pp.532, 575, 591; *Papers of James Madison Volume XII*, eds. C.F. Hobson *et al.* (Charlottesville, 1979), pp.225–9.
25 *Ibid*, p.200; *Works of Fisher Ames*, ed. S. Ames, 2 vols. (Boston, 1854), i, 35, 56.
26 *MS*, 21 May 1789, p.3.
27 *T*, 24 Sept 1789, p.2, 26 June, p.2; *Jefferson*, xv, 281; *MP*, 15 July 1789, p.2.
28 *PR*, xxvi, 447.
29 *Ibid*, 291; S. Romilly, *Observations on a late publication entitled 'Thoughts on Executive Justice'* (1786); *AR*, 1789, p.203; *T*, 27 Mar 1789, p.4.
30 Browning, ii, 220–1; *The Torrington Diaries*, ed. C.B. Andrews, 4 vols. (1935), ii, 52.
31 *Ibid*, ii, 87–8.
32 Young, p.157; Morris, i, 130; Roberts, p.123; Browning, ii, 230.
33 BN, 13713, ff.15, 17; Young, p.156.
34 *D'Arblay Diary*, iv, 290–1; *T*, 4 July 1789, p.3; *Burke Correspondence*, vi, 27.
35 Young, p.158; *T*, 3 July 1789, p.2.

Chapter 7

1 *Jefferson*, xv, 190; Young, pp.155, 161; Browning, ii, 222–3.
2 Morris, i, 127–8; Bessborough, *Georgiana*, pp.150–1.

3 Browning, ii, 224–6; Morris, i, 128; Bessborough, *Georgiana*, p.150; *Groenvelt*, p.108.
4 Bessborough, *Georgiana*, p.150; AN, KK, 641, f.261.
5 Young, pp.162, 166.
6 Hobson, *Papers of Madison XII*, p.288; Montjoie, *Conjuration*, ii, 39–40.
7 Morris, i, 143.
8 *T*, 4 July 1789, p.2.
9 *T*, 6 July 1789, p.3, 10 July, p.2, 13 July, p.3; *MP*, 17 July, p.3.
10 *Jefferson*, xv, 243–54; Add, 33541, ff.55–6.
11 Browning, ii, 232; Montjoie, *Conjuration*, ii, 12–13, 33–51; *Souvenirs*, p.82; Browning, ii, 231.
12 *Souvenirs*, p.83; *T*, 14 July 1789, p.3; Browning, ii, 232–3.
13 *Ibid*; J.A. Creuzé-Latouche, *Journal des Etats-Généraux*, ed. J. Marchand (1946), pp.164, 192–3; Browning, ii, 229.
14 S.F. Scott, *The Response of the Royal Army to the French Revolution* (Oxford, 1978), p.62; Young, p.172; *T*, 6 July 1789, p.3, 7 July, p.3.
15 *MS*, 17 Sept 1789, p.3; Hobson, *Papers of Madison XII*, pp.275–6.
16 *NYJ*, 2 July 1789, p.3; I.N. Phelps Stokes, *The Iconography of Manhattan Island 1498–1909*, 6 vols. (1915–28), i, 388; v, 1235–7; *NYJ*, 20 Aug, p.2.
17 *Maclay*, pp.90, 83, 68; Hobson, *Papers of Madison XII*, p.293n.; *NYJ*, 9 July 1789, p.3.
18 Stokes, *Manhattan Island*, i, 373, 376–7; v, 1235; *NYJ*, 5 Nov 1789, p.3.
19 *Jefferson*, xv, 239–40, 255; Morris, i, 136–7.
20 *Jefferson*, xv, 260, 335; Simpson, *Waiting City*, p.102; A. Williams, *The Police of Paris 1718–89* (Baton Rouge, 1979), pp.200–1.
21 *Journal and Correspondence of Lord Auckland*, 4 vols. (1861–2), ii, 331; *Groenvelt*, p.127.
22 *Ibid*, p.128; *Auckland Correspondence*, ii, 329; Morris, i, 146.
23 Grace D. Elliott, *Journal of my life during the French Revolution* (1955), pp.1–5; AN, KK, 641, f.307; Campan, *Marie Antoinette*, p.205n.
24 *Groenvelt*, p.129.
25 Roberts, pp.126–8.
26 *Auckland Correspondence*, ii, 330–1.
27 Browning, ii, 239.
28 Crèvecoeur, *Duquesnoy*, i, 221; Droz, *Règne du Louis XVI*, ii, 249.
29 *Groenvelt*, pp.143–4.
30 *Souvenirs*, p.86; *Groenvelt*, pp.145–6.
31 *Ibid*, pp.168–9.
32 *Souvenirs*, p.86; *T*, 16 July 1789, p.2, 20 July, p.2, 21 July, p.2; *SJC*, 18/21 July, p.4; *Historical Manuscripts Commission Reports 42, Carlisle*, p.666.
33 *PR*, xxvi, 451–7.
34 *MP*, 21 July 1789, pp.2, 3.
35 *Mémoires de Besenval*, ii, 357; Montjoie, *Conjuration*, iii, 25–27.
36 *Memorials and Correspondence of Charles James Fox*, ed. Lord J. Russell, 4 vols. (1853–7), ii, 361; *MP*, 29 July 1789, pp.2, 3.
38 *T*, 14 July 1789, p.2, 15 July, p.2, 24 July, p.2, 2 Aug, p.2, 8 Aug, p.3, 21 Aug, p.2, 5 Oct, p.2.
38 *Ibid*, 8 Aug 1789, p.3, 16 July, p.2; *MP*, 15 July, p.2; Browning, ii, 250–1; *Auckland Correspondence*, ii, 340.

39 *AP*, viii, 287–8; Hampson, *Social History*, p.80; *T*, 5 Aug 1789, p.2.
40 *Ibid*, 11 Aug 1789, p.3; Young, pp.190, 195, 224.
41 *T*, 25 Aug 1789, p.2, 14 Aug, p.2; Namier and Brooke, *Commons*, iii, 397.
42 *NYJ*, 16 July 1789, p.2; *Jefferson*, xv, 327.
43 *Ibid*, 359.
44 *Ibid*, 360.
45 Young, pp.199, 200.
46 Lefebvre, *Great Fear passim*; Young, pp.186–7, 209.
47 Roberts, pp.140–1; Hampson, *Social History*, p.81.

Chapter 8

1 *PR*, xxvi, 413, 449–51.
2 *Jefferson*, xv, 329; *PR*, xxvi, 278–80; *Life and Correspondence of Major Cartwright*, ed. F.D. Cartwright, 2 vols. (1826), i, 182–3.
3 Young, pp.164–5, 185.
4 *Jefferson*, xv, 105; *T*, 4 July 1789, p.3, 3 Sept p.2; *D'Arblay Diary*, iv, 298–9.
5 *GUSA*, 2 Sept 1789, p.161; *MS*, 21 May 1789, p.3, 12 Nov, p.3, 12 Nov, p.3; *Papers of Alexander Hamilton*, eds. H.S. Syrett *et al.*, 27 vols. (New York, 1961–87), vi, 335–7; Hobson, *Papers of Madison XII*, p.258.
6 *Proceedings of Congress*, p.637; *Maclay*, pp.112, 121; *Washington*, xxx, 363, 370–1.
7 *Jefferson*, xv, 269.
8 Furet, *Mirabeau: Discours*, p.85.
9 *Souvenirs*, pp.102–4, 276; C. D. Casaux, *Simplicité de l'idée d'une constitution* (1789), p.119.
10 Fitzmaurice, *Life of Shelburne*, ii, 373; Jarrett, *Bowood Circle*, p.33n.
11 *Ibid*, p.121; *Life of Romilly*, i, 272.
12 *Jefferson*, xv, 291, 366; Morris, i, 162.
13 *AP*, viii, 285–7; *T*, 3 Sept 1789, p.2; *Auckland Correspondence*, ii, 345–6.
14 *AP*, viii, 343–4.
15 *Ibid*, 350.
16 *T*, 11 Aug 1789, p.3, 3 Sept, p.2.
17 *D'Arblay Diary*, iv, 340.
18 *T*, 21 Aug 1789, p.2; *GM*, 1789, p.950.
19 J.Q.C. Mackrell, *The Attack on 'Feudalism' in Eighteenth-Century France* (1973), p.175.
20 *Souvenirs*, p.97; *Analytical Review*, July 1789, pp.332–7.
21 *AP*, viii, 417; Furet, *Mirabeau: Discours*, p.101.
22 *Jefferson*, xv, 366–7.
23 *Maclay*, p.97; *Works of Fisher Ames*, pp.35, 48; Hobson, *Papers of Madison XII*, pp.334–5; *Proceedings of Congress*, pp.707, 766.
24 *Jefferson*, xv, 354; Furet, *Mirabeau: Discours*, pp.105–18; *AP*, viii, 563, 566–7.
25 *T*, 9 Sept 1789, p.2; Browning, ii, 259–60, 261; *London Gazette*, 12/15 Sept 1789, p.597.
26 Morris, p.217.
27 *Ibid*, p.216; Young, p.226.
28 *Ibid*, pp.209–10.

29 *Life of Romilly*, i, 272; Morris, p.184; *T*, 6 Aug 1789, p.1, 8 Aug, pp.2, 3, 1 Sept, p.1.
30 *Ibid*, 3 Sept 1789, p.2, 31 Aug, p.3; *Jefferson*, xv, 449.
31 *London Gazette*, 26/29 Sept 1789, p.625; *PPS*, No.7546.
32 *T*, 24 July 1789, p.2; *SJC*, 3/6 Oct, p.4; *PPS*, No.7553; *T*, 2 Oct, p.2, 21 Sept, p.2.

Chapter 9

1 *Jefferson*, xv, 424–6, 452, 458–60; *T*, 21 Sept 1789, p.2.
2 *Ibid*, 10 Sept 1789, p.2.
3 *MG*, 28 Jan 1790, p.2; *AP*, viii, 642.
4 *Ibid*, viii, 643–4; ix, 4, 23.
5 Browning, ii, 261; Roberts, pp.157–60.
6 *AP*, ix, 34; Roberts, p.170; Scott, *Response of Royal Army*, pp.74–5.
7 Browning, ii, 262–3.
8 Roberts, p.178.
9 Campan, *Marie Antoinette*, p.223.
10 Browning, ii, 266.
11 *SJC*, 8/10 Oct 1789, p.4, 13/15 Oct, p.1, 17/20 Oct p.4; *T*, Oct, p.2, 17 Oct, p.2; *MP*, 12 Oct, p.2.
12 Browning, ii, 267; *Later Correspondence of George III*, ed. A. Aspinall, 5 vols. (Cambridge, 1962–70), i, 446; *SJC*, 20/22 Oct, p.4.
13 *Souvenirs*, p.142; Browning, ii, 272–5.
14 Aspinall, *Later Correspondence*, i, 448; *T*, 15 Oct 1789, pp.2, 3.
15 *Life of Romilly*, i, 282, 285; *Correspondence of George, Prince of Wales 1770–1812*, ed. A. Aspinall, 8 vols. (1963–71), ii, 47, 57.
16 *PPS*, 7548; *MP*, 19 Oct 1789, p.3; 22 Oct, p.3.
17 *T*, 5 Oct 1789, p.2; *Burke Correspondence*, vi, 24–6, 9–13, 29–30.
18 *Souvenirs*, p.111.
19 *Ibid*, pp.109–10, 142, 291; MD, 17, ff.36–7.
20 Blount, 'Bentham, Dumont and Mirabeau', pp.163–64.
21 *Life of Romilly*, i, 283–5.
22 *Souvenirs*, p.122; Bacourt, *Correspondance Mirabeau–La Marck*, i, 400.
23 Bacourt, *Correspondance Mirabeau–La Marck*, i, 364–81, 406; Morris, pp.250, 252, 256; *T*, 31 Oct 1789, p.2.
24 Bacourt, *Correspondance Mirabeau–La Marck*, i, 407–17.
25 Furet, *Mirabeau: Discours*, pp.179–83.
26 *AP*, viii, 370; *T*, 19 Aug 1789, p.2, 23 Sept, p.2; Bacourt, *Correspondance Mirabeau–La Marck*, i, 410.
27 Roberts, pp.187–8.
28 Young, pp.203–5, 245.

Chapter 10

1 Young, pp.246–7, 261–2.
2 *Ibid*, pp.247–8, 251.
3 *Ibid*, p.255; *Groenvelt*, pp.181, 186.
4 *Ibid*, pp.186–7.
5 Browning, ii, 256–7.

6 *MG*, 17 June 1790, p.1.

7 *T*, 30 July 1789, p.2; *MG*, 4 Feb 1790, p.2.

8 *T*, 22 Aug 1789, p.2, 31 Aug, p.2, 7 Sept, p.2; *GUSA*, 30 Sept 1789, p.193; Bacourt, *Correspondance Mirabeau–La Marck*, i, 360, 432.

9 *Burke Correspondence*, vi, 31–4, 39–50.

10 *PPS*, 7624; *PH*, xxviii, 355; *PPS*, 7627.

11 *Burke Correspondence*, vi, 85–92; *The Debate on the French Revolution*, ed. A. Cobban, 2nd edn. (1960), p.64; *PH*, xxviii, 467.

12 Bessborough, *Georgiana*, p.169.

13 *PH*, xxviii, 361–2.

14 *Souvenirs*, p.147.

15 Morris, i, 246, 263.

16 Syrett, *Papers of Hamilton*, v, 483, 486; R. Buel, *Securing the Revolution: Ideology in American Politics 1789–1815* (Cornell, 1972), p.31.

17 A.L. Burt, *The United States, Great Britain and British North America* (New Haven, 1940), p.107; Washington, xxx, 498.

18 *Freeman's Journal*, Philadelphia, 7 July 1790, p.3; Syrett, *Papers of Hamilton*, vii, 49–50.

19 Cited C.D. Hazen, *Contemporary American Opinion of the French Revolution*, (Baltimore, 1897), p.144; *GUSA*, 16 Dec 1789, p.281.

20 *MS*, 15 Oct 1789, p.3.

21 *Ibid*, 24 Dec 1789, p.2; *T*, 24 Sept 1789, p.2; 24 Aug, p.2; 7 Sept, p.3.

22 *Freeman's Journal*, 6 Jan 1790, p.2; 16 Dec 1789, p.2; *MG*, 14 Jan 1790, p.2.

23 *T*, 5 Sept, p.2; E. Burke, *Reflections on the Revolution in France* (1790), p.321.

24 H. Aptheker, *Negro Slave Revolts* (New York, 1943), pp.213, 42.

25 *Writings of Jefferson*, ed. P.L. Ford, 10 vols. (New York 1892–99), vi, 154; Buel, *Securing the Revolution*, pp.168–9, 138.

Index

Abingdon, Lord 72
Accarias de Serionne 19
Act of Settlement (1701) 172
Adams, John, President of U.S. (1791–
 1801) 188; as Vice-President 52, 72,
 90, 113–14, 119, 146
d'Aiguillon, duc 83, 150
d'Albon, comte 19–20, 21
American Mercury 185
Ames, Fisher, of Massachusetts 115,
 154
L'Ami du Peuple 163
Analytical Review 153
Annual Register 15–16, 24, 42, 85
Arles, Archbishop of 94
Armstrong, John 47, 51
d'Artois, comte, brother of Louis XVI
 27, 131, 132, 138, 167; flees from
 France 161; Royal Council 112;
 Secret Council 98; supporting
 nobility 120–1
Assembly: *assignats* 173–4;
 bankruptcy 160–1, 172; church 173,
 178–9; constitution 121–2, 148–51,
 153, 171; counter-revolution 170;
 extremists 182; Jacobins 175–6;
 Jefferson 129; Louis XVI 134, 159,
 163, 164; Mirabeau 147; Necker 132;
 royalty 120, 162; troops 125; veto
 155–6; wealth seized 177; *see also*
 National Assembly
assignats 173–4

Astley's amphitheatre 157
Austrian Netherlands 14, 60; *see also*
 Joseph II
'Austrian woman', alias for Marie-
 Antoinette 26

Bailly, Jean-Sylvain, Dean of Assembly
 100–2; mayor of Paris 134, 162;
 Tennis Court Oath 111
bankruptcy threat to France 15, 25, 37,
 160–1, 172
Bastille 137, 139, 143, 146, 168, 186;
 falls 133–4; American reaction to fall
 185; as London entertainment 157
Beaufoy, Henry: Bill to celebrate
 centenary of Glorious Revolution 41,
 56, 87–8, 116, 143–4, 145
Beckwith, George 184
Bentham, Jeremy 72, 93, 169; *Draught
 of a New Plan* 169; international
 hopes 75–6, 77; and Mirabeau 74–5,
 124; *Political Tactics* 65; support of
 French people 62–3
Bergasse, Nicholas 73–4, 125
Berkeley, Lord 152
Besenval, baron de 27, 84, 132, 133,
 136
Blackden, Samuel 124
Booth family 42
bourse, Paris 37, 74, 76
Bouthillier, marquis de 98, 99

bread: cost of 38, 75; distribution to poor 58; riots 80; shortage 123, 124, 125, 136, 160–1, 162
Bréhan, marquise de, sister-in-law of Moustier 48
Brézé, marquis de 85
Bright, Richard, dissenter, 87
Brissot, Jacques-Pierre 28–9, 48–9, 50, 73, 147; *France and the U.S.* 21; returns to France 52; Rhode Island 11–12, 127; on U.S. economy 77, 173
British Riot Act 175
Broglie, maréchal de 118, 120, 126
Brown, Mr and Mrs; aliases for Louis XVI and Marie-Antoinette 26, 31
Buisson, bookseller of Rue Hautefeuille 72
Burke, Edmund 63, 88, 135, 186; Beaufoy's Bill 87–8; George III 119, 137; *Inquiry into the Sublime and Beautiful* 64; Mirabeau 75; monarchy 180–1; *Reflections on the Revolution* 179–83, 187; regency 56–7, 59; revolution 168, 178–80, 181–2, 182–3
Burke, Richard 179, 181
Burney, Fanny, writer 152
Byng, John 117–18, 152

Cade, Jack (rebel) 137, 168, 178
cahiers de doléances 69–70, 83, 122, 150–1
calendar reforms 13
Calonne M., French finance minister 25–6, 27, 29, 37, 74, 178
Camaran, M. de, governor of Provence 34
Casaux, marquis de, 148
Castaing, M. 187
Cavendish, Lord John 43
Cavendish family 42, 46; *see also* Devonshire, duke of
centenary celebrations of Glorious Revolution 40, 41–6, 47, 117
Champ de Mars troops 132–3
Champaretz, Madame de 59
Charles I, King of England (1623–49) 27, 53–4, 111, 155
Charles VII of Bavaria, Holy Roman Emperor (1742–45) 26
Charlotte, Queen of England, (1761–

1818) 145, 180–1; George III's health 55, 103, 119, 167
Charter of Rights 100
Chastellux, marquis de 21
Chatham, William Pitt, 1st earl of 18, 64, 123
Church of England 9, 41, 179, 182
Cincinnati, Order of the 50–1, 128–9
Civil Constitution of the Clergy 174
Clavière; Etienne 50, 76, 77, 99, 112, 125, 166; *France and the U.S.* 21; Gallo-American Society 28; Mirabeau 92; Society of Thirty 82–3
Clermont, Lady 44
Clermont Tonnerre, M. de 34
Clinton, George, Anti-Federalist 65–6, 78
Commercial Treaty 27, 116, 184
Common Council 128
Commons, House of 69, 88–9, 90, 107, 149, 180, 181, 184; crime and punishment 116–17; flour exports 123–4, 135–6; George III 43–4, 71, 79–8, 105, 116; Lansdowne 65, 83; members 68, 73–4; Mirabeau 75; pattern for Estates General 91, 94–6, 101; Pitt 44, 54–5; Portland Whigs 43–4; Regency Bill 56–7; revolution centenary 41, 87, 143–4, 145; successor to James II 13–14
Commune 132, 134
Condé, prince de 98, 156
Condorcet, marquis de 35, 47
Congress 21, 69, 91, 114, 185; constitution 12–13, 115; cost 128; debt stock 77; Declaration of Rights 154; disbanded 48; procedure 89–90; and Washington 89–90, 145–6
Conti, prince de 98
Convention Parliament 13
coronation oath 10
Coutts, Thomas, banker 54–5
Creuzé-Latouche, M. 126
Crèvecoeur, St Jean de, consul at New York, 21, 66
Cromwell, Oliver, Lord Protector 90, 136, 137, 168, 178
Curtius, M. waxwork museum owner 130

Dalrymple, General William 183–4

Darcy family 42
Dauphin, son of Louis XVI 161, 163, 164; illness and death 100–1
Declaration of Independence 10, 32–3, 47, 100, 110, 129, 154
Declaration of Rights (France) 116, 129, 147, 149–50, 153, 154–5; King's sanction 163–4
Declaration of Rights (U.S.) 154–5, 187
Déficit, Madame (alias for Marie-Antoinette) 26
Depont, Charles-Jacques-François (also known as Picky Poky) 179, 180
Desgouttes, marquis 173–4
Desmoulins, Camille 131, 169
Devonshire, duchess of, 26, 31, 43, 46, 120–1, 181; and the Prince of Wales 54–5, 167; flees from Paris 138
Devonshire, 5th duke of, head of Cavendish family, 43, 46, 138
Devonshire, earl of 42
Domine Salvum Fac Regem 165–6, 169
Dorset, duke of (British ambassador) 43, 85, 126, 156, 177; Assembly 109, 121, 149–50; *cahiers* 69; Calonne 26; commerce 27; Dauphin 101; *doublement* 53; economics 96–7, 125–6; Estates General 78, 91; famine 118; Geneva 75; George III 46; grain 123, 125; Hailes 39; Mirabeau 95–6; Necker 26; Orléans 70, 120; Paris 138–9; Plenary Court 31; poaching 117; poor relief 58; provinces 33–5, 74; Prussians 60; ratification 31–2; third estate 52, 105; uprisings 68–9, 84, 133; Versailles 93, 100
doublement 36, 38, 53–4
Duer, William 76–7
Dumont, Etienne 26, 77, 95, 105–7, 109–10, 153, 157, 166, 168–9; Bastille 133–4; and British 166–7; Estates General 92–3, 101; Mirabeau 75–6, 85, 96, 106, 108, 112, 125, 134, 147–9, 169–70; National Assembly 121; Necker 86, 99, 130; Paris 176–7; *Reflections* 182; riots 132; Royal Council 111–12; Society of Thirty 83–4; Tennis Court Oath 111; Versailles 97
Dupont de Nemours 150
Duport petition to King 125

Duquesnoy, Adrien 95, 101
Duroveray, Jacques-Antoine 77, 83, 171; and the British 166, 169–70; destroys pamphlets 168–9; Mirabeau 75–6, 92, 105–6, 112, 125, 170; Necker 99, 110

Eden, William 17, 21, 130–1
Elgin, Lord 108
Elliott, Grace, mistress of Orléans 131–2
Elsworth, Senator of Maryland 146
d'Eprémesnil, Duval 84, 162
Estates General 30, 46–7, 69, 75, 89, 103–4, 106–7, 109–10, 132, 139, 145, 149; British pattern 16; constitution 35–40, 51, 52–4, 70, 73–4, 115; deadlock 71, 90, 100; delay 92–4; electorate 66; financial deficit 15; Lafayette 28; Necker 58, 78; opening 82–3, 85–6, 86–7; provinces 32; Versailles 80–1, 85–6

Fall of Faction; or, Edmund's Vision, The 63
Ferrières, marquis de 138
Fishbourne, Col. Benjamin 146
Fitzgerald, Lord Robert 139, 156, 163–4, 165–6
Flahaut, comtesse de, mistress of Morris 170
Flanders infantry regiment 162–4
flour exports 123–4, 135–6
Foullon, Joseph-François 136
Fox, Charles James 143, 180, 183; and Beaufoy's Bill 87; duc d'Orléans 136, 137, 167; regency crisis 43–4, 47, 55–6, 58–9
Francis, Philip 181
Franklin, Benjamin 51, 64, 65, 134
Freeman's Journal 186
French Guards 126, 130–1, 133
Frith, John 180

Gallo-American Society 28
game 69, 117, 145, 152, 153, 156
Gates, Horatio 47
Gazette of the U.S. 23, 79, 145, 178
Gentleman's Magazine 80, 85
George III, King of England (1760–1820) Burke 137, 180; illness 14, 46,

George III – *contd*
54, 55, 56, 59, 63; Lansdowne 26, 43–
4; de Lolme 72; Mirabeau 106;
Orléans 165–6; Parliament 32, 54, 71,
89, 105, 114, 116; recovery 59–60, 64–
5, 79–80, 103, 118–19, 144, 147, 157;
Regency Bill 14, 64; and US 10, 23,
128; veto 108; Whigs 88
Germigny, comte de 141
Gillray, James 158
Glorious Revolution (of 1688) 9–10,
13, 14, 18, 44–5, 181; Albon's view
19–20; Burke's view 56–7; centenary
celebrations 41–2, 56, 87, 144
gold reserves of England 17
Graham, Catherine Macaulay 184
grain: hoarding 25, 38, 61, 133;
shortage 80, 122–4, 136
great storm (of 1788) 24–5, 34
Grégoire, abbé 155

Hailes, Daniel 30, 34, 36, 37–8, 39
Hamilton, Alexander 146, 184, 185
d'Harcourt, duc, governor to Dauphin
100
Hardy, Jacques-Philippe 74–5
Hardy, Siméon-Prosper 80–1
Hare, James 181
Hastings, Warren, impeachment 88
Hawkesbury, Lord 155
heatwave in New York 127–8
Henry VI, King of England (1422–61)
47
Henry, Patrick 49
Hôtel de Ville 132, 134, 135, 163, 176
Huber, Bartholomew 130–1, 132
hunting 69, 119, 137, 156, 158, 159

Independence Day banquet 128–9
Inquisition 185, 186, 187
Invalides, Les 133
Isabel of Bavaria 26
Izard, Senator Ralph, of S. Carolina
89–90

Jackson, James (Georgia) 90
Jacobin club 175–6
James II, King of England (1685–88) 9,
42, 45, 57, 122; catholics 14, 87–8,
182; choice of successor 13
Jay, John 12, 145–6

Jefferson, Thomas (U.S. ambassador
to Paris) 12, 48, 66, 89, 109–10, 120,
144; breaking deadlock 99–100;
British 17, 115–16, 140, 157–8;
burgled 129; constitution 21–2, 60,
147, 149; debt stock 77; Declaration
of Independence 129; Declaration of
Rights 153–4; Estates General 51–2,
91; George III 145; grain shortage 124;
King's veto 155; Moustier 48; Price
144; Prussia 160; ratification 31–2;
Shay 16–17; sugar 140; in U.S. 183,
185, 187
Jenkinson, Robert 155–6, 162
Johnstone, Sir James 116, 135
Joseph II, Holy Roman Emperor
(1765–90) brother of Marie-
Antoinette 14, 26, 166
Justi, Johann von 22

Keeper of the Seals 93, 97, 99, 100, 107,
109

La Chaise, M. 187
Laclos, Choderlos de 169
Lacoste, marquis de 172
Lafayette, marquis de 28, 30, 125, 158,
170, 184; breaking deadlock 100;
Declaration of Independence 33;
Declaration of Rights 129, 147;
Estates General 28–9, 35; grain 124;
Louis XVI 155, 163–4; Mirabeau
170–1; Morris 113, Paris 130, 134–5;
Society of Thirty 83
la Luzerne, M. de 130
Lamarck, comte de 170, 171, 178
Lamballa, princesse de 135
Lambesc, prince de 131
Langres, Bishop of 161
Lansdowne, Lord 35, 65, 93, 110; and
Bentham 62–3; Burke 88, 179–80,
181; Dumont 148; Duroveray 171;
Geneva 75–6, 77, 99; George III 26,
43–4, 64; Mirabeau 74–5, 124, 168,
169, 170; Price 143; reforms 83, 117;
Repository 72; Romilly's patron 95;
death of wife 148–9
La Rochefoucauld, duc de 33, 83
Launay, marquis de 133
Lauzun, duc de 83
Lawrence, Dr 181

Le Chapelier, Isaac-René-Guy 93–4, 95, 175
Leeds, duke of 42
Leguen de Kérangal 150
Le Jay, Madame 168
Liancourt, duc de 83, 104, 112, 133
Locke, John 9, 10, 16
Lolme, Jean Louis de 72–3
Loménie de Brienne, Archbishop 37–8
London Gazette 156, 158
London Revolution Society 14, 41, 87, 144, 179
Long Parliament 27, 111, 155
Lords, House of 54, 68, 90, 148, 178; attendance 89; George III 105, 116; Glorious Revolution 13, 87, 144; Hastings impeachment 88; Long Parliament 155; Mounier 153; as pattern 31, 91, 96, 108; Plenary Court 73–4; regency crisis 56–7, 62–3; taxation 71
Louis XVI, King of France (1774–93) 15, 23, 26, 27, 28, 117, 162, 166, 180, 185; army 118, 125–6, 132; Assembly 39, 109–10, 112, 120–1, 138, 158–9, 162–3, 172; attacked 165, 168; Bastille 133; British 18–19, 46, 53–4, 135, 137; counter-revolution 170, 174; *doublement* 53, 71; electorate 66–9; Estates General 35, 80, 82, 85–6, 93, 100, 144; etiquette 145–6; grain 122–3; in hiding 129; hunting 119; Mirabeau 168, 178; Necker 25, 38, 98, 130; Orléans 131–2, 136, 167; Parliamentary reform 29–32; Plenary Court 33, 37; role 99, 147, 151; Royal Council 111; Saint-Antoine riots 84; sons 100–1, 161, 163, 164; submission 134, 164, 175; Tennis Court Oath 112; third estate 52; U.S. opinion 23–4; Versailles 96, 97, 160–1, 164; veto 107–8, 155–6
Luxembourg, duc de 178

Maclay, Senator William, of Pennsylvania 12, 49, 113–14, 128, 146, 154, 185
Madison, James 16, 21–2, 32, 127; Congress 89, 91; Declaration of Rights 153–4; and France 33, 52, 53, 66, 149; and the people 114–15, 116; Washington 49, 145–6
Magna Carta 31
Malesherbes, M. 35
Mallet du Pan, Jacques 72
Malouet, Pierre-Victor 101, 105, 108
Marie-Antoinette, Queen of France (1774–93) 44, 99, 121, 138, 141, 147, 166, 180–1; Assembly 120, 123, 132; George III 46; Necker 25–6; Orléans 131; public opinion 26–7, 163–5, 167, 175; Royal Council 53; secret council 98; son's death 100
Marx, Karl 188
Mary II, Queen of England (1689–94), wife of William III 13–14, 56–7
Maryland Gazette 161, 177, 186
Massachusetts Spy 90, 115, 127, 185–6
Mawbey, Sir Joseph 143
Mercier, Louis Sebastian 21, 130
Mercure de France 72
Milne, Dr (Revolution sermon) 45
Milton, Cromwell's secretary 168, 169
Minchin, Humphrey 79
Mirabeau, comte de 74–5, 106, 116, 166, 168–9, 179–80; *Analysis of English Newspapers* 172; anglophilia 147–8; Assembly 107, 169, 171–2; *assignats* 173; bread shortage 125; counter-revolution 170–1, 174, 178; Declaration of Rights 153; *The Estates General* 93, 95; Estates General procedure 94, 101, 149; Genevese 75–6, 95, 110, 148; grain shortage 124; *L'Histoire Secrète* 74–5, 82, 84; King 112–13, 134, 174, 178; King's veto 109–10, 155–6; *Letters to Constituents* 95; Necker 99, 105–6, 172; Orléans 134, 154, 162; pamphlets 168–9; recommends moderation 96–7; Society of Thirty 82–4; Versailles 92
Montesquieu's encomium on English 20
Montjoie, M. 155
Montmorin, comte de, Foreign Secretary 82
Morellet, abbé 35, 51, 64, 65, 75, 148
Morning Post 55, 124, 167–8; on Paris riots 135–8, 165

Morris, Gouverneur 80, 85, 113, 120,
129, 131; ambassador 183–5; army
and war 118, 121; constitution 149,
156, 157; grain shortage 123; Necker
77–8, 170
Morris, Robert 77
Mortemart, duc de 162
Mounier, Jean-Joseph 35, 36, 107, 125,
147, 149, 153; King's veto 155–6;
*New Observations on the Estates
General* 73; Tennis Court Oath 111
Mountmorres, Lord 152
Moustier, comte de 47–9
Mühlenberg, Frederick 128

National Assembly 109–12, 113, 138,
185–7; attacks on property 139, 141;
Declaration of Rights 154; delay 93;
food supplies 124; French Guard 126;
Mirabeau cleared 169; opposition of
Queen 123; procedure 116, 121, 144–
5; Tennis Court Oath 111; *see also*
Assembly
National Guard 163–4, 175–6
Necker, Jacques, Genevese banker 25–
6, 38, 52, 57, 93, 158, 172; Assembly
100, 132; bi-cameralism 88–9; delay
99, 101; dismissal 147; Duroveray
110; Estates General 53, 58, 80, 86;
exile 130–1; French bankruptcy 96–
7; grain shortage 123, 124; Mirabeau
105–6, 108; mobs 118, 134;
opposition 147, 170, 171; secret
council 98; U.S. debt 77–8; Versailles
144–5
Necker, Madame 98, 130
New York Daily Advertiser 155
New York Journal 13, 78, 127, 139; on
France 23–4, 28, 31, 51, 129
Newton, Sir Isaac 62
Noailles, vicomte de 150
North, Lord 87

Orange, Prince of 14, 17
d'Orléans, duchesse 58, 120
d'Orléans, duc 158, 160, 161–2, 165–6,
169; *cahiers* 69, 70; conspiracy 27–9,
120, 131–2, 134–5, 137, 140; enciting
riots 122, 136, 164; grain 125; King's
veto 155; in London 165–6, 167;
National Assembly 121; Necker 38,

123; poor relief 58; Prince of Wales
135; regency crisis 44; Saint-Antoine
riots 84–5; supporters 141, 153–4; *see
also* Palais Royal (his home)
Osborne family 42

Paine, Tom 63, 147, 157–8, 160
Palais Royal (home of duc d'Orléans)
104, 120, 121, 131, 161, 176, 177;
mobbed 109, 126, 130–1, 163
Parker, Daniel 76–7
Parlement of Paris 20, 30, 31, 33–4, 49,
54, 62, 74; Estates General 35, 38, 39,
52; and monarchy 51, 71; and riots
84: Society of Thirty 82–3
Pennsylvania Packet 185
Picky Poky (alias of Depont) 179, 180
Pitt, William, Prime Minister of
England 44–6, 72, 139, 158, 169, 180,
185; centenary celebrations 41, 87;
export of flour 123–4; financier 116;
George III 54, 64, 105; in press 136,
137; regency crisis 47, 55–8, 59;
supporters 143, 155, 182; U.S. opinion
65
Plenary Court 30–1, 33, 37, 71, 73
poaching 117, 152
Polignac, duchesse de 121, 138
Portland, duke of 43–4, 46, 55, 183
Price, Richard 6, 143–4, 166, 179–80,
181, 183
Priestley, Dr Joseph 62, 64, 65
Provence, comte de (brother of Louis
XVI) 27, 53, 170
Prussia 60, 74, 160, 166

Rabaut St-Etienne, Jean Paul 94, 100
ratification in U.S. 31–2, 65, 127
regency crisis for George III 14, 46, 54–
60, 62–4, 65, 73, 149; French support
73, 135; Queen's opposition 167
regency of Isabel of Bavaria 26
regency proposed for Louis XVI 26
Repository, The 65, 72
Representatives, House of 13, 65, 69,
89, 115, 154–5; and the President 78,
90, 91, 114, 146
Réveillon riots 84, 85, 126, 129–30
Revolution banquet 40, 56
Revolution Clubs 41, 43

Revolution Commemoration Bill 116, 143–4; *see also* Beaufoy
Revolution families 42, 44, 46
Revolution House 42–3
Revolution sermon 45
Reybaz, Etienne Salomon 92, 125
riots 80, 84, 118, 123, 126, 129–30, 163–5, 167
Robespierre, Maximilien 95, 97, 163
Rochambeau, commander in U.S. war 33
Rodney, Admiral 68
Rolliad 64
Romilly, Samuel 95, 99, 117, 157, 167, 169, 170; book on House of Commons 149
Royal Allemand regiment 131
Royal Council 53, 111–12
royal session 115, 116, 118, 120–1
Rush, Benjamin 11, 12, 49, 51

Saint-Antoine riots 84–5
St Huruge, marquis de 161
St James Chronicle 56, 58, 135, 158, 165
St Lazare corn found 133
St Paul's Cathedral 41, 79–80
Salis-Samande, regiment of 126
Salon des Princes (club) 131
Sarsfeld, count de 95
Sauvigny, Berthier de 136
Selwyn, George 135
Senate 13, 31, 49, 115, 154, 184; Tonnage Bill 146; and Washington 78, 90
Shakespeare, William 115
Shay, Daniel 11, 16, 21, 66
Shelburne, earl of, *see* Lansdowne, Lord
Sheridan, member of Parliament 180
Sherman, Roger of Connecticut 155
Short, William 183, 187
Sièyes, abbé 71, 86, 101, 105–6, 107, 108–9; Society of Thirty 82; Tennis Court Oath 111, *What is the Third Estate?* 70, 72
Sillery, marquis de 121, 131, 162
slavery 11, 48–9, 65, 67, 88, 140, 187
Smith, William, member of Parliament 41

Society of Mechanics and Tradesmen 128–9
Society of Tammany 128
Society of Thirty 82, 83, 84
Stainville, maréchal de 33
Stanhope, Earl 41, 144
Steuben, baron de 50–1
Stevens, John 72
Strafford, 1st earl of 27
Sumter, Thomas 114
Swan, James 124
Swinburne, Mrs 26

Talleyrand-Périgord, Charles-Maurice de (Bishop of Autun) 29, 170–1, 172, 173
Target, deputy for Paris 150
Tennis Court Oath 111
Thurlow, Lord (Lord Chancellor) 54
Times, The: Bastille entertainment 157; Beaufoy 56; British constitution 74, 109; Burke 168, 178; *cahiers* 70–1; Church 172, 186; Dorset 138–9; Estates General 87, 103; French colonies 127; French constitution 137–8, 149, 151–2, 155; French in London 177; George III 59, 63, 79, 145; grain shortage 80, 124; Louis XVI 119, 158–9, 161, 165; Mirabeau 125, 168; Necker 57–8, 86, 171; negroes 187; Orléans 135; Pitt 55, 56, 57–8; Prussians 60, 160, 166; Triple Alliance 166; U.S. 60, 115
tobacco 28, 49, 127
Tonnage Bill 146
transportation 116–17
Tucker, Thomas Tudor 90
Turberville, George 49
Turgot (reforming minister) 20
Tyler, Wat (rebel) 137, 168, 178

unemployment 176–7
Utrecht, treaty of 161–2

Vaughan, Benjamin 65, 91, 148
Vaux, maréchal de 34
Vergennes (French foreign minister) 18–19, 63
Versailles 114–15, 142, 149, 151, 166, 178; Assembly 112, 116; Bretons 96; Estates General 80–2, 85–8, 90–2, 97–

Versailles – *contd*
8, 100, 103–4; King's veto 107–8;
Louis XVI 134, 160–1, 164, 170;
march on 118, 166–7, 168, 184;
Mirabeau 169; Necker 130–1, 144;
Orléans 132; palace 40; poaching 117;
royal session 113; troops 125, 126,
162–3
veto of monarch 107–8, 148, 155–6,
171
Vining, John (of Delaware) 146
Voltaire, François Marie Arouet 20,
182

Wales, Prince of (later King George
IV) 44, 103, 119, 135, 144, 167;
regency crisis 14, 46, 54–60, 63
War of American Independence 12, 22,
25, 33, 183–4, 187; debt 11, 76
Warren, Dr John (Bishop of Bangor) 144
Warren, Richard, doctor to George III
55, 144
Washington, George, President of U.S.
(1789–97) 11–13, 30, 47, 128; and
Britain 63, 115, 184, 185, 188; French
constitution 33, 184–5; illness 113–

14, 119, 145–6; Lafayette 28, 134;
Morris 77; as President 50, 78–9, 80,
89–90, 90–1, 147; ratification 32;
Virginia 37, 48–9
Wilberforce, William 88, 123
William III, King of England (1689–
1702) 9, 14, 17, 18, 33, 42, 122, 182;
accession 13–14; 56–7
Willis, doctor to George III 55
Wilson, Arthur 8
Windham, William 135, 168, 181
women's riot 163–5, 167
Wraxall, Sir Nathaniel 59
Wycombe, Lord 65, 148

Yates, Robert 66
Young, Arthur 15–16, 37, 138–9, 141,
144–5; Bretons 33–4; *cahiers* 122;
estate in France 173–4; French
electorate 66–7; French Guard 126–
7; game 156–7; Louis XVI 119;
National Assembly 109, 112; Necker
118; Orléans 120; in Paris 103–5, 175–
6; Royal Council 112; Tennis Court
Oath 111; trade links 27; Versailles
103–5, 107